HISTORY OF PADIHAM

BY

JACK NADIN

Acknowledgements

I am grateful to a number of people who assisted me in this enormous project on the History of Padiham. I would like to thank Duncan Armstrong of Padiham for all his help, Molly Haines, and Margaret Jones for their very special wisdom of old Padiham and their delightful little books on the town. Mike Rothwell's book on the Industrial Archaeology of the district was also invaluable. I would also like to thank Ken Spencer of Burnley for pointing me in the right direction on a number of occasions, and the help he always gives without question. The information contained herein is also from other reliable sources such as newspapers of the day, census returns and trade directories—every effort was made to be as accurate as possible. However, I am only human and apologise and beg forgiveness in advance for any mistakes, which I hope are few or better still non-existent. A general index is included at the back of the book as well as a surname index for the sake of family historians.

Jack Nadin
2015

Copyright © Jack Nadin 2015

ISBN 978-1-911138-00-6

Published by Nu-Age Print & Copy
289 Padiham Road, Burnley. BB12 0HA

CONTENTS

CHAPTER ONE
Padiham, the early history.
The Neolithic Period, the Romans, the Doomsday Book, and the Anglo-Saxons. How Padiham got its name, the early roads. The Norman Conquest and Ightenhill Manor House. Details of Padihamers in the early years, food, drink and attire. Common lands, field names and Padiham corn mill. The Civil War and the Skirmish at Old Read Bridge. Wages, the Padiham Overseers, the Poor Laws, and Padiham Workhouse. John Wesley and his visit to Padiham in 1761.

CHAPTER TWO
Church, Chapel and Religious Matters
The Parish Church of St Leonard's, St Matthews' Church ('The Iron Church') St Anne and Elizabeth Church, Burnley Road Baptist Chapel and the Sabden Baptists influences and its history. Cross Bank Chapel, The Congregationalists, Hall Hill Chapel and the Methodists, Owd Mary Monk and her cottage on Old Chapel Street, Pendle Street Baptist Chapel, Ebenezer Chapel, St Philips R.C. Church and St John's R.C. Church.

CHAPTER THREE
School days and Education
British Schools, Padiham National School, Padiham County Primary School, Padiham Green School, Partridge Hill School, Private Schools, St John's School, St Leonard's School, The Technical Institute, Gawthorpe High School.

CHAPTER FOUR
Industry, The Cotton Trade, Mining, Engineering etc.
The cotton mills and sheds, and the cotton masters, bankruptcies, mill fires, strikes and disputes. The coal mining industry, Opencast Mining, stone quarrying, engineering, foundries, blacksmiths and lesser industries. Hill 'Special' cycle, Padiham Aerated Waters and Hill's 'Pop' works, Bertwistle's Saw Mill, Ropewalks and Tripe dressing.

CHAPTER FIVE
Strikes and disputes
Strikes and Riots in the Cotton Industry, The Cotton Strike of 1852, The Cotton Strike of 1859, The Strike of 1878, The Strike of 1883, The Strike of 1885, Mining and Engineering Disputes.

CHAPTER SIX
Essential Services, Electricity, Gas, Sewerage and Water, The Post Office.
Electricity supply at Padiham, Padiham 'A' and Padiham 'B' Power Stations, The Gasometer at the Old Factory, The first Padiham Gas Company, Fatal accident taking a boiler to Padiham Gas works, Padiham's new gasworks. The first water supply and Wall Green Reservoir. Leeches in the drinking water, the building of Churn Clough Reservoir and the accidents at the 'shanty town' there, the tunnel through Black Hill, and pure water at last for the town of Padiham. The Post Office.

CHAPTER SEVEN
The Railway, Bridges
The idea of a railway running from Rosegrove to Blackburn is put forward. The costs involved, and the difficulties. The first goods trains and passenger services. A runaway train, fatal accidents on the line and the end of the railway. The new linear park. Padiham Bridge and other bridges around Padiham.

CHAPTER EIGHT
Leisure and Entertainment
Padiham Memorial Park, the Fountain, and Whitegate Park. 'The Alexandra' Theatre, Fred Lichfields 'Alhambra' Theatre. The Grand and the Globe Cinemas. Roller Skating and Ice Skating and the Empress Skating Rink. The Recreation Ground, tennis courts and bowling greens. Padiham Races, Travelling Circuses and a Killer Elephant. Padiham Pool and the Skateboard Park.

CHAPTER NINE
Banking, Padiham Building Society.

Penny Bank, Craven Bank, (Top Bank) Manchester and County Bank (Bottom Bank) Padiham Building Societies.

CHAPTER TEN
The Padiham Co-operative Movement.
The early Co-operative movement, The First Padiham Co-operative premsises, Branch stores, The Co-operative in court over employing girls, the Co-operatives main store on Burnley Road, the Co-operative take over the old National School.

CHAPTER ELEVEN
The Fire Service at Padiham
An early fire at Padiham, The various brigade headquarters, Testing a new extinguisher, The Fire Brigade under the Local Board, The first Fire Station, Testing a new Fire Engine, The Brigade becomes part of the National Fire Service, The new fire station and the first lady fire fighter.

CHAPTER TWELVE
A Few Notable Padiham Buildings
*Crossways, Knight Hill, Osborne Terrace, Cross Hill (*Trevelyan House)

CHAPTER ONE

Padiham, the Early History

Padiham is a small township around three miles west by north from Burnley with a population in 2001 of 8,998 souls. The little town of Padiham we see today is largely a product of the Industrial Revolution, which can still be testified by the rows of terraced houses laid out in a grid fashion, and the relics of many old mills and factories. However, the presence of mankind in this area goes back much further than the Industrial Revolution—much, much further back. Neolithic (4,000-2,200 BC) tools in the form of stone axe heads and other cutting implements have been found on Burnley moors and around Pendleside. An early Bronze Age burial site has been excavated near Mereclough, in July 1950, revealing burial urns and other artefacts, and also another site at Worsthorne revealed more finds.[i]

The Romans of course, were also present in this area of East Lancashire, although no Roman finds have been recorded in the immediate vicinity, there have been finds not too far away and camps recorded at Ribchester, Portfield near Whalley, and other places. While at Wheatley Lane in the Pendle Forest *"Great numbers of coins"* were found dating from the Roman period.[ii] When the Doomsday Book was compiled in 1086, this area was part of the Blackburn Hundred, yet there was no mention of Padiham—in fact very little was said about the Blackburn Hundred in general. That does not mean that Padiham did not exist at that time of course. The suffix 'ham' as in Padiham, Higham and many other place names often relate to Anglo-Saxon origins.[iii] It is generally accepted that the origin of the name Padiham then is "The home (Ham) of Padda, or Paddi"[iv] Thus we can assume that this area was also inhabited in Anglo-Saxon times, although again no archaeological evidence of settlement in this area prior to the 13th century exists. It's probable that Padiham as a settlement only exists at all, due to its important position on the River Calder and the river crossing there. At first, the early settlers chose the higher ground near the present day church, and along the ridge towards Hargreaves (Hargrove) and High Whitaker, forsaking the boggy flood prone land nearer the river. The area around the church developed more rigorously and an open air market bustled and traded around the outer walls of the church. Many years later the market stalls and other obstructions to the pavements caused comments in the local newspapers.

One correspondent in August 1879 said:

"Until I saw your last impression that the police of Padiham had obtained a conviction against the Parish Bell ringers for obstructing the footpaths, I was under the idea that Padiham was outside the peals of civilisation, and that its police had no authority to maintain order, as in other towns, for I have often driven through the place and found the principal streets blocked up with stalls, fruit and fish carts &c., so as to make it quite dangerous for carriages to pass through. But it appears that the Local Board allow and encourage these obstructions during the week, and that the police only take action on Sundays, and then only when people are sheltering under cover on the footpaths...."

Markets often developed near the church as it was often believed that no unfair dealings would take place near a holy edifice such as the church or market cross. It's known that a cross existed in St Leonard's Churchyard many years ago, but this has since disappeared—to where forever remains a mystery. Annual fairs had also been established by the early seventeenth century, and a number of shops were also in existence by this time. Names we still use today gives an indication of what the land was like hereabouts. To the north of the church the land was clayey, and not much use for agriculture as in 'Clay Bank' and further on was wastes and moorland reached by 'Moor Lane' and you really could catch partridge and other game birds on Partridge Hill.

The view from the church tower would have been very different to what we would have seen today. Open moorland or common land would have stretched away to the north and towards Padiham Heights, broken only by an odd farmstead such as Slade, with perhaps glimpses of Foulds House and Hargrove. Eastwards, the land sloped quickly away towards the River Calder, more fertile land with sandy sediments and pasture. In the distance we would see a managed and wooded area around Gawthorpe Hall, and to the right Stockbridge House, and further over The Green, beyond which was all open countryside up to the present day Hapton village and beyond. To the west was Craggs and Isles House with more open countryside beyond, to the south the land dipped steeply down 'The Banks' to the River Calder. Many of these houses had been rebuilt in a more attractive style, whilst later ones were much more basic and often whitewashed to make them more attractive.

Attached to the main farmhouse or close by would be a small cottage or two for the farm hands. The very earliest crossing of the River Calder here would have been a simple ford, a footbridge, or even stepping stones, and would be passable only in the driest of weather. No-one then can really say for certain just when the first Padiham Bridge was built, but in 1457 Sir Thomas Walton bequeathed 14 shillings towards the making of the bridge at Padiham. Like all stone structures the bridge needed care and maintenance, and in 1647 when in *'a state of collapse'* it was repaired at a cost of £10 at a burden to the parish. In 1754-55 the Padiham Bridge became part of the turnpike road leading from Blackburn to Burnley thence on to Yorkshire, and the Lancashire coast thus ending that burden on the parish. The direct route to Whalley only came about with the construction of an entirely new road in 1810. Prior to this the way was by Moor Lane, on past Slade and the entrance to Huntroyde straight across at Trapp Lane and then along the old back lane through Read, onto Read Bridge and the Old Roman Road before dropping down to Whalley.

The way to Sabden and Clitheroe was very much the same as today, reaching Clitheroe over the Nick O' Pendle. There was a footbridge linking Padiham with Hapton, then a separate parish over Green Brook, formerly Lodge Brook which was mentioned in 1602—Green Brook itself is fed by another small stream flowing off Hambledon Hill named Shaw Brook. 'Shaw' being the old word for woods, so the brook must have been surrounded by trees at one time. Travel was by no means a pleasure in these early days, most went by foot, and those who could afford it rode a horse. Only the very wealthy could afford to travel in a litter slung between two horses. As late as the 1860s, one correspondent to the local newspaper stated that *"If anyone has the misfortune to travel there* (Padiham) *then they would have to wade through mountains of mud, and encounter the most obnoxious stenches from ashpits, pigsties, slaughterhouses and donkey stables that are reared up against many houses, the occupants of which consider themselves respectable and reforming citizens of our town"*.

Indeed as late as 1875, Richard Suddal, the landlord at the Black Bull Inn, besides the Parish Church, who was also a butcher there, was charged with keeping pigs for killing in a cote just under the bedroom window of the inn. He was fined ten shillings and costs, with a further five shillings to be incurred for every day the pigs remained in the cote.[v] In the heat of the summer months the smell must have been atrocious.

The roads themselves, if we could call them roads started out as little more than footpaths, and merely increased in width by the increased traffic. They rarely kept to a straight course and turned here and there to avoid areas of crops, wet and boggy land, the odd barn or cottage, an old field quarry or even coal-pit shafts. Coal mining is recorded around Padiham as early as 1434, but we shall hear more of this in a later chapter. [vi] The road from Burnley to Padiham used much the same route as today, only instead of going up the present day Westgate, at Burnley, the traveller went up Sandygate, thence left up Coal Clough Lane, if going to Halifax and beyond, or carried on past the Angel Inn towards Gannow Top and down into Padiham. There were no houses to be seen on this old road save for a few outlying farms or an odd barn. The Tim Bobbin was an early farm, and Palace House was also of some antiquity. Following a private Act of Parliament in 1754 the new road connecting Blackburn, Burnley Colne was permitted.

This road left Burnley via the present day Westgate, thus avoiding the steep descent down Sandygate—and through Padiham it took the route up Mill Street, Moor Lane, West Street, or as it was also known Owd Back Lane, thence through Altham and on to Blackburn. After the Norman Conquest (1066), Padiham became part of the new administration centre set up at Clitheroe, and later still came under the jurisdiction of Ightenhill Manor House (GR 8186-3399), but still responsible to Clitheroe. The Lords at Clitheroe for the greater part of the earlier Medieval period were the de Lacy Family. The castle at Clitheroe was actually built by Robert de Lacy around 1186. Burnley, Habergham, Extwistle, Little Marsden, Cliviger, and Worsthorne also came under the jurisdiction of Ightenhill Manor House, but after 1399 and until 1660, the Honor of Clitheroe became the property of the Crown. Ightenhill Manor House was by all accounts a substantial building and it stood in a commanding position above the River Calder between Ightenhill Park Lane and the present day Padiham Road—happily we still have some details of it. The Manor House was built in the 12th or 13th Century, the main building faced south-west and was rectangular in shape, with outside measurements of twenty yards by ten yards. A courtyard in front was twenty yards square, and a well was situated outside the hall at the north-east corner. Some thirty yards north of the main building there are foundations of what might have been a chapel, which measured ten yards by eight yards.

Fifty or sixty yards to the west there is an earthworks, possible a deer trap, into which the deer were driven into at certain times of the year. It was roughly triangular in shape, with one side about thirty yards long. Foundations of smaller buildings which may have been barns or huts can still be seen. The main house was very strongly built, and had carved door jambs and window mullions[vii]. Ightenhill Park Lane which lay a short distance away from the ancient Manor House is also in fact part of another ancient highway connecting Lancashire and Yorkshire via Burnley, Ightenhill, up towards Higham and on through Sabden. The other way was via Cowden or Coal Clough Lane on over Limers Way at Clowbridge, and over into Yorkshire to Halifax and beyond. I mention here a rather remarkable instance that occurred at Higham in the year 1743. It appears that a large hog killed here in December weighed in at 29 score and 2 lbs, all saleable stuff which at 14 lbs to the stone made it 41 stone and 8 lbs, thought to have been the largest ever known at that time.

The importance of the Ightenhill Manor House can be seen in the fact that the then Lord of the Manor, Edward II (1284-1327) paid a visit to the house in 1323. The Ightenhill Manor House served as the administration centre for the small farming communities mentioned above, taking in the rents and also acted as court dealing out fines, and acting as mediator in petty crimes. The Ightenhill Court Rolls mentions the cuckstool at Padiham in 1572, but there were no stocks in 1596, although there were stocks in later years near by the Parish Church, and they are mentioned again in 1612. Perhaps the last time that the Padiham stocks were put to use was in late November 1858, when a man was placed there for six hours for breaking the Sabbath. On the previous Wednesday another man was placed in the Padiham stocks for a similar offence. If it was meant to have been a punishment it did not have much effect on the person being punished! He declared that he *"Cared nothing much about it—if anything he had plenty of rum and tea whilst he was in, supplied to him by the spectators and passerby's".*

A cuckstool was a plank of wood pivoted near its centre with a stool at one end, and was erected near a fairly deep pool of water in the river—in Padiham's case the River Calder. The person to be ducked was strapped into the stool then dropped in and out of the water by pulling on the other side of the plank.

The cuckstool was a punishment usually applied to scalds, or quarrelsome women, and of course witches. Interestingly, there still is a Cuckstool Lane running down from Wheatley Lane village to the river in the valley bottom. Padiham even had its own witch, not as famous as the Lancashire witches, but still worth recalling. Her name was Margaret Pearson, and she stood trial in 1612 at the same time as the Lancashire witches, but happily did not suffer the same fate. She was however committed to be pilloried on four consecutive market days at Padiham, Lancaster, Clitheroe and Whalley, thus escaping hanging—but she was also sentenced to a year in jail. Margaret's crime was that of supposedly bewitching a horse, a crime for which she was arrested by the constable employed by the Gawthorpe estate. On the subject of crime and punishment we record here that on 12 March1536, William Haydocke, a monk at Whalley Abbey along with two others was tried for treason at Lancaster Castle, for which they were condemned to death. Haydocke was executed at Padiham, possibly at The Green or Guy Gate. *"He was allowed to continue suspended for some time entire".* The other two were put to death at Lancaster, where they were also hung drawn and quartered, and their remains distributed to other towns as a deterrent. On the subject of the town constable there was an interesting report in the Blackburn Standard in January 1837 on this matter:-

"A meeting of the ley-payers of Padiham was held at the church for the purpose of electing a constable at a salary of £10 per annum. The Rev., S.J.C. Adamson was in the chair—the candidates were John Ashworth who was proposed by Le Gendre Nicholas Starkie of Huntroyde, seconded by Mr Dugdale of Lowerhouse Print Works. John Hargreaves, the late constable was reported to have given great dissatisfaction to the respectable inhabitants of Padiham by improper conduct in his office. This person was proposed by a weaver named Pate and seconded by Nicholas Stevenson a hawker—but he lost his election by a large majority. The result is considered a great triumph by the friends of order in Padiham and district."

The inhabitants of the Padiham area in 1258 consisted of eight cottars, twenty five serfs, nine or ten tenants at will, and one free tenant named Gilbert. A serf was the most common type of peasant in the Middle Ages.

They had more rights and were of a higher status than the cottars, but were under a number of legal restrictions that differentiated them from the freeman. Villeins generally rented small homes, with or without land. As part of the contract with their landlord, they were expected to use some of their time to farm the lord's fields and the rest of their time was spent farming their own land. Cottars, on the other hand, were often the poorer members of the local classes, and would rent a cottage around which would be two or three acres of land at an annual rent of 6d. They also had the right to use the common lands, which around here lay towards Northtown and Padiham Heights.

By 1311 the cottars had appeared to have ceased to exist as a class in the Padiham area and elsewhere, but by this time there were two free tenants, John of Whitaker (High Whitaker) and Richard, the son of Matthew. High Whitaker was also the place where the priest Thomas Whitaker is reputed to have been caught and taken to Lancaster goal where he was found guilty and hung drawn and quartered. Interesting to note here, that High Whitaker, always spelt with one 'T' was acquired by the Shuttleworths of Gawthorpe Hall comparatively recently in 1878. In 1332, the following people at Padiham paid the subsidy, Richard of Whitaker, Richard of the Wood, William of Mikelbroke, Thomas son of Henry, Roger the Leadbeater, Adam of Augrim, and Henry son of John. In 1313, William of Goukthorpe (Gawthorpe) gave up 9 ½ acres which he had cultivated, and it was not until 1342 that a new tenant could be found, and then only at a much reduced rental of 2/2d a year. The Shuttleworth family appear to have settled at Gawthorpe around 1388 or 1389, when land was surrendered by John del Eves to the use of Ughtred de Shuttleworth. [viii] Interesting to note that there still is an 'Eves Barn' which may have some connection with the above John del Eves near Stonemoor Bottom to this day.

The tenants at this time were also expected or obliged to grind their corn at the Lord's mill, there was one at Burnley, named *"The King's Mill"* and the one at Padiham was in existence by 1253 when an inquiry was ordered as to the value of the wheel there by which a man had been killed. In 1311 the mill was worth *"40s yearly beyond repairs"* and in 1324 various persons were fined for not repairing the mill pond.
Padiham corn mill
Repairs included in 1333 mending the axel, the mill itself, repairing the miller's house, the mill wheel, and the *'floodyates'*.

The Padiham manorial corn mill was on the site of today's Padiham Youth Centre and the adjoining shops, formerly the Padiham Liberal Club. The mill was water powered—water from the River Calder was captured in a weir not far upstream from Padiham Bridge and conveyed to the mill in a channel, known locally as the 'Goit'. This shouldn't be confused with the goit, which ran near Wyre Street—the corn mill goit took its water from further down the river near the present day Lune Street. The water filled a mill pond behind the corn mill and once the water had powered the waterwheel it ran back into the River Calder downstream just below the bridge on Station Road. Much of the Padiham corn mill goit has now disappeared as the town developed—but behind Padiham clinic a gate leads out onto a small patch of grassy land, with the River Calder on the left hand side, and on the right hand side here can still be seen a large stone archway with a trickle of blackened water running out. This is what remains today of the goit. The Padiham corn mill was advertised to be let for a term of 21 years at the Hall Inn, at Burnley on 8 July 1799, and was described as follows:

> *"The corn mill and kiln at Padiham (is) supplied by a powerful stream of water (At all times of the year) out of the River Calder, with goits, wears, water-wheel, gears and utensils thereto belonging, and other conveyances required to carry on an extensive concern. The premises are a small distance from the Leeds and Liverpool Canal and from the market town of Burnley, three miles, and from Blackburn nine miles. The farmers within the township of Hapton under Charles Towneley are bound by their lease to grind their corn at the said mill".*

In December 1815 there was a fierce fire at the corn mill and an adjoining factory which gutted the premises and claimed the life of Matthew Wilkinson who was helping trying to clear an adjacent cottage when the gable wall collapsed onto him. Two others were seriously injured. The old corn mill must have been rebuilt, but almost forty years later corn milling came to end in 1852, when a severe flood caused a great deal of damage to the property. The last miller here was Henry Preston who was obliged to sell off all his machinery including the grindstones.

After this the old Padiham corn mill was used for various other purposes, notably by Messrs Watson for storage, and eventually the new Padiham Liberal Club was built on the site in 1898. What was life like in the 1300s? Walter Bennett, author of "History of Burnley" parts I and II, page 60-61 gives his impression of life at that time, and if his impressions applied to Burnley, then it must also have applied to Padiham, just three miles away.

"Many were very poor and dressing in evil smelling clothes of leather, rough skins or course woollen cloth. Ignorant and hard working, the vast majority knew no comfort. They lived in huts that were little better than hovels, sometimes made of turf, sometimes made of wattle and clay, with thatched roofs and earth floors... One common type of house was made by splitting lengthwise two bent trees, to provide two bent pairs of 'crocks' or 'crutches' for the four corner posts of the house. The tops of the two inverted 'V's so formed were joined by a ridge pole. Cross bars and upright stiles formed the framework of the walls which were filled with wattle and clay. The roof was thatched with straw or rushes. In this one roomed house, with a hole in the roof to let out the choking smoke from the wood or peat fire, and often with no window at all, the family ate and slept in summer and winter alike. There was no furniture as we know it, and rough planks and sawn tree trunks served for table and chairs, while a bundle of straw or bracken was used as a bed. Around the hut was a croft. Here was the garden, a dilapidated shed that housed anything required for fieldwork and a small enclosed space for the pig and a few hens. The better type of farm was made of stone, and had the living quarters with chamber and buttery, barn and ox stalls all under one roof. The house part was separated from the farm section by a wide passage known as the 'Threshold' where corn was threshed...The food of the poor was very simple consisting mainly of porridge, bread made from barley or rye, pork and bacon, and ale made from barley was the chief drink..."

As we entered the Tudor Period in history, twixt 1485 to 1603, things do improve slightly for the commoner albeit slowly. Padiham had by this time begun to develop into a scattering of house and small shops and farms, even large enough to be called a hamlet. At the shops you could purchase candles, fabrics, bread, buttons, soaps and honey to sweeten your gruel. These shops were located on the present day Guy Street, and stood side by side to the ale-houses, pig sties and cattle sheds.

The buildings would have been made of stone, or a combination of stone, wood and plaster, and all, or most would have had thatched roofs. Importantly, a number of larger houses and farms on the outskirts were also being built around this time, or rebuilt to a higher standard. The names of some of these Yeoman dwellings are still recognisable today—Hargreave (Hargrove) The Green, Stockbridge, Brookfoot, High Whittaker, Cophurst, Wallgreen, and Slade. From the parish records we can even say who lived at these places at various times. Thomas Ryley was living at the Green in 1594, when his daughter Maria was baptised, and perhaps the very same Thomas Ryley of the Green, the aforementioned was buried in St Leonards churchyard in 1634. The Ainsworths lived at Brookfoot in 1619, and Thomas Whittaker lived at Cophurst in the early 1600s, and Johnis Hey lived at Wallgreen Whilst at Stockbridge House was Robertus Roe whose death occurred in 1594[ix]. There is even evidence of a place named Padiham Hall, for there was a house on the right hand side of Hall Hill three or four doors from the gate of the old chapel that used to stand there with cylindrical shafts on the door jambs.

This is perhaps the reason for the name Hall Hill. It was supposed that this was the home of the incumbent of Hall Hill chapel which was built on *"Tithe Barn Croft"* a large garden belonging to the house sloped down to what is now North Street. A 'Tithe' is a tax, one tenth, usually of the annual crops of the workpeople and levied to support the church—the *'Tithe Barn'* was the building where these taxes were collected. The vicar of the Parish Church lived in the *'Parsonage'* at the top of Moor Lane, which also had a potato field and a croft behind. The 'Parsonage' was eventually built over and two streets took their place—one named John Street, and the other named Adamson Street after a former incumbent at the Church, the Rev., Sandford John Cyril Adamson. [x]

Many Padiham surnames reoccur time and time again, names such as Webster, Helm, Wilkinson; a Thomas Wilkinson was the towns constable back in 1641, Starkie, Sagar and Jackson are other names. Apart from the tradesmen, the masons the shopkeepers and alehouse keepers, most of the residents at Padiham at this time, as at Burnley, would have been involved in agriculture and/or horse and cattle breeding in one form or another. However, others also had something to do with textiles, albeit on a small loom in an upstairs room, or a cottage spinning wheel. For instance, John Roo of Cross Bank was a clothier.

Interestingly too, is the fact that Edmund Starkie of Huntroyde, gent, who died in 1619 had a spinning wheel and two looms at his house. Lancashire's last handloom weaver was probably William Wade who was born around 1805 in some cottages near Cock Bridge at Read. He ended his days at Old Moss on the Higham Road off Slade lane. Most handloom weaving had ceased by the 1860s, but William stubbornly carried on the handloom weavers' trade. We think he died around 1890, but not before he took his handloom to the Manchester Exhibition and gave a demonstration there on the dying art of handloom weaving. By 1650, the population of Padiham was 232 families, or 1,106 persons, and fairs were held yearly on 29th April and 27th September. Rushbearing ceremonies were also a popular affair, they were fixed for 12 August, and often lasted two or three days. There was a report in 1867 of Padiham rushbearings, which gave us a great insight into the goings on of the day.

"The celebrations lasted from Monday through to Tuesday and Wednesday, the stalls being on Church Street outside of St Leonards, a church of which the Starkies of Huntroyde had been patrons since 1730. The gaiety of the hobbyhorses, the swing boats and shooting galleries were on the Bank overlooking the River Calder. All the mills and other workplaces had ceased work for the duration of the three day ceremony, and the weather was fine and extremely hot. The town was somewhat quiet during the daytime and did not assume the aspect of a fair until evening was approaching. Of course this was a religious ceremony, and the local chapels and church competed for the best day out. The Wesleyans, the Baptists and the Unitarians all went to Windermere in the Lake District, 500 in all. The Hapton Wesleyans went to Blackpool and they numbered around 340. Even the miners employed by the Hapton Coal Company were treated, they too went to Blackpool, the fares being paid for by their employers, the Hapton Coal Company. They all left via Hapton Railway Station in the morning and returned in the late evening, so that upwards of 2,300 left Padiham that day out of a population of about 6,000 inhabitants"

The town must have appeared to be like a ghost town. Common lands which were situated close to the village, included the following, and these all had names. *'Padiham Field'* was on part of Church Hill, and consisted of *'Townwall'*.

This *'Townwall'* is probably a corruption of *'Townwell'* as there were a number of wells in this area. *'Padiham Hey'* was closer to Gawthorpe, whilst *'Stockbridge'* was nearer Padiham Bridge, and perhaps the old name for *'Green Bridge'* where the 'stock' or cattle was brought to market? Hargrove had fields named *'Sands' 'Ringyard'* and a strangely named field called *'Gadweyne'*. Parts of these commons were enclosed in 1526, including Stockbridge (40 acres) Church Hill (32 acres) Townwall Bank (40 acres) Hargrove (40 acres) Lawrence Shuttleworth was the largest freeholder with about 120 acres to the East of Padiham. The wastes consisted of around 378 acres situated on Padiham Heights reached by a lane now named Moor Lane. In 1618 these wastes were allotted to 28 landowners. [xi]

During the Civil War (1641-1651) the two most prominent families in Burnley and Padiham were on opposing sides. The Towneleys of Towneley Hall, Burnley, were Royalists and supported King Charles I, but Burnley supported the Parliamentary forces and several local battles and skirmishes took place in the area at this time between the Royalists and the Parliamentarians including the Battle of Read Bridge (GR 7536-3535) on 20th. April 1643. This was a significant event because it helped to turn the tide of the Civil War in Lancashire in favour of the Parliamentary forces. Richard Shuttleworth of Gawthorpe Hall was a former High Sherriff of Lancashire, and was for the war against the King—he became a Colonel in Cromwell's army. There are a number of accounts of this conflict. The scene of this skirmish was close by to Read Old Bridge, where Old Roman Road dips down into the hollow. A scouting party of about 400 local militia men and Parliamentarians led by Richard Shuttleworth had left Padiham by Moor lane, and on reaching Read Old Bridge and Cabcar Nook positioned themselves behind the walls. When the first shot was fired an advance party of the Troopers of the Royalists thought they had been lured into a trap, and swung their horses round and fled. The noise and the commotion as they raced down Whalley Brow caused such a concern among the main body of men stationed near Whalley Abbey and church that many of the footmen dive into, or waded across the Calder, abandoning their cause for the sake of life itself. The Royalist Cavalry troops hastened to make a stand, but they too were driven back by the Parliamentarians, which had by this time had moved forward from Padiham.

The 400 local militiamen were able to claim victory of nearly 4,000 Royalists troops that day and in the process saved Padiham and Gawthorpe from the 'enemy'. [xii] Metal detectorists can still find musket balls in this area around Read Old Bridge even today. The following year, on 2 July 1644, near Long Marston, Yorkshire Charles Towneley was killed at the battle of Marston Moor; local tradition says that Oliver Cromwell himself helped Mrs Towneley to search for the body of her husband in the blood and gore of the battlefield. The other prominent family within the area the Starkies of Huntroyde also played an influential role in the areas civil war struggles. When Sir Gilbert Hoghton of Hoghton Tower and his Royalist troops moved against Blackburn, having taken Whalley, Colonel Shuttleworth of Gawthorpe Hall and Colonel Starkie of Huntroyde together raised a force of 8,000 and routed the king's supporters. The following year, after Parliament's forces attacked Preston, Colonel Starkie laid siege to and took Hoghton Tower itself. Local tradition also states that Cromwell and his men were regular visitors to Gawthorpe and also stayed at Isles House Padiham, which is near the bottom of Arbory Drive, but the not at the building we see today of course. The Isles House we see today dates from 1806, although it was largely altered in the 1830s. We know that Isles House was 'newly erected' in 1806, because an advertisement telling us this appeared in the Blackburn Mail that year, when the house was owned by William Robinson—this is reproduced below.

BLACKBURN MAIL
December 3rd, 1806
"TO BE LET BY TICKET FOR A TERM OF YEARS
At the House of W. Waddington, the Starkie's' Arms in
Padiham in the County of Lancaster, on Wednesday, the 17th
Day of December next, between the Hours of four and six in
the Afternoon. All that capital newly erected MESSUAGE or
MANSION called Isles House together with the Garden and
the Barn, Stable and other Outbuildings and two Acres or
thereabouts of rich Meadow land and one Acre and a half of
Pasture Land, customary measure, near to and in Part
adjoining the said Messuage. Isles House is pleasantly
situated near the Town of Padiham .aforesaid, a short distance
from the Turnpike Road leading from Burnley to Blackburn
and is distant from the former place about three miles and is a
desirable situation for a genteel family or a manufacturer.

*The possession of the Premises may be had and further
Information obtained on application to Mr William Robinson,
at Isles House, the owner, or at the office of Mr William Shaw,
Solicitor, in Burnley aforesaid.
Burnley. November 22nd. 1806"*

The William Robinson mentioned above married Miss Robinson of Crags (sic) the farm not far away in 1805. William Heap the cotton manufacturer was living at Isles House in the 1840s, but by the 1850s Isles House was the home to yet another cotton manufacturer, James Helm. James was a member of the well known Helm family who were cotton manufacturers who started at up at Grove Mill on Grove Lane and at Padiham Old Mill around the end of the 18th century and the beginning of the 19th century. The firm greatly expanded in the 1830s to become one of Padiham's largest employers running mills named Smithy Gate, Padiham Old Mill, (also known as 'Guy Yate Mill') and Victoria Mills. Padiham Old Mill still survives in part on Factory Lane where a date stone can still be seen which reads "H. Helm 1807". James Helm continued to live at Isles House until his death in 1866—his widow Eleanor afterwards left the large Isles House and went on to live at 75 Windsor Terrace on Church Street in the town, she died in 1887. We know that one of James and Eleanor's children, Ruth Ward Helm 'married into more cotton' as it was said at the time, when she wed Henry Watson of the Padiham firm of cotton manufacturers Watson and Sherburn on 20 June 1860 at the Wesleyan Chapel at Padiham. Following the death of James Helm, Isles House became the home of the Nottinghamshire born land agent for the Starkies of Huntroyde, Daniel Howsin and his family.

By the period 1650-1750 men's dress of the more upper classes consisted of a long coat with large cuffs to show off the lace ruffles of his shirt. He also wore a cravat, a long waistcoat and knee length breeches—wigs were worn, powdered and perfumed on special occasions and a three cornered hat completed the outfit. Men of the working class wore a low crowned hat with a broad brim, a short coat or jacket made of woollen material and a waistcoat. A pair of breeches buttoned at the knee made from fustian and sheep leather with strong shoes with hob nails to complete his outfit.

The women's dress hardly changed at all in the working classes, it consisted of a flannel gown with sleeves to the elbow and a petticoat of the same material, with an apron made of linen to match. The young women by tradition wore their hair down their back, but married women wore mobcaps. Strong leather shoes were fastened with buckles or straps. Eating habit improved slightly, but the poor still lived on porridge, with salt pork beans and fat bacon, with black puddings and berry pies. The richer classes ate white bread and butter, jams cakes and fresh meats of all kinds, and wines. Ale and beer was the drink of the working class, safer than spring or river water due to the boiling process in its making.

Wages during the years 1650-1750 varied, but those of the workings classes were very low. A journeyman weaver might earn four pence a day with meat and drink—eight pence a day without. An average weaver might earn £2.10d per year, a skilled weaver £3.00 per year. A farm labourer might earn a shilling a day in summer, and 10d a day the rest of the year. Masons, carpenters and other semi skilled were paid 10d per day. Many families had a small enclosed field attached to their cottage on which they might keep a pig, a few hens, and perhaps even grow a few vegetables of their own. A rabbit or two, even a deer might be 'acquired' to supplement the diet with no questions asked. For the really poor, Padiham like other towns had its elected Overseers who dealt out help and charity to the sick and the infirm, the handicapped and the orphans and the illegitimate. There were seventeen such persons in Padiham during the term from November 1710 to April 1711. These included Widow Kirkham, Widow Kelley and Sethson (s) lad. An account for this period exists, and included:

"To Mr Brockden for cloth and thread for a coat for Widow Kelley 2s.0d
For clogs for Sethson(s) Lad 0s.4 ½ d
Two shirts for Jer; Denbigh Lads 2s.3d
Makinge and thread 0s.3 ½ d
For old widow Kirkam for a smock making and thread 2s.1d

It was quite natural for the ratepayers to object to paying for paupers they considered to be another parish's responsibility which resulted in the Settlement Act of 1662. This restricted people to getting any relief in a place where they had a legal settlement.

This usually meant the place where they were born, had served an apprenticeship, or in the case of a wife, where her husband lived, or a place where a person had lived for more than one year. If a *'foreigner'* came into the village, one likely to be poor and chargeable to the rates, then a Removal Order was obtained from the magistrates, and the prospective offending person would then be unceremoniously removed to the parish boundary and handed over to the officers of the adjacent township. Thus casual labourers would only be taken on for just short of twelve months to save the burden on the ratepayers. It is known that a workhouse existed at Padiham by 1730, but just where it was is difficult to say—in any case it was probably just a common house, rather than a purpose built structure. On the first day of November 1736 it housed just ten persons. The inmates appear to have been well looked after, and earned their keep with a bit of spinning, weaving and housework. The Masters account at this Padiham Workhouse for Christmas Day 1737 gives us the following information on supplies for the workhouse;

Four loads of Coles	*1s-4d*
One li. Chees at Baxters	*1s-10d*
Two strik of Wheat	*4s-0d*
A peck and half of Meal	*3s-6d*
Beef at Willm. Robs.	*4s-0d*
Beef at Thos. White	*3s-0d*
A strik of Aples	*0s-6d*
Milk	*1s-2d*
Two buter and Grout	*1s-0d*
Threed and brinding	*0s-2d*
Suger and peper	*0s-5d*
Black peper	*0s-1d*

An account exists for this workhouse in 1798, but it probably ceased to be soon after this date. On a number of occasions, such as in 1757 and 1782 arrangements had to be made for the pauper to be taken in at the workhouse in Newchurch-in-Rossendale—this may however, have been due to overcrowding. [xiii] The local gentry helped out at times, such as in February 1780, when;

> "Le Gendre Starkie of Huntroyde, near Colne in Lancashire lately distributed with his own hands to the poor of Padiham, Symonstone, Higham and Hapton 30 pieces of good Knaresboro' linen made into shirts and shifts. The situation in that part of the country is rendered pitiable not only be the distress occasioned by the madness of the late mobs in destroying those inventions which were means of procuring them bread but also by sickness—the fever having raged in such a manner as may in some measure be compared to the destroying Angel in Egypt, for there is hardly a house where there is not one sick or dead" [xiv]

Also, December 1805, when *"At Padiham near Burnley on Thanksgiving Day Le Gendre Starkie of Huntroyde gave 1,336 poor persons in the neighbourhood of Padiham and Symondstone one pound of solid beef each, and to those who attended divine service each had one quart of ale added to regale themselves with".*

A Governor and Governess for the Padiham Workhouse was wanted and advertised for in the Blackburn Standard of April 1837 who must show themselves as being as *'Man and wife without children'* It was also stipulated that the applicants must understand weaving. The fear of ending ones days in the workhouse was upmost in the minds of every decent working class man or woman—even into living memory. To die in the Institution as it was called and without money meant being buried in an unmarked pauper's grave. The parish records at St Leonard's Church tells us that a number of people passed away at Padiham Workhouse, including Ellen Varley who died aged 83 years old and was buried 17 January 1853—likewise, William Pilling aged 87 was buried on 28 March 1853. The old workhouse was replaced by a new one on the Blackburn Road in 1832, which was known as *'Workhouse Farm'* (GR 7799-3341) and in fact it is marked on some maps as *'Workhouse Farm'*. The advertisement below appeared in the Blackburn Standard (28.9.1842) about a runaway inmate from Padiham Workhouse. The Governor, James Ashworth though, appears to be more concerned about the loss of the bed-gown, stockings and petticoat;

*"LOST
Strayed, or Runaway
A FEW DAYS AGO,
From the Workhouse at Padiham
A WOMAN, 70 years of age, belonging to the township of
Marsden, in the Burnley Union, in the County of Lancaster.
Had on when she left, a blue printed bed-gown, blue worsted
stockings, and a blue petticoat, with tied clogs. She also has a
mark on her right cheek, and her name is Ellen Bateson.
Whoever will give information to JAMES ASHWORTH, the
Governor of Padiham Workhouse, will be handsomely
rewarded"*[xv]

In the 1850s the Governor at the Workhouse was Joseph Ashworth, and Mary/ Ashworth who were probably related to the above mentioned James Ashworth. In 1837, the new Burnley Poor Law Union took over the old workhouse building in Royle Road Burnley, and the Blackburn Road Workhouse at Padiham—between them they catered for over 300 places. [xvi] It is likely that Workhouse Farm was in operation until the opening of the new Workhouse in Briercliffe Road Burnley in 1876, when the inmates from Padiham appear to have been moved there. Certainly, the 1881 census indicates that Padiham folk were in residence at the Briercliffe Road Workhouse. These included people like Richard Heap aged 58, a cotton weaver from Padiham, and 44 year old Jane Pilling, who was classed as an 'imbecile'. Sadly, the Blackburn Road Workhouse Farm is now a dilapidated building which it seems is unlikely to survive, even though it is a grade II listed building. It stands in the corner just beyond Shuttleworth Link Road and on the Blackburn Road. Burnley Borough Planning Services gives us this description of the former workhouse in its listings:

"Workhouse and associated farmhouse, probably early C19, altered, now (1984) mostly unoccupied. Sandstone rubble, stone slates roofs, the farmhouse having a ridge chimney and gabled chimneys, the barn attached to it gable copings with a finial at the north end, and the former workhouse range a single chimney cowl on the ridge. L shaped complex, the farmhouse gable to road on north-south axis with linking cart-sheds and barn in the same range, and the former workhouse range joined at right angles to the west side of the barn.

Single depth low two storey of random rubble in five bays in length, with a single storey lean to at west end, the partitioned 5th bay lofted with a flight of external steps to a raised doorway, and another door below. The remainder has rectangular windows, some with glazing bars, and others variously altered or damaged. Adjoining under the same roof at the east end is a projecting porch with wagon doors to the barn. The interior of the workhouse has been gutted, but a small fireplace remains at first floor level of the partitioned walls to the 4th and 5th bays. The barn at the south end of the east range is three bays and two higher storeys, its formerly colonnaded left window now filled in. Linking the left gable wall of the barn to the farmhouse is a small set back two storey cart-shed with open segmental arch spanning the full width and a window at first floor. The farmhouse is three bays and two storeys with two plain doorways, and three windows on each floor, mostly sashed but damaged except coupled four paned sashes in centre of ground floor. The rear has four 4-paned sashes on each floor. HISTORY: Unusual survival of parish workhouse pre-dating Poor Law Amendment Act of 1834".

By the 1800s, the population of Padiham had reached over 2000 souls, and was to continue rising to reach a peak in the next hundred years, all brought about by the Industrial Revolution. Baines' in his *'History, Directory and Gazetteer of Lancashire'* published in 1825, had this to say about the town.

"Padiham is a large populous village and chapelry, 3 ½ miles west of Burnley. The place is beautifully situated on an eminence rising from the North bank of the Calder. It is probably of Saxon origin, and has in its surrounding scenery at striking resemblance to Padua, the birthplace of Livy. The Church dedicated to St Leonard is the oldest place of worship of the new foundation in the extensive parish of Whalley. The living is a perpetual curacy in the patronage of Le Gendre Pierce Starkie of Huntroyde Esq., and the Rev. Sandford John Cyril Adamson is the incumbent. The Methodist and the Unitarians have each a chapel here. There is a free school of which Mr John Wilkinson is the master. Coal and stone abound in the district, and the Leeds and Liverpool Canal passes at a distance of little more than a mile. The cotton trade which prevails to a considerable extent, has occasioned a great influx of strangers, and the number of inhabitants in Padiham with its dependencies of Simonstone, Hapton and Higham must now amount to nearly 6,000"

This 'great influx of strangers' reached almost epidemic proportions by the mid 1840s, and something needed to be done about the chronic shortage of housing for the working population. To this end in November 1845 the Padiham Building Company was formed with a capital of £5,000 in 500 shares of £10 each. The company was formed in consequence of the extensive and pressing call for dwelling houses in the town, in particular for cottage type dwellings for the operatives and workers. The provisional list of shareholders in the company read like a book of who's who in Padiham at that time. William Waddington, timber merchant, William Wilding, cotton spinner, James and Henry Helm, cotton spinners, Christopher Lawson, the corn miller, James Whitaker, post master, John Dewhurst, gentleman, Richard Webster, farmer, Thomas Holt and George Thompson, surgeons, John Waddington, grocer and John Waddington builder, etc. The company went on to acquire land for the building of the new cottages 'within 150 to 200 yards of the quarries at Padiham'. Whether this company was dissolved after completing the cottages is not known, but there are no other known references to the Padiham Building Company after this date apart from a company of that name who constructed the Jubilee Mill in 1887.

The Methodists mentioned above in Baines Directory, had a long standing in Padiham. The introduction of Methodism into Padiham was due to a petty chapman named William Darney, colloquially known as *'Scotch Will'*. He visited Padiham about 1744. (Or 1746?) John Wesley, (1703-1791) also preached in the town. Wesley recorded in his journal on Monday 13 July 1761 *"About five I preached at Padiham, another place eminent for all manner of wickedness. The multitude of people obliged me to stand in the yard of the preaching house. Over against me, (at) a little distance, sat some of the most imprudent women I ever saw. Yet I am not sure that God did not reach their hearts, for they roar'd and would have blush'd if capable of shame".*

On another occasion, while preaching in Padiham in 1766, he noted that he was approached by a man with a long white beard—*"In all other respects, he was quite sensible"* Wesley said. *"But he told me with some concern, you can have no place in Heaven without a beard, therefore I beg you, let yours grow immediately".* [xvii] We shall hear more of the Wesley Methodists later, as well as the established church and other religions.

The population of Padiham at the time of the first census return in 1801 was put at 417 families living in 385 houses. [xviii] We have details of some of the residents of Padiham at this time. The postmaster was James Whittaker, the stop off point for the post coach was at the Starkie Arms. We know that the Starkie Arms was there in 1816 when landlord Mr Waddington died in that year. A Samuel Wilson also ran a coach between Preston and Burnley via Whalley and Padiham in the mid 1850s. There was Richard Hargreaves, a hat manufacturer, and Agnes Harris, milliner. The corn miller was Miles Heap, and Thomas Marcus was the village wheelwright. Sam Nutter was the village painter, whilst James Smith was the plumber and glazer, and William Taylor the local ironmonger. William Wilkinson was an earthenware dealer, and John and Thomas Wood were both sizers in the village. And thus the main needs of the little village were catered for. The Black Bull besides the Parish Church was being run by landlord Richard Webster, a grand old Padiham name. The Clock Face another old inn was somewhere close by, possibly on Mill Street, and this was run by Richard Clegg. The George and Dragon higher up Church Street was run by landlord James Holker, and the Hare and Hounds by Jeremiah Stephenson. The Swan near the George and Dragon was run by John Tunstall. The landlady of the Starkie Arms was Mary Waddington, and the landlady at the King's Arms was Ellen Anderton. The Shuttleworth Arms recalling the family at Gawthorpe Hall was kept by T. Robinson, this may have been an earlier name for the Hand and Shuttle? The shuttle is included in the crest of the Shuttleworths of Gawthorpe.

The village in 1825 had no less than three blacksmiths, William and John Emmot, no doubt related, and N. Waddington. But just nine years later there were just two blacksmiths, George Ainsworth and Elijah Waddington. By the beginnings of the 1850s though there were no less than five blacksmiths in the little village of Padiham. John Ainsworth had a smithy on Mill Street, which may have given its name to Smithy Gate, John Ashworth worked on North Street, Robert Pickles on Church Street, James Sagar on Burnley Road and Billy Waddington had his smithy on Bank Street. The smithy named James Sagar died in September 1852. The blacksmith was one of the most important craftsmen in rural England in any village. His skills varied from making swords and armour to the repair or assembly of all manner of agricultural and farming equipment.

Padiham folk it appears liked their meat, for there were also seven butchers in the town, and an abundance of shopkeepers, thirteen in total. Cotton manufacturers included James Bridge, H. & E. Helm, James Hoyle, John Hudson, and James Pollard. Cotton spinners were John Dugdale and Brother, H. & E. Helm and B. And R. Walmsley. In the Mannex Directory published in 1854, the growth of the township is confirmed—and it was commented that *"...Several new streets have been formed, and many mills and dwelling houses have been erected within the last few years, so that it now presents the appearance of a small town..."*

Crime was never a serious problem at Padiham, although of course there was the usual petty crime and misdemeanours. These might include Rachael Dearden, who in January 1809 was charged with stealing one silk handkerchief, the property of John Eastwood of Burnley and was sentenced to six months imprisonment. At the Lancaster Assizes in March 1810, John Law and Thomas Ryan were brought up on a charge of stealing from a dwelling house at Padiham. Fined one shilling and imprisoned for one month. The reports of more serious crimes came up every now and again. In August 1808, John Smith of Padiham, labourer was committed to Lancaster Castle by the Coroner on a charge of killing and slaying Benjamin Sagar at Padiham.

In June 1816, a young gentleman returning from Carr Hall was stopped on Padiham Heights by four footpads who seized the horses bridle and holding fast his leg demanded the man's name, watch and pocket book. The former of which he refused to give, but produced some loose silver, at length they released their position and allowed the man to go on his way. In the more petty cases we might record the case of three lads, William Hays, Thomas Blezard and John Holgate who were brought up before Le Gendre Nicholas Starkie on a charge of throwing stones at doors and windows in 1840. "The little fellows on promising to be better behaved in future were ordered to pay a shilling each and costs and were discharged". In 1895 William Marsden was brought before the courts at Burnley on a charge of attempted wife murder. It appears that Marsden of Shakespeare Street in the town struck his wife with a hatchet while she lay in bed. She managed to escape and fled to a neighbour's house where she collapsed in a pool of blood. Tragic accidents also find their way into newspaper reports of the day.

In October 1815, an old cottage at Padiham, which on account of its ruined state was being prepared by the mason to be taken down and it suddenly fell. A girl aged about seven year who happened to be playing in the building was taken out dead from the ruins. A mason and several other children narrowly escaped similar fate. In April 1817, Richard Cook of Higham near Padiham left his father's house in good health and a short time later was found dead in a brook near his house. The previous day had been fixed for the young man's marriage but for some reason it had been put off, and was then intended to take place the following Monday. It was thought that he went out for the purpose of washing himself in preparation for the occasion when he was overcome by a fit. There were two incidents involving children within days of each other at Padiham in September 1817. On the 9th inst, a child about four years old was killed by a chaise—the driver of which appeared to be free from blame, whilst on the 11th inst, a child just able to walk was killed by a cart at Padiham. The child had been placed in the care of an elder brother, who in pursuit of other amusement left the child in the road when the accident happened. In April 1819, an inquest was held at Padiham on the body of a man named Helme aged 32 who was found dead in a field in the neighbourhood. He was subject to having fits and was supposed to have died in one.

The obituary of George Cockshutt (Burnley Express 8 February 1908) gave some interesting recollections of old names around Padiham around this time, and a glimpse into the lifestyle and perhaps the stubbornness of the working classes. *"On Thursday last there was laid to rest in Padiham Church Cemetery, one of the more robust, vigorous and older type of Padiham inhabitants in the person of the late Mr George Cockshutt of Cobden Street. He was born June 24th 1831 in what was then commonly known as 'The Rake' immediately opposite the police station in Bank Street, in one of two houses that stood back from the road near the site upon which St Leonard Street now stands. The front portion of the house was flagged, and after the days washing was always scrupulously clean, but the place known as the back kitchen had a mud floor surface. When the landlord of the estate decided to have the property pulled down, to give place for Leonard Street, no magnate could have more highly prized his mansion or palace than did the mother and sister of the late Mr Cockshutt, who were there living alone, he having entered into married life.*

All means were tried, both by the agent of the estate and Mr Cockshutt to induce them to remove but so tenaciously did they cling to their old homestead that it was not until the actual operations had been commenced and the roof stripped that they could be convinced of the inevitable and prevailed upon to leave..."

By about 1800, the chief form of employment for the masses in the town appears to have been that of handloom weaving, and twenty years later the township officers estimated that there were 1241 looms between a population of 3060 families.[xix] By the time of the 1841 census, the first real census to be of any help to either the historian or the genealogist just over 50% of the population, or at least of those who gave details of their employment said that they were working in the cotton industry. This consisted of handloom weaving, spinning and block printing, which were soon to be susceptible to mechanisation through various inventions. The village that was once Padiham was now about to change forever, from a small rural country gathering of just a few houses into an industrial cotton mill town. Sweeping changes were about to happen to Padiham, but the town rose to greet the problems that were forthcoming, and welcomed the benefits of new changes. Thousands flooded in to the small town, as it offered employment in the new mills and factories, the census returns indicate people coming from Yorkshire, Northumberland and Staffordshire.

In fact the author's great great grandfather James Thoms came to Padiham around 1871, from Luton in Bedfordshire, settling in Calder Street, the family all finding employment in the local mills as operatives. The Church Cemetery opened in June 1852 on Blackburn Road. A Local Board was formed in 1873 from part of the townships of Padiham and Hapton, and powers to supply water and gas were granted by Acts in 1874 and in 1876. In 1894 the local board district was made a separate township, or civil parish, the remainder of Padiham, the rural part becoming a new township called North Town, part of which was added to Padiham in 1896. This new township was governed by an Urban District Council of fifteen members, chosen equally from five wards in the town, named Bank House, Clay Bank, Partridge Hill, Stockbridge and Green. The Parish Church of St Leonard was rebuilt in 1869, and the new railway brought more prosperity when it came in 1877—the future was now looking bright for the little town of Padiham.

The persons mentioned in Padiham's past are but a few of the thousands of people who must have lived and worked in Padiham at any one time in history, doubtless there were many tens of thousands of others not recorded, the ordinary smithy, the common agricultural labourers and workers, the pig and cattle breeders, the wheelwrights, alehouse keepers, the market traders, and the general labourers, who like many others before them in history, although not by choice, now remain anonymous and forgotten in Padiham's past.

CHAPTER TWO
Church, Chapel and Religious Matters.
St Leonard's Church Parish Church

The Parish Church of St Leonards stands proud upon a hill overlooking the town—the rustic browns and beiges of the fine stone tower can be seen from most vantage points throughout Padiham. The church we see today was built in 1869—but there is little doubt that the first place of worship here was the chantry chapel of St Leonard, which was founded around 1455 by John Marshall. John was a native of Padiham, and an official of Cardinal Langley (1363-1447)

In 1452 he obtained the King's license to purchase lands to support a chantry priest at the Church or Chapel at Padiham. As the lands were 'for the use of a chantry priest at the church or chapel of Padiham,' there must have already been some sort of chapel already in existence, and Marshall may have built it for his purpose.

The 15th-century chapel appears to have been rebuilt about the time of Henry VIII, but the nave having become ruinous was pulled down, and a new one built in 1766, 'with an attention to economy not very laudable among so opulent a body of parishioners.' The Public Advertiser of 8 March 1863 said 'A Brief has passed the Great Seal to the inhabitants of the parochial Chapel, or Township of Padiham on the Parish of Whalley in the County of Lancashire to rebuild their Chapel'. The old tower, however, was left standing, and was described in 1866 by Sir Stephen Glynne (1807-1874) a Conservative, landowner and historian of church architecture as 'of the local Perpendicular type, of ordinary character with battlement and pinnacles.' The original early 16th-century east window had also been retained, but everything else was 'modern and bad.' This building, however, had already been condemned and was pulled down the same year, when the foundation-stone of the present church was laid. The building, which was not finished till 1869, was of stone and consisted of a chancel with north and south aisles, north and south transepts, clear storied nave of five bays with north and south aisles, south porch, and tower at the west end of the south aisle. It is a good example of modern Gothic 15th-century style, with high-pitched slated roofs and embattled tower with lofty pinnacles. There are galleries in the transepts.[xx]

The clock in the tower was a present of the vicar, the Rev., S.J.C. Adamson in 1869. The timepiece was for over sixty years in the charge of 'Billy' Shaw, the Padiham watchmaker whose shop was on Church Street. From the date of the presentation the clock went well—its' 'ting tang' chime reminded Padiham folk of the passing of time, but after a few years it started going wrong. Good willed men with more public spirit and less clockmakers skills climbed the tower and tinkered with the mechanism and only made matters worse. One November night in 1883 the clock went twenty minutes wrong, and the following morning a delegation from the Urban District Council was on the doorstep at 'Billy' Shaw's shop offering to pay for the upkeep and maintenance of the clock.

It was in 1902 that 'Billy' and his brother made a set of Westminster chimes and fitted them to the clock so that the very same bells that were rung to summon folk to church also chimed the passing hours. Perhaps 'Billy's strangest callout to the clock was when an overtired pigeon came in to roost alighting on the hour hand on Burnley Road. So sleepy did the bird become that it failed to notice the minute hand creeping up, and it got caught between the two hands. Only 'Billy's' quick and timely intervention in turning back the hands saved the birds life.

The finest relict from the churches historic past is the old octagonal stone font donated to the church by John Paslew, the last abbot of Whalley Abbey in 1525 which has been preserved. Its sides are panelled and carved with emblems of the Passion, and the sacred monograms in shields. There was an alarming case of Sacrilege at the church in September 1826. John Lees, surgeon, Robert Pilling, weaver and John Lucas were charged by Colonel Clayton and John Hargreaves Esq. to be committed for further examination to the house of correction at Preston on the charge of being the persons who took on the 4th of September from the parish church at Padiham, a gown and a cassock the property of the Rev., S.J.C. Adamson and two surplices and a Bible the property of the Parishioners and defacing and destroying the register books. Later Lees was sentenced to 14 years transportation, Pilling was discharged, and Lucas it appears was never tried. In 1838 a *'small but neat organ built by Henry Lonsdale cabinet maker of Padiham was opened at the parish church by Mr Hacking of Bury and a select choir'* The Blackburn Standard informed us on 22 August 1838.

In August 1864 a meeting was held at the National School to consider the best means of raising funds for the new Chapel at Padiham. The Rev., H. A. Starkie presided and was supported by the Rev., W. Stocks the senior curate, L.G.N. Starkie (the patron of the living) The Rev., S.J. C. Adamson and a number of the manufacturers of the town. The following manufacturers volunteered to act as a committee to raising funds for the new church. Mr Thompson, John Waddington, John J. H. Sherburn, H. G. Booth together with the incumbent, the curator, churchwardens and Mr Le Gendre Starkie and Major Starkie. The present chapelry contained 9,000 inhabitants and only one small church capable of holding 63 persons.

The proposed new church was to be capable of holding 1,000, 600 free sittings, the inhabitants being extremely poor. The incumbent made an appeal to the parishioners and landowners to aid him in his work which was most generously responded to by Mr Le Gendre W. Starkie who gave the site £1,000 an endowment fund and £1,000 towards the building—leaving £2,000 still required towards the cost of the new church.

The last service in the old church was held in some style on 13 May 1866—the congregations were unusually large both in the morning and in the afternoon, but in the evening 'the aisles were literally thronged'. Worshippers gladly availed themselves of resting on the steps of the prayer desk and the pulpit, others finding it impossible to gain admittance were left at the doors of the church. The sermons in the mornings and afternoon were preached by the Rev., H. A. Starkie, the youngest son of the Starkie family of Huntroyde and late incumbent of Padiham, and the collections made at the end of the day totalled £70. The design for the new church was by the Burnley firm of William Waddington, although the actual architect would have been Angelo Waddington, who two decades previous had also designed the All Saint's Church Habergham. The workmen chosen to do the job include Cornelius Anderton, the building work, Mr J. Sherburn was to make most of the pews as well as the alter, and it was said that one of Mr Bertwistle's joiners, and loyal member of the church discreetly carved his name on one of the seats. Throughout the whole of the rebuilding programme the little chapel named 'All Saints' at the Church Cemetery on Blackburn Road was used for Holy Communion, and the National School on Mill Street used for other services.

The date 28 of June 1866 was chosen to lay the foundation stone for the new church—and what a day it was. The sun shone down, all the mills in town were laid idle, men women and children dressed all in their Sunday best as crowds lined the road from the church to Padiham Bridge—all waiting in anticipation for the great event. Flags and buntings flew from the church tower, the only remaining piece of the old building still to stand, spectators peered from roof tops and high windows to catch the best view of the forthcoming proceedings. Children's laughter and adult banter filled the air as the procession grew nearer. The first to arrive at the Arbories from whence the procession was to begin was the band of the 84th Rifle Volunteers, led by Major Dugdale.

Then came the scholars proudly dressed in Sunday attire—700 in all. Then came the police, the Padiham Britannia Band, the Free Gardeners' four abreast, the Joiners' Club, four abreast, as were the Oddfellows' Club and the Lodge of Foresters. Then came the Tradesmen and the Farmers, two abreast, followed by the Sunday Schools, Gentlemen and Friends. Next came the churchmen; The Rev., Perpetual Curate of Padiham, the Rev., Curate of Hapton, the Rev., and Rural Dean of Blackburn—and so it went on. Bringing up the rear was Captain Starkie with the bearer of Trowel and Mallet and Provincial Officers. The procession itself numbered two thousand people, and to count the crowd was almost impossible, the whole town appeared to have turned out for the occasion. After saying a few prayers, the vicar the Rev., J. Hamilton Fox moved forward to lay the stone in true Masonic fashion. The treasurer leaned forward with a bottle containing a book of prayer, a portrait of the late L.G.N. Starkie, coins of the Realm and copies of local newspapers. The inscription of the stone read;

"The corner stone of this church, dedicated to St Leonard, was re-laid by the patron, Le Gendre Nicholas Starkie, Esq., M.A. Captain 2 D.L.M., P.G.S.W.E.D.C.L. the 28th day of June, being the 29th anniversary of the Coronation of Queen Victoria".

And then—Captain Starkie was presented with a silver trowel and a mallet of polished mahogany with which to laid the foundation stone. The building work went on for two and a half years, there were doubts whether the parish could afford the spiralling costs, or whether they would be left with a church built without a tower. In the end the new church was opened on Thursday 8 January 1869. The bells, six in all when the church first opened rang out in jubilation from seven in the morning until eight at night. On the first Sunday after the opening there were so many parishioners turned up for the service, that the church, built to seat a thousand people had to turn many away. The evening service too was full to capacity. At the time of its opening the debt incurred by the church stood at £400, by the beginning of January 1872 this had shrunk to £175. A 'Christmas Tree' later that month raised another £145, which left just £30 to go and wipe out the debts altogether.

On Sunday 11 February 1872 the two curates, the Rev., Miles Greenwood and the Rev., William Claytor preached a service and the target was achieved. The following Saturday the bells once again pealed out in celebration of the happy event.

But the new church was not going to just sit back and rest on its laurels, the new church, the school and the three clergymen might have sufficed thirty years previous but now the was a large increase in the population. In the 1801 census returns there were then 3,394 souls in the district under St Leonard's, but by 1871 there were 8,816 which also included those in the new parish of Habergham Eves. In 1870 plan was put forward to build a new 'offshoot' church in the Partridge Hill district of Padiham—see that entry. Fund raising also went on for other causes—the grand bazaar of 1900 had as one of its objectives to raise money 'for the general improvement of the Church and Belfry, an addition of two bells and an introduction of the Cambridge Chimes at the Church of St Leonard'. In March 1886 there was a farewell sermon given to the Rev., J. A. M. Johnstone who had been vicar at the church for the previous seven and a half years. Later that year in August a handsome alms dish of polished brass was given to the church by Mrs Starkie of Huntroyde Hall. Colonel Le Gendre Nicholas Starkie was the patron of the church—the inscription on the dish read *"The gift of the Dowager Mrs Starkie to St Leonard's Church, Padiham on her 77th Birthday, 16 August 1886"*

There was another gift from the Starkies of Huntroyde in 1888 by way of a handsome marble tablet in memory of the late J. P. Chamberlain Starkie. The inscription on this read *"In Memory of John Peirce Chamberlain Starkie, second son of Le Gendre Nicholas Starkie of Huntroyde, and Anne, his wife. He was born 28 June 1830, educated at Eton and Cambridge where he graduated LL. B., 1857, LL, M., 1869, was a Justice of the Peace for the County of Lancashire and represented the north east division of that County in Parliament 1868 to 1880. In public affairs of his native country in which he took an active part his uprightness of conduct geniality and kindness of disposition gave him the respect and confidence of all and justly earned for him the title of a man without an enemy. He married 1861, Ann Charlotte, daughter of Harrington Hudson of Bessingby Hall county of York and died at Ashton Hall County of Lancaster 12 June 1888.*

Also in Memory of Anne Elizabeth only daughter of Le Gendre Nicholas Starkie and his wife. Married to the Rev., G.W. Horton vicar of Wellow County of Somerset where she died 29 January 1869 aged 37 years"

Interesting to note here that the daughter Anne Elizabeth gave her name in remembrance to her to the church on Hapton Road, Padiham. Another memorial to the Starkie family was unveiled on Sunday 9 August 1903, which bore the following inscription;

In Memory of Le Gendre Nicholas Starkie Esq., of Huntroyde, Lancashire, M.A., J.P. and D.L. Born January 10th 1828 died April 13th 1899. He was High Sheriff 1868, M.P. for the borough of Clitheroe 1853-56, and Colonel commanding the 5th Royal Lancashire Militia (Now the 3rd East Lancashire Regiment) 1882-1890. Provincial Grand Master of the Free Masons of Lancashire. He laid the foundation stone of this church 28th June 1866. On October 15th 1867 he married Jemima Monica Mildred, second daughter of Henry Tempest of Lostock Hall. By his express written request, dated May 16th 1893 he desired that a tablet of marble should be erected to his memory in the church of St Leonard's, Padiham on which no elaborate inscription or laudatory epitaph should be written but this text. "To everything there is a season, and a time to every purpose under Heaven, a time to be born, a time to die" This tablet was erected by his widow and his two sons, A.E. Le G. And P.C Le G. Starkie"

The place where these memorials to the Starkie family were situated in the church was to be known as, and still is the *'Starkie Chapel'*. The fundraising continued, the 1904 bazaar raised £2,000 towards the building of the new St Leonard's School, in 1918 there was the 'Big Gun Week' and so it went on. There are other memorials in the church, the Reredos in the Parish Church was erected in November 1926 in memory to those killed in WW1 in the town. The Chancel Screen made of carved oak was dedicated by the Lord Bishop of Blackburn on 7 November 1927. It was given by James Wilkinson, a Burnley Road butcher in memory of his father, and a James Wilkinson who had once been a church warden.

The screen was designed by Taylor and Young, Manchester architects. In March 1929, the organ which utilised a water powered blower was in a bad sate of repair, and it was advised that it would cost £410 to repair and modernise it including providing an electric blowing apparatus. The organ was 'reopened' on 16 July, when it was felt that it had 'a great range and depth in effects'. [xxi]

In more recent times there was a very serious setback at the church when in September 1972 a fire was discovered which destroyed part of the main roof and the organ. The blaze started in the vicar's vestry, and the organ which had a complete refurbishment only seven years previous at a cost of over £8,000, was intended to last another 100 years. Ironically, the organ pipes acted rather like a flue in the fire which was believed to have been started by children. Happily all the treasures of the church, the silver and priceless document were saved from destruction. It was Albert Young who raised the alarm, he had a grocers shop just across Church Street and on noticing smoke coming out of the roof phoned the fire brigade. A restoration fund was started almost immediately for £20,000 to repair the damage done in the fire. Four centuries of tradition proudly arose again and the people of Padiham rallied round—support came from Guy Le Gendre Starkie, patron of the living at the church, and from Lord Shuttleworth of Gawthorpe Hall whose family had been connected with the church for generations. It came from the ordinary workers, such as the employees at Main Gas, from individuals who held jumble sales to raise cash, from pensioners, from rich and poor alike. It was not only from Padiham folk, or even from just the Anglicans, but support came from many denominations and from folk throughout the land and beyond, as far afield as Japan, Australia and America. Today the church, known as 'Owd Peg' still stands proud upon the hill overlooking Padiham and she seems to dwell rather smugly as she gently ages upon her proud past, and 'Owd Peg' is sure to be looking forward to serving many more generations of Padiham folk. Good 'Owd Peg'!

St Matthew's Church
On Wednesday 23 November 1870 the still chill of a winter's day in Padiham was broken by the merry peal of the bells from St Leonard's Church—the timing was unusual, but it soon transpired that there was a reason for the pealing of the church bells.

It was all part of the welcome to the Bishop of the Diocese who on that day had come to open the 'Iron Church' at Padiham. This new church, a mission church to St Leonard's was built at a cost of £320 by public subscription and could seat about 200 worshipers. The site of the new church which was behind Garden Street was given by Sir J. Kay-Shuttleworth, Bart.

St Matthew's Sunday school outing at Padiham station

At three o'clock the Bishop made his appearance at the new church, and after delivering a short sermon the church was declared to be open. The new church was looked upon by the vicar of St Leonard's Mr Fox as one of his great achievement, here was a church with no pew rents. For he believed that the new church was for every man and every woman and child who had a soul to be saved. The new church was lined with stained and varnished deal, the same as was the commodious pews. There were four large windows on each side and a larger East window. By the time the building was finished there was only £160 left in debt to pay off. Bertwistle, the local joiners were once again employed to do the joinery work and the choir stalls and the lectern was constructed by them. 'The chancel was a delight, and the Communion Table was covered in crimson cloth...and the floor area scrumptiously carpeted.

The pulpit had previously been used at the Partridge Hill School, and the lighting at the new church was by 'gas stars' suspended from the ceiling. A collection on the day raised £43. There was a rather unusual occurrence at St Matthew's Church in 1903, perhaps unique, a strike by the choir. It appeared that on the Sunday evening, the choir simply did not turn up, because some 'difficulty' had arisen over the singing of the hymn each Sunday in Lent after the evening services. The Rev., J. Gornall, the curate-in-charge requested the choir to sing, and the choir owing to its length suggested that they sing it in parts. So, accordingly to these differences of opinion the choir did not turn up. Some arbitration did succeed, for by the following Sunday all but four of the choir turned up for evening song. St Matthew's Church was always known locally as the 'Iron Church' and was always meant to be temporary. In July 1919 it was announced that "Owning to parochial difficulties the St Matthew Mission Church had been closed". The final service at the church took place on Sunday 29 June 1919. In the morning the Vicar of Fence, the Rev., G. R. Cook was the preacher. A scholar's service was given in the afternoon, addressed by Mr D. M. Taylor of Whalley, and the evening song was conducted by the Vicar, the Rev., F. Wilkins. The final services aroused many memories among the congregation, many having been connected with the *'T' owd iron church'* since it was put up. It had weathered the storm for just short of fifty years, but its time had come to an end. The church authorities deemed that it was inadvisable to incur the large expenses that were required for repairs to the old church. The site of the old church was cleared by 1930, and today its place is taken by an open grassed space behind Garden Street and Berkeley Crescent.

St Anne and Elizabeth.
This lovely little former church stands at the start of the Hapton Road Padiham facing The Green. The foundation stone for this then new church was laid on 16 July 1874 on land given by Major Starkie, and the whole cost of the structure was defrayed by the Starkie family. The idea of this edifice was first thought of by Le Gendre Nicolas Starkie, and it was he who gave £2,000 towards its erection, £1,000 for the building and £1,000 towards the endowment. The new church was to be dedicated to St Anne and St Elizabeth in memory of the only daughter of Le Gendre Nicholas Starkie, she had died 29 January 1869. The style of the church was to be Gothic and to a design of Stevens and Robinson of Derby.

The schools were to be built by subscription and to a design by John Thompson. The stones of the new church were laid with Masonic honours—a Freemasons Lodge was opened about one o'clock by Lieutenant Colonel Dugdale, assisted by Mr Alexander of the Silent Temple Lodge, and Mr Holden of one of the Accrington Lodges. The procession left the Starkie Arms at half past one headed by a band of the 5th R.L. Militia, and after the Freemasons came the children. The pomp and ceremony of the day was all gone through in typical Masonic style before the foundation stone was finally laid over a bottle containing papers and coins of the realm. The Rev., H. A. Starkie presented his brother Major Starkie with a mallet and the foundation stone was checked for level and square before completing the occasion. Songs were sung, and then they all moved off to the new school where a similar stone laying ceremony was performed this time by Edmund Arthur Le Gendre Nicholas Starkie, son of Major Starkie. The Major then addressed the crowd before adjourning for lunch at the school followed by a banquet at the Starkie Arms. It was however to be 8 January 1881 before the church was finally dedicated, and it was February 1889 before a new organ was dedicated. St Anne and St Elizabeth Church served the community for 130 years before dwindling numbers of worshipers caused its demise. In October 2003 the church was closed down marking the end of an era which many still recall. In the following year in February it was announced that a bid of over £50,000 had been put in for the old church, and in May 2004 an application by Peter David Broadley was put before the Burnley Planning Offices to convert the church into dwellings and garages. In 2006 the church was advertised for sale as 'The Priory' but at the time of writing its future appears to be uncertain.

NON-CONFORMISTS
Assemblies of God, Ightenhill Street
Also known as Pentecostals worshipped in what was thought to have been an old foundry which was converted to religious use around 1807 on Ightenhill Street and used until the late 1970s. They vacated the place fully in 1980, when they may have amalgamated with the Queensgate Pentecostal Church at Burnley?.

Burnley Road Baptist Chapel
The Baptist faith in Padiham has a long and proud history—it began in 1840 at a meeting place in Moor Lane, and a room in Dove Street, and Adamson Street. The history of the Baptist movement was given in an excellent article in the Burnley Express on 1 June 1940, to mark the centenary of the Baptist movement in Padiham as follows:

"The pioneers were the Sabden Baptists, and soon there were 'stations' at Red Rock, Simonstone as well as Padiham by 1841. These were probably founded by the Sabden members living in those districts, or by individual residents keen to spread the word and teaching beyond their own village. The latter appears to have been the case in Padiham, as the following resolution from the Sabden Baptist minute books seems to indicate.

> *"That we hereby record our hearty gratitude to the Divine head of the Church for having put into our heart of our dear brother, George Foster, to build a house for the worship of God at Padiham, and a room for the instruction of the young both on the Sabbath and during the week..."*

The entry continued. *"In 1840, a few members of the Baptist Chapel in Sabden took a room in Moor Lane in which a Sabbath School was commenced and the public worship of God conducted".*

At the end of two years it was found that their efforts had been so far blessed as to require a larger place. Meetings were held on the subject and after due consideration it was found desirable to enlarge our borders and a wish was manifest to build. Mr Foster J.P. of Sabden then undertook the management of the affair and the result was the erection at his own expense. The (Burnley Road) was chapel was commenced in November 1844 and completed at the beginning of October 1846. It was designed by Mr J.T. Emmett, the dimensions were 50 feet by 24 feet. On Thursday 8 October 1846 this chapel was opened for worship. On the following Lord's Day hundreds were unable to gain admittance, collections were made for the British Day Schools and £60 was raised. Within a few months of the opening the first resident pastor, Mr Fisher was appointed, but this office was terminated on his death in November 1848. In 1849, the Rev., J.H. Wood recently returned from Jamaica became minister.

At a church meeting in August 1849 it was resolved that in consequence of the low state of the church funds collections should be made once a month instead of as previously once a quarter. Until the baptistery was erected in the schoolroom in 1851 or 1852 those wishing to be baptised had to go to the Sabden Chapel or to Burnley and Sion Chapel there—or to the old Watergate in the River Calder at Padiham Bridge. From its foundation to its dismissal in 1852, the Padiham Church was a branch, or mission of Sabden Church. The first person baptised by the independent church was Abraham Broughton. In 1858, the chapel was enlarged at the expense of Mr George Foster, and further costs were met by friends, the debt being cleared at once. From 1857 to 1865 the Rev., Richard Brown was minister, and the month following his departure the Rev., George Hinton Griffin was appointed. In June 1866, the Rev., Thomas Ryder became minister and remained for four years. His successor was the Rev., B. May who served until 1877. The Rev., H.C. Bailey began in 1878 and concluded in 1881. In 1883 the Rev., W.M Thomas was elected and stayed for five years and retired through ill health. Burnley Road was without pastor from Mr Thomas's resignation until 1893, when the Rev., D. Muxworthy was accepted. His influence was felt immediately, and he seemed to have been a man with great ideas, as well as an ability to get things done. In 1895, members of another 'off-shoot' church began holding services in the Temperance Hall in Ightenhill Street, and later decided to build Horeb Church on Victoria Road. Burnley Road Baptist was once again without a minister from 1895 until 1897 when the Rev., J.S. Langley was appointed. This was the beginning of the longest ministry at Burnley Road, and right from the start the church benefited from Mr Langley's enthusiasm. In 1898 the church joined the Burnley and District Baptist Union. In 1901 it was decided to close the day schools and through a bazaar in 1905 the debt was cleared off. One aspect of Mr Langley's work was the training of young men for pulpit work, and a local preacher's class was held, and three Mr D.M. Patterson, Mr J.C. Lee and Mr Joseph Cardwell became ministers. To mark the tenth anniversary of Mr Langley's ministry in 1907 it was decided to beautify and renovate the church and the work was completed in 1908, the pulpit was also remodelled. In 1910 great efforts were being made to clear off the debt on the shop premises built in 1890 attached to the building, and the members showed their loyalty by hard work and self-denial. As a result £1,000 was raised. Mr Langley's ministry ended in 1922 after 25 years service.

He was a great man who undertook great work and was held in high esteem as a true Christian gentleman. Until his death some years after the close of his ministry he took a keen interest in the church and his kind thoughts and Christian teaching would always be remembered by those who knew him. From October 1925 to January 1929 the Rev., Ralph Holme was minister, and the Rev., W. J. McBride who became pastor in December 1934 left in December 1939 to serve as a chaplain with the Forces". [xxii]

Thus concluded a general history of the Baptist Church at Padiham up to 1940—we can now add further information on the chapel. The Burnley Road Baptist Chapel had a new school attached to it on the right hand side, erected in 1890 to hold 120 pupils—it was at this time the shops in front of the chapel, now occupied by Bertwistles' Bakery and other were also added. Today only part of these schools exist, the chapel itself being demolished in 1971, but the archway which gave access to the chapel also still exists. Although the chapel and school were erected by George Foster J.P. of Whin House Sabden, it still belonged to him although he let the trustees of the chapel and school use the buildings free of charge. All this changed in July 1880, when the ownership of the buildings was transferred to the trustees for full use of the Baptist Church and denomination. Only one condition was attached to the transfer and that was "That the church and congregation erect or purchase a house for use of the minister". To this end a house on Albert Street was purchased off Mr J. Thompson for the sum of £410. During WW1, in February 1915 a 'Tipperary Room' was opened at the Burnley Road Baptist School, in a room kindly lent by the officials there. Among members of the Committee were Hon., Rachel Kay-Shuttleworth, Mrs Noble, Mrs Grant Jones and Mrs Worswick. "The room was tastefully decorated in patriotic colours and was for use of soldiers and sailors dependants. There will be stationary provided for dependants to write to their husbands or sons who are in the forces". In August 1968 it was reported that the officials of the Burnley Road Baptist Chapel were looking into acquiring the old Pendle Street Baptist Chapel for their own use as the Burnley Road Chapel had too many steps for the elderly. In November 1969 they moved into the old Pendle Street premises, and two years later Burnley Road Baptist Chapel was demolished.

Congregationalism
A congregational place of worship was opened on 29 July 1880 in Webster's Buildings facing Burnley Road and Moor lane in a room being rented at £20 a year from John and Paul Webster. The services were previously held in a cottage at Stone Moor Bottom, and the first service was preached at the Assembly Hall on 14 March 1880 by the Rev., G. J. Knox. But the cottage at Stone Moor Bottom proved to be totally inadequate and there was a need to look for larger premises. [xxiii] The foundation stone for a new Congregational Mission room was laid on 27 May 1882 by Mrs Weston of Burnley. The cost of the new building was expected to be £550 and would cater for between 200 and 300 worshippers. The congregation then was around 90, and until the new building was up they would worship in the Assembly Rooms. The room at Webster's Buildings had to be vacated on 1 February 1883, in order to make way for the Conservative Club who had effectively been kicked out of their premises on Mill Street by the Local Board. Later the Congregationalists moved to the north side of Guy Street into a row of cottages which later became known as Bethel Independent School Chapel. Later still this became the Salvation Army Hall after they took up residence in 1890, and remained as such until it was demolished in or around the 1940s. All traces of these old cottages and the school have now disappeared, replaced by a steep grassed embankment. The Congregationalists always remained a minor sect in Padiham, although the full title of the Horeb Chapel on Victoria Road was 'The Horeb Union Free Congregational Chapel'

Cross Bank, Wesley Street
Many Padiham folk will still miss Cross Bank Chapel, more so the school for those who went there. The Chapel which fronted Wesley Street was only demolished in 1991. The chapel dated from 8 September 1871 when the Rev., W. O. Simpson preached the opening sermons. On the first Sunday after opening the Rev., John Jeffreys of Manchester preached both in the morning and evening. The new building could accommodate 500 to 600 and had been built and fitted up at a cost of £1,000, only £300 of which was outstanding as a debt. By 1891 the chapel had been outgrown by its worshippers, and there was a need for a new and larger chapel. In late June 1891 the memorial stones for a new chapel were laid to be built at a cost of around £3,200 which would cater for 750 persons.

The proceedings began with the children of the district arriving at the chapel where the Rev., A. White was waiting. There was a large gathering including the Rev., C. W. Cook, the Rev., Thomas Brackenbury, Rev., I. Pollitt Messrs F. Helm, W. Waddington, A. Waddington, J. Gregson, J. Blezard, J. R. Smith and others. Mr John Dean then presented Mr Helm with a mallet and a handsome trowel which bore the following inscription.

"Presented to Mr F. Helm by the trustees on laying a memorial stone in the Wesley Chapel, Cross Bank Padiham June29 1891"

The new building was to be built to a design by W. Waddington and Sons of Burnley, and was in the Italian style. The main body of the chapel was to be 64 feet long by 43 feet wide with a central vestibule which opened right and left to give access to stairs and the gallery. The far end of the building was provided with a band room, choir vestry and ministers vestry, over which was arranged the organ chamber and orchestra. All the internal woodwork was of pitch pine and the ceilings panelled with plaster, and the windows relieved with margins of lead and colour. The new chapel prospered, and in August 1922 it was time to honour two past members of the congregation by unveiling portraits of them at the chapel. The framed portraits were to honour the late Mr John Dodgeon, who was a lifelong worker for the Cross Bank School.

Cross Bank Chapel

In January 1908 a presentation was made to Dodgeon for completing 50 years service with the Sunday School there. Miss Emma Dodgeon his sister had died in September 1920, she too was a lifelong supporter of the Cross Bank Chapel. However, by the 1970s the membership of all three Methodist Chapels in Padiham was on the decline, and it was decided to amalgamate the chapels into one and thus Trinity Chapel became the new name for Cross Bank. But even that was not to last, in 1991 Cross Bank Chapel was demolished, and the Padiham Methodists had to find other headquarters. The Minister the Rev. Michael Sparrow and his congregation were able to secure the building belonging to the former Unity Working Men's Club on Ribble Street. The new 'church' was dedicated in March 1992, when a 'time capsule' that was buried in the foundations stones of Cross Bank Chapel was also put on display.

In November 2009 the Methodists moved out of Ribble Street and joined up with Ightenhill Methodists and together renamed Padiham Road Methodist Church.

Ebenezer Chapel, Hill Street
This neat little former chapel still exists on the corner of Hill Street and Thompson Street and dates from the laying of the foundation stone in 1883. Today the little chapel is used as a children's nursery, but in the past it was also used as an ambulance station. The laying of the foundation stone was marked by a large presence that had first assembled at the Oddfellow's Hall, from whence they marched to the site of the new chapel, where another large gathering of people had already assembled. The stone laying ceremony was begun by the singing of a hymn given out by the Rev., G.E. Lloyd of Brierfield. Alderman Whitaker of Burnley then laid the first of the memorial stones, and Mr John Baldwin laid the second, with the third being laid by Mrs J. Hindle. Each of those who laid the stones was presented with a beautifully bound book on the history of the Primitive Methodist connexion. The ceremony then concluded with the singing of hymns before making its way back to the Oddfellow's Hall—here tea provided for nearly 300 persons. The new chapel was to consist of one large room and seven classrooms with seating for teaching and worship for about 450 persons. It was to measure 19 yards by 15 yards and substantially built of local stone. The masons work was to be carried out by Mr Anderson of Padiham, the joiners work by Robert Brown of Burnley, plastering and paintwork by Mr Shuttleworth of Burnley, the slating was done by Mr Stanworth of Burnley. The chapel was built to a design of Mr T. Dean of Burnley. The chapel survived as such until April 1935 when it became a St John's Ambulance Station, the keys to the building were handed over by the Padiham Ambulance Queen Miss Monica Wynne. In 1995 it became 'Kinderbear' nursery which it still is at the time of writing in 2015.

Hall Hill Chapel and the Methodists
Padiham Methodists go back a long way and first appeared in the town in 1744 thanks to the efforts of a man named William Darney, also known as 'Scotch Will'. The population of Padiham at this time was barely 1,000 souls, but enough to make 'Scotch Will' want to save them all. Darney, like the movements founder John Wesley preferred preaching in the open air.

However on the first occasion he was driven away by a mob led by the parish clergy, who by all accounts had been drinking in a local alehouse before the arrival of 'Scotch Will'. His subsequent visits continued to attract opposition, but the Methodist movement was eventually established, and they first met at the house of John Hunter in the year 1748 in an old thatched cottage that used to stand where the old Unitarian Chapel stood at one time on West Street. The members met here and preached services until the first of the Methodist Chapel was built in 1758, opening in November that year at the top of the town on what was known as Old Chapel Street, now West Street. This is the section of highway between the Hare and Hounds and Arbory Drive. The chapel was on the Haworth Round, and the first preacher was the Rev., William Grimshaw, the vicar of Haworth in Yorkshire, a place now more famed for the Bronte' sisters. The new chapel could accommodate 230 persons and was built at a cost of £186. Segregation was strict—there were two entrances to the chapel, the females going in at one door and the males going in at the other. The pulpit was fixed between the two doors and served to separate the two sexes, males on one side, and females on the other.

There was an interesting tale told of the time when this chapel was being constructed. The builder was a man named Whitehead, a member of the society, and his fellow worshipers arranged for him to make two cottages into one and make it into the preaching room for the society. Thus he began, and to start off he built the outside walls first, whenever someone asked him why he was doing it that way, he replied that he wanted to get the outside walls up and the roof on before the onset of the winter weather. In this way the building was erected and the licence got before anyone knew its purpose. Sometime later a dwelling house was built for the living quarters of the preacher, and at the back was a stable for the preacher's horse, which was reached by a passage from the Chapel. The room over the stable was the sleeping quarters for the preacher, the heat from the horse's body providing a sort of central heating for the bedroom. Worship continued at this small chapel for 21 years until the year 1779, when it became too small for the growing congregation. It was decided to go forward and construct a new chapel to be named Hall Hill. The foundation stone of this chapel was laid on 1 October 1778. During the construction of the new chapel a dispute arose between the trustees and a gentleman named J. Willion over a certain boundary line between his property and the land on which the new chapel was being built.

As the masons worked during the day the walls were pulled down during the night, many weeks went by with no progress being made at all on the new building. At last the trustees appointed a night watchman until the chapel was completed and the dispute settled. The old cottage fell into disuse. The first sermon was preached at the new Hall Hill chapel by none other than John Wesley himself on the Tuesday afternoon of 13 April 1779. Wesley recorded the following in his journal *"I preached at nine to a crowded audience in the new house at Bacup, at one in the shell of the new house at Padiham"*. The new chapel was still without doors or windows, and even a roof! It was some time after Wesley's sermon that the place opened for public worship. It is recorded that John Wesley visited Padiham six times;

20 May 1757. *"Preached at Craggs Fold near Padiham at eight in the morning to a large and wild congregation"*.
13 July 1761. *"About five I preached at Padiham, a place eminent for all manner of wickedness"*.
29 April 1776. *"I preached at Padiham in a broad street to a huge congregation"*
29 July 1776. *"I preached in the evening near the preaching-house at Padiham"*
13 April 1779. When he preached in the new shell of the chapel at Hall Hill, he also recorded *"I preached at Padiham, Burnley, Southfield (Nelson) and Colne"*

The cost of building the new chapel at Hall Hill was put at £419-12-. There was a gallery round on three sides seating 246 persons, the main body of the chapel was fitted with forms without backs and seated 334—making a total seating capacity of 580 persons. The year 1798 saw the completion of two cottages on the east side of the chapel built at a cost of £171. One of these old cottages may have become the home of *'Owd Mary Monk'* who had a cottage on Old Chapel Street on the left hand side going towards Whalley Road. She was Mary Whitehead before her marriage, and was born at Padiham around 1823. She married John Monk, a Great Harwood lad at St Leonard's in 1844. John was a contractor, and the couple lived at the old cottage for many years, and Mary bore John a number of children.

The eldest was Whitehead Monk, named after his mother's surname, which was quite common at this time, then came George, and then the daughter Nancy who married William Shaw. Padiham was in the Haworth Circuit from 1747 until 1775, and then it was in the Colne Circuit from 1776 until 1809, and then the Burnley Circuit until 1861 when it became a Circuit of its own. By 1845 the congregation had outgrown the chapel at Hall Hill, and in November that year a scheme was started to built a new chapel. The foundation stone for the new Chapel on Church Street was laid 1 January 1846 by William Hopwood of Burnley. The ministers, friends, trustees and children of the Wesleyan Methodist Sunday School attended the appointed place at two o'clock and totalled in number 500 for the laying of the first stone. Mr Hopwood was presented with a very elegant silver trowel to lay the first stone. Several hymns were then sung and excellent sermons given by the ministers, after which they retired to the new school-room to partake in tea. A collection was made towards the cost of the new building which amounted to £30. The total cost of this fine building including the land was put at £3,038-6-7 ½ the workmen erecting the chapel got the following wages. Joiners and masons 21 shillings per week, labourers 15 shillings per week. The working week being 62 hours. The new chapel opened for public worship on Friday 30 July 1847 with two services being held in the afternoon and evening. The debt remaining after the chapel was opened was £1,150 and was not cleared until the year 1868. The first marriage at this new chapel was that of Mr Nicholas Thompson and Miss Moorhouse, both of Padiham on Saturday 15 1849— the happy couple were presented with a handsome Bible. Extensive alterations were carried out in 1882 mainly to the front of the chapel. [xxiv]

The Hall Hill site which was sold off after the new chapel was built was bought back for use as a Mission and was eventually demolished in 1955. The only other incident here was in December 1927 when part of the roof collapsed at the Hall Hill Chapel causing a great deal of damage. Once again the congregation rallied around and the repairs were carried out. No further repairs or alterations were needed at either Hall Hill or the Church Street Chapel until 1945 when an inspection of the roof at the latter revealed that the main beam was about to give way, and the whole roof was in danger of collapsing. The trustees were supported in the cause for these repairs which cost over £200.

With declining membership the Church Street Chapel was closed down in 1969, and was eventually demolished in 1972. Today new housing known as the 'Mews' has taken its place—the old burial ground at the Hall Hill Chapel was landscaped in 1952, some of the headstones can still be seen against the walls. [xxv]

Horeb Chapel, Victoria Road
This chapel still exists, although no longer used for the purpose for which it was built. It is now used as a day nursery, but it was also used as the Employment Exchange, renamed Jobcentre in the not too distant past. The closure of the old chapel as a Jobcentre was announced in October 1998, when all the 260 clients on the books would have to go to places like Burnley, Accrington, Nelson and Clitheroe. However a free telephone was installed in Padiham library to help claimants to contact other Jobcentres. It could also be said that Horeb was built out of anger. The Rev., Daniel Muxworthy was a former minister from September 1893 with the Burnley Road Baptist Chapel—he was a popular minister and during his first couple of years attracted a large number of new members who were baptised at the Chapel as well as a number of former members who chose to come back. Trouble appears to have started when it was decided that the Chapel should take more interest in the workings of the school known as the British School attached to the Baptist Chapel. Although housed within the range of the Baptist Chapel buildings, the school had been presented to the trustees in July 1880, along with the Chapel itself by George Foster of Sabden. It was George Foster who built the Baptist Chapel and schools in the first place at his own expense, but gave the trustees full use of them, until he passed ownership over to them in 1880. However, relationships between the school and the Chapel had been a source irritation for a number of years. The British School was in fact run as a separate establishment and catered for children of all denominations. The grants from the Department of Education hardly covered the teacher's wages, and practically nothing went towards the expenses incurred towards fuel bills and other expenses. Mr Muxworthy had been critical of these affairs in the past, he even went as far as accusing those in charge of misappropriation of the Chapel funds in favour of those for the school. Letters of claims and counterclaims appeared on the local newspapers, and the deacons in charge of the school considered suing Muxworthy for slander.

To avoid scenes of a highly scandalous nature, it was decided to call in the Lancashire and Cheshire Baptist Association to act in arbitration—for two months they checked over the accounts and questioned those involved in the running of the school and the bookkeeping. At a meeting in April the arbitration body declared that there was no case to answer and completely exonerated those in charge of the school funds. There was uproar, Muxworthy tried to stand and make a statement but was told to sit. On the advice of the police, who were there at Muxworthy's request, the hearing was adjourned but the arguments continued outside. Muxworthy and the headmaster duly resigned, although the headmaster, Mr Wallington was later reinstated.

A large body of the Baptist members chose to leave with Mr Muxworthy and a few days later gathered at the Gospel Temperance Hall on Ightenhill Street to hear him preach to them. It was decided to form a 'breakaway' church with its own Sunday school and choir, and their numbers soon swelled to well over two hundred. The Temperance Chapel was too small for these numbers and it was decided to build their own chapel. Land was purchased totalling three hundred square yards off Sir Ughtred Kay-Shuttleworth and the Gawthorpe Estate on the corner of Shakespeare Street and Victoria Road for the new chapel. The cost of the land and the chapel was about £2,000, and the new chapel was to be built to a design of Virgil Anderton. The corner stones of this new chapel were laid on 19 October 1895. The new building was to consist of one large room and eight smaller rooms to be used as classrooms. It was to be built of best Yorkshire points, and would accommodate 750 persons. Benjamin Naylor was responsible for the mason work, Messrs Waddington and Bertwistle did the joinery work, the slating was done by Foster and Sons and the plastering by James Nutter. The new chapel was opened the following March, the opening ceremony being performed by Miss Hitchon of Clayton Manor, Wilpshire. All the members of the congregation formed at the Temperance Hall, and headed by the Volunteer Band and followed by Mr Muxworthy and others marched to the new chapel in good style. The new Chapel was to be known as Horeb Union Chapel, and was open to Baptists and others from various denominations. From the end of WW2 the former Horeb Chapel was used as the Employment Exchange—in 1999 a proposal was put forward by Ben Leaver to use the old chapel as a childrens day nursery, a proposal accepted by Burnley Council.

Kingdom Hall, Bank Street/Higham Street
This chapel still exists on Higham Street, and was built in 1992 and remarkably it was built over two weekends employing literally hundreds of Jehovah's Witnesses using a method called 'quick build' a system they developed for themselves, the system started with pioneering two day building programs in America and Canada before being extended to three days and six day program to suit local conditions. The first such hall in Europe was built in Northampton in 1983, and since that time has been used by the church throughout the world. Prior to this the congregation of Jehovah Witnesses held their meetings at Padiham at a 110 seat hall in Bank Street until they acquired the new site in June 1991. These premises on Bank Street used to be the former Crown Hotel. The new Kingdom Hall had a capacity of over double the old hall and could seat 240 persons. We might record here that Padiham also had a Spiritualist Church which was run single-handed by Mrs Jean Bindoff until 2003 when it was forced to close due to her illness. The 'church' was on Mill Street and later became a jazz venue and wine bar named the Empire.

Mount Zion Chapel, Pendle Street
In 1866 an 'off-shoot' Baptist church, now known as Mount Zion was founded by a breakaway group from the Burnley Road Baptists. The members first worshipped the Assembly Rooms in Guy Street before moving to Morley Street in 1870, into a tinner's shop where the old Unity WM Men's club used to stand. *'Three sermons were preached to celebrate the opening, in the morning and evening by Mr Vasey of the Baptist College, and in the afternoon by the Rev., G.W. Oldring of Burnley. Collections were made to defray the costs of fitting up the room'.*
By 1876 land had been purchased to build a brand new chapel on Pendle Street. At half past two on 10 August 1876 the laying of the corner stone for the new chapel took place performed by G. Shephard of Bacup. The architect for the new building was Mr Bertwistle, it was to be a plain substantial building and built to a cost of about £1000 of which the friends had already donated £200. The building was 63 feet 6 inches long by 41 feet 6 inches, and contained two small vestries. The church members at this time numbered thirty. At the close a public tea was provided at the Assembly Rooms, followed by a public meeting at the same place, when the Rev., J. Harvey was called to the chair.

Addresses were also given by Revs., J. Lee senior, A. Pickles, D. Geyrge of Lumb, E. Pickles, J.T. Marshall and others. *'The chapel choir gave select pieces, and Mr Graham presided on the harmonium. The proceedings of the day were of a most interesting character'*

In July the following year the building was completed at the new Baptist Chapel and school. Time to celebrate; firstly a public tea party was provided in the schoolrooms, when about 250 sat down to all the good things provided. After tea a public meeting was held in the same place—the chair being occupied by Councillor Altham of Burnley. The following gentlemen also addressed the meeting, Councillor Whittaker of Burnley, Rev., A. Pickles of Rochdale Rev., J. Naylor of Oswaldtwistle, Rev., J. Higham of Padiham, Mr B. Hargreaves of Burnley, and Mr Fenwick of Accrington. The choir gave selected pieces, and collections amounted to £39. 3s. 3 ½ d. A report went on to state that the chapel and school were substantial buildings and capable of holding about 500 persons. It was pewed in the centre, and had a platform, pulpit and a baptistery and two vestries. It was situated in the midst of a rapidly growing population, and was erected at a cost of about £1,100, towards which the friends had raised in subscriptions £406. Mr Jonas Bridge was the contractor for the masons work and the joiners work was by Mr Richard Bertwistle, the plasterer, Mr William Foster, and the plumbing and glazing was by Mr Job Pollard. The larger addition at one end of the building was built in 1892 as stated on the datestone, which also recalls some names connected with the past.

The Pendle Street Chapel prospered until 1948, when it was sold on to the Co-operative Society, and its members reverted back to the Burnley Road Chapel. In 1968 church officials at the Burnley Road Chapel realised that the premises needed drastic alterations—there was also a possibility that the chapel might have to be demolished to make way for a new road. The Baptist Minister, the Rev., G.W. Rasmussen heard that the Co-op might be selling the former Mount Zion Building on Pendle Street which they had been using as a store and bakery. He asked the council if they would like to buy the Burnley Road Chapel, and they agreed enabling them to purchase the Pendle Street Chapel. What followed was a lot of hard work. First a huge fridge used for storing frozen meat had to be dismantled, and the building was sandblasted and pointed.

Parts of the chapel had to be plastered, new stairways installed and new toilets, and a good lick of paint all round finished off the job which all in all took over a year to complete. For some of its members, it was like returning home being former members of Mount Zion, but from then on the chapel would be known as Padiham Baptist Chapel (Pendle Street) The main hall would have chairs, not pews so that they could be removed for sales and concerts, and could seat about 200 people. Central heating installed in the Burnley Road Chapel three years previous was removed and taken to be refitted at Pendle Street. A marble plaque commemorating church members who fell in WW1 which was moved in 1948 to Burnley Road from Mount Zion was returned to its original place at Pendle Street. Today, the Pendle Street Chapel still serves for worship of the Baptist faith.

Salvation Army
Almost everyone knows that the Salvation Army was founded by General William Booth. At first it was called the Volunteer Army, but this was changed in 1878 to the Salvation Army when one of Booth's valued supporters George Railton objected to being called a 'volunteer' and declared 'I am a regular or nothing'. It may come as some surprise then that the Salvation Army was established in Padiham just four years later. The local newspaper of 9 December 1882 gave this report on the matter for its readers, which appears to have been more like a mini invasion;
"The Salvation Army. This organisation of revivalists under the direction of General Booth commenced operations in Padiham on Sunday last, a captain and a lieutenant arriving on Saturday. They sang into town about ten o'clock assisted by about ten of their soldiers and others, marching on to the fairground where upwards of 1,000 of those requiring their services were gathered expecting their arrival. Here they sang and prayed and delivered short addresses, and then marched through the town singing and proceeded to their barracks, the Assembly Rooms which had been taken by General Booth for 12 months to carry on the work of his Christian Army It is a long time since Padiham was so thoroughly roused, for thousands were in the street during the procession. In the Assembly Rooms there were during the day, large gathering of the rougher elements of the town, and in the afternoon they appeared at one time to claim the direction of the proceedings.

During the day three services were conducted in the room, which were continued on Monday evening, assistance being furnished again from Burnley. Again the rougher element were present, and demonstrative, and one young man got into the hands of the police. The meetings so far have been under the direction of the Captain and Lieutenant sent to Padiham, and their addresses have been pointed, earnest, and such that might be delivered by any earnest Christian evangelist addressing similar audiences..."

The 'Army' continued for a number of years at the Assembly Rooms until May 1890 when General Booth purchased the (Bethel) Independent Gospel Chapel on the north side of Guy Street for his use. On the opening of the new premises a public tea-party was held when about 250 sat down. In the evening there was a grand procession led by two bands formed to receive Major Kyle, the new district officer for the Preston Division. He was accompanied by Ensign Batteridge of the junior soldiers, War Major Brunner and others from Burnley, Nelson and neighbourhood. There were also large meetings the following day, and on the Monday at three o'clock, Major Kyle conducted a holiness meeting after which around 100 officers and friends sat down to tea. After the tea about 50 officers from Preston had a procession through town headed by a brass band from Burnley. By 1911 the Salvation Army had secured premises on Mill Street according to a directory, although there is some other evidence which points to the fact that the Salvation Army continued to use the Gospel Chapel until it was demolished in the 1940s.

Temperance Mission Hall, Guy Street
This hall was erected in 1883 by the Rev., Knox at a cost of upwards of £800. It was intended to be used as an independent chapel, but soon afterwards was taken for a term by the Gospel Temperance and Blue Ribbon Committee, for public services and a reading room. The chapel was formerly opened in March 1883, when an impressive temperance sermon was preached by the Rev., Duncan McCallum of Burnley. By all accounts there was a good congregation that night, when Mr John Hartley presided on the harmonium. In the evening of the same day a public Blue Ribbon meeting was held, addressed by Messrs R. Cronshaw, Thomas Oxley, A, Hollins, and V. Lucas.

Mr Lucas also contributed a solo, and led the singing. The Temperance Gospel Mission Hall had closed down by 1890 and was bought by the Salvation Army—see that entry.

Unitarian Chapel, Spring Gardens / Church Street
The origins of Unitarianism in Padiham goes back a long way to the birth of a man named Joseph Cooke. He was born on 8 May 1775 at Dudley in Worcestershire to Methodist parents. He became a local preacher quite young, his first two stations being at Burslem and Merthyr Tydfil, from where in 1803 he moved to Lancashire. He was then aged 28, and on his removal to Lancashire was appointed to be one of two preachers on the Rochdale Circuit. Joseph Cooke was later described by the Rev., C.J. Street as being a man of considerable promise. He seemed to have been gifted with a clear mind and was able to express his thoughts with winning eloquence. He also rebelled against that arrogant spirit which boasted that it assured men of their salvation. However, his plain down to earth speaking led to him being expelled from the Methodist movement at a conference in August 1806. But by expelling Joseph Cooke the Methodists had not silenced him. A number of Methodists had embraced his views, and before long a chapel was built for him at Rochdale, and soon a congregation of 1,000 gathered every Sunday to hear him preach. To gather more into his flock every fourth Sunday Joseph went to Newchurch-in-Rossendale, and the following Monday and Tuesday he went to Padiham and Burnley as well as the occasional visits to Todmorden, Haslingden and other places. This new sect soon became known as the 'Cookites'. Soon another chapel had been built in Newchurch, but the man who had founded the movement Joseph Cooke died on 14 March 1811 a victim of consumption. His death was a heavy blow to all his followers, but the work was still carried on by a loyal band of preachers. The Society at Padiham was started in the year of Joseph Cooke's expulsion, 1806 and the friends here were honoured by a monthly visit, but the main work in Padiham was carried on by two local preachers named James Pollard and John Robinson. They met every Sunday in a small upper room reached by a back door in a cottage in Back Lane, now called East Street. It was the year 1820 when the congregation started thinking about having a religious place of their own at Padiham. The population of the town at that time was estimated to be around 3,000, the places of worship then, were the Church, the Methodist Chapel and Unitarian Meeting house.

At the annual meeting of the Unitarian Methodists at Rochdale the following year and application was made for help for the new chapel. Over £12 was collected that day at the meeting, and the very next year 1822 a piece of land was acquired and building work commenced at the chapel at Spring Gardens, West Street. To give stimulus to the movement the annual meeting of the Unitarians was also held at Padiham that year, the services being held in the open air. The cost of the new chapel which was opened in 1823 was put at £419.16s.6d. It was a plain rectangular chapel with the simple text above the entrance doorway *"To us there is but one GOD, even the FATHER"*. There was some forethought put into the chapel even at this time, for although the galleries were not yet installed the stairs leading up to them were. The galleries were actually added in 1836 when the chapel was enlarged and a graveyard was also added at that time—although this was short lived and was forced to closed as such in 1855. A sundial was also attached to the chapel at this time too. On 10 May 1994 planning permission was granted by Burnley Borough Council for this old disused chapel to be demolished for the erection of some new housing—little thought was given to the remains of the fathers of the congregation, James Pollard and the Rev., John Robinson that remained buried in the little graveyard, nor to the fact that this part of Padiham was in the Conservation Area. James Pollard who died first was buried beneath the pulpit at a spot marked by a simple slab of stone with the inscription 'J.P.' This stone and one to the Rev., John Robinson who both died in the year 1848 were later removed to the new Chapel on Church Street, but their bones still lie in the grounds of their chapel in West Street, where others keep them company. One further inscription is worth quoting that inscribed to John Astin who died in 1846 aged 20 years:

> *"He was born of humble parents, processed of a strong mind, of a studious disposition and passed through many difficulties in the pursuit of knowledge. As a Sunday School teacher he was revered and loved. Desirous of benefiting others by the spread of knowledge, he bequeathed all of his books to the chapel library..."*

Another stage which marked the growth of the Unitarians at Padiham was the erection of the new church on Church Street near the junction with the Blackburn Road—the old chapel being found too small for the growing congregation.

The land for the new chapel had been bought at a remarkably low price of £420. The style of the architecture was to be Gothic, the building to measure 66 feet from the front to the chancel and 38 feet wide. The tower was to be 14 feet square and rise to a total height of 95 feet. It was to be built of local grit stone from Mr Anderton's quarry at Read, the inside stonework and the doorways constructed from stone from the Padiham quarries. There were a number of gift donations by local people—the font was given by Henry Helm, and the Gothic pulpit was given by James Pate of Padiham. Another welcome gift was the work done by a member of the church and the services of the architect Virgil Anderton. Cornelius Anderton was the contractor for the masonry work and his services too were given at a minimum charge. The three stone crosses on the roof were worked by masons engaged on the building, Joseph Anderton, Andrew Wilkinson and Fergus Anderton, who then donated them to the church. The actual building operations on the church were begun in the Spring of 1872, the corner stone being lid by John Grundy of Summerseat, Bury on the Good Friday of that year. A 'time capsule' containing the usual coins and newspapers was placed in a cavity of the stone by Jabez Robinson, the son of the first Minister of the chapel. The cavity was then covered with a copper plate bearing the inscription *"The cornerstone of this chapel dedicated to the exercise of religious worship and to the services of the Almighty God, was laid by John Grundy Esq., of Summerseat, on this 28th day of March 1872"*

The building took two years to complete and was opened for public service on 30 April 1874. A number of memorial tablets were removed from the old chapel to the new chapel in January 1874. These included the one to the memory of the Rev., James Pollard who died 19 October 1848 aged 82 years and the one to the Rev., John Robinson who died 26 November 1848 aged 73 years. Today the Unitarian Chapel at Padiham thrives on still—perhaps because its door are often thrown open to other organisations and groups who hold special events at the church. These included the taking part in the Heritage Open days held in September 2010, by which its doors were once again thrown open to the public. There was also a concert given in aid of the air ambulance with songs from the amazing 12 year Grace O'Malley in June that year. We will be hearing more of Grace in the future that I am sure.

ROMAN CATHOLICS
St John the Baptist Church
The Catholics first became established in Padiham at an upstairs room in a building on Wyre Street in 1863. The building belonged to Job Pollard and the downstairs was used as a workshop and warehouse for his occupation as a plumber. The Catholics came from all parts as did many others to seek out regular employment in the mills and factories of East Lancashire. They arrived from the Yorkshire Dales, from Cumberland, Staffordshire, and increasingly after the Potato Famine in the 1840s from Ireland. To cope with this increase the foundation stone for a new Catholic Chapel was laid on land adjoining the cemetery on what was to become St Johns' Road on 11 May 1863. The site was actually that of some old cottages in Laneside View, this in 1914 became St Johns' Road. The present church, or what we might term the new church was begun in 1880, and was to be constructed of ashlar or dressed stone in the Gothic style and was to seat 600 persons. The total cost of the building was put at £3,600 and there was to be a bell turret 88 feet high surmounted by a plain cross. The new church was to a design of Edward Simpson of Bradford, the masonry work by W. Crowder of Brighouse, the joinery by J. And S. Copley of Bradford and the only local contractor was J.H. Harrison who was in charge of the plastering. The whole operation was under the sole charge of Rev., Father Jones, the priest in charge of the Mission.

The laying of the corner stone took place on 1 August 1880. The new church was solemnly opened 27 March 1881 by his Lordship the Bishop of Salford, followed by a sermon by Rev., Father Anderton of Stoneyhurst College, and thus the Catholics in Padiham were content. Tales were told of one priest Father Francis Hart, who often stood his own ground, and did not at times see 'eye to eye' with the authorities. One time he was having trouble getting an 'official' Catholic burial ground at the new cemetery below the church. To which he took matters into his own hands and knocked a hole in the party wall between the church and the cemetery in order to gain direct access. As part of the Silver Jubilee of the parish (1863-1913) events went on for a whole year. The local authority also noted the events and the following year changed the name from Laneside View to St Johns' Road. After 1932 plans were put into effect for the church extension, and every item used was second hand.

The stone came from old mills being demolished, notably Lowerhouse Mills, the timber for the sanctuary, the sacristy and the confessionals came from the "Mauretania" "The Empress of France" and other large ocean liners being broken up at the time. All the services were installed by the parishioners, joinery by Willie Towers, plumbing by Jerry Mitchell, plastering by Tom Bleasdale and Tom Lord. At the back of the 'old church' a new choir gallery was erected and the organ was transferred from the Hall. Finally the completed Church was opened in September 1937 by the Bishop.[xxvi]

St Philip the Apostle Church
It was a packed congregation that filled an empty shell of a building at the new St Philip's Church on Slade Lane in Padiham on Saturday 25 June 1955. The crowds stood upon a bare concrete floor in the windowless building to hear the Very Rev., Joseph Canon McEnery of St Alban's Church Blackburn bless the altar and the foundation stone of the new building. The sun shone down to give the day an added serenity and warmed the crowds outside that peered through the windowless gaps that would soon be filled with glass as the rich colours of the clergy robes clashed with the brick and stone. The Rev., Michael Canon Fitzgerald was there too, formerly of St Mary Magdalene's Church at Burnley, and remarked that it was one of the finest demonstrations of faith that he had seen in his lifetime. *"It is a red letter day in Padiham in the history of the church"* continued Canon Fitzgerald. Before the service a procession led by Father Reynolds set out from St John's Church and walked through the town to the new building. As they marched a pipe band played music and the crowds were flanked by choirboys carrying candles—then came the May Queen seven year old Elaine Dyer and her attendants. Also in the Procession were the Knights of St Columba of Burnley, and the Children of Mary. It was a day to remember by all who attended. The church was officially opened on 18 December 1955 by the Right Rev., J. Cunningham, St Philips Church still survives and indeed prospers on Slade Lane Padiham. In August 1998, Father Denis Dwyer of St Philip's RC Church in Slade Lane, Padiham was appointed Rural Dean for an area covering Burnley, Pendle, Padiham and Todmorden. The first marriage at the new church was that of Miss Joan Margaret Standing of Scott Park Road Burnley to Harry Rawstron of Colne Road Burnley in January 1957.

Just over ten years later there was a serious case of subsidence at the church. In June 1967, Father P. Reynolds was shocked to find that there was a case of sliding in the damp proof courses at the church which was going to cost about £2,500 to remedy. Steel buttresses had to be put in to arrest further movement which was also attributed to underground workings in the area. One of the more unusual events in the churches history took place in 1957, when Wilfred and Mabel Pickles the radio and television stars opened a fashion show for raising money for St Philips Church at Padiham Town Hall. How did that come about? Most of the 350 people present were wondering how they would be able to get Wilfred and Mabel to travel the 40 odd miles from Blackpool to make a brief appearance before dashing back to their Blackpool show at half past five. There happened to be a chance meeting between Mr and Mrs Pickles and Father Fletcher of St Philip's at Southport several months previous. The priest introduced himself and they had a merry chat, during which was mentioned St Philip's £23,000 debt—immediately the famous couple volunteered to help. Father Fletcher was able to thank the couple at the opening ceremony on 10 September 1957. Wilfred responded by saying that if they ever wanted them again to help in any way they only had to ask, and *'It wouldn't cost them a sausage'*. The church has had many other celebrations since that time such as in June 1997 when Father Denis Dwyer, who had been at St Philip's since 1975, celebrated his 40th anniversary of ordination. We might also recall here the oldest D.J. in town, Kitty Sumpton of Padiham who in July 2003 at the age of 93 was still spinning records at the dances held at St Philip's Church every Wednesday, and at the dance held at St John's Padiham each Saturday night. "The dances keep me going" she said "it's something to look forward to and something to get dressed up for".

CHAPTER THREE
Schools and Education.
    The first indications we have on education in Padiham are in 1605 when a levy was made on some properties in Padiham to pay for the construction of a schoolhouse, however it is not known where this school stood, although it may have been in the church grounds. Towards the end of the 17th century a schoolhouse was built on land behind St. Leonard's church which also comprised a room for the schoolmaster on the ground floor and a schoolroom above.

Up to 1830 this served as a school for the children of Padiham, Higham, Hapton and Simonstone, and it was run by trustees from each township. It was better known as Padiham Parish or Charity School. Further information can be gleaned from *'A History of the County of Lancashire'* Volume 6, by William Farrer and J. Brownbill published 1911 which says *"A schoolhouse was built about 1680, (fn. 87) but no endowment was provided until about 1756, when a fund was raised by the efforts of Richard Webster of Hargreave"*.

This 'Hargreave' we know today as 'Hargrove', which was associated with the Webster family for centuries, and is still a grand old Padiham name even today. By the year 1811 a society with the long title of *'The National Society for Promoting the Education of the Poor in Principles of the Established Church throughout England and Wales'* was established. This society's aim was to encourage the building of National Schools that would provide poorer children with an elementary education at a cheap weekly rate as well as teaching the faith of the established church. [xxvii] Padiham's first National School, on Mill Street also included a schoolmaster's house and a playground, it being very tiny was constructed in 1830, although the rainwater head on the downspouts on the building today bears the date 1822. The Parish or Charity School on land behind St Leonard's Church remained in use until the 1820s, when it appears to have been replaced by a new National School. It is thought that the 'old school' was demolished by the 1840s probably for St. Leonard's Church graveyard extension. In any case Chapel Sunday Schools were also being established around this time, for we know that Christopher Hudson the master at the Methodist Grammar School at Padiham was wed to Alice Hartley of Padiham in 1836 at All Saints Church Wigan. There was an interesting reference to an old Padiham School in the Burnley Express 22 February 1936. This old school was formerly known as Club Street School, Club Street being the old name for St Giles Street, and was believed at that time be more than a century old. It had in its time been an elementary school, a mission school and then the headquarters of the Blue Ribbon movement—it was last used as a joiners shop. The reason why it was in the newspapers was that it was about to be demolished as part of the slum clearance in Padiham. As in previous chapters we will deal in alphabetical order with the individual aspects of education in Padiham.

British Schools

In 1814, the 'British and Foreign School Society' was formed, non-conformist schools like those attached to chapels became known as 'British Schools' One 'British School' at Padiham was the school attached to the Burnley Road Baptist Chapel, this and others like it were maintained by voluntary contributions, low school fees paid by parents, and collections made in church and chapel. This was in addition to grants made by Government. The chapel and school at the Burnley Road Baptist Chapel was built in 1846 by Mr Foster of Sabden, the school being on the ground floor of the chapel. It was a 'British School' as an application had been made to the British and Foreign School Society for funding. You may recall that a serious rift about funding of the British School led to the departure of the Rev., Muxworthy and the founding of Horeb Chapel—see also that entry. A baptistery was also in use in the schoolroom here from around 1852. The schoolrooms were also used on occasions to hold lectures, such as in July 1849, when;

> *"The members of the Burnley Philharmonic Society had a grand concert of sacred music in the British School Rooms at Padiham. The programme comprised of music from Haydn, Handel, Mozart etc., and on the same evening a public examination of the scholars in connection with the above school took place, and the manner in which they acquainted themselves was proof that Mr Smith, their instructor had bestowed much attention in their instruction"*

Nancy Nuttall and Joseph Yarnold were the teachers at the British School in 1851, and in 1883 the master at the British School was Alfred Wallington—he lived at 20 Sweet Home Buildings in 1881 and at 31 Albert Street in 1883. The rooms which have now been converted into a private house and which still exist on the corner of Factory Lane and Ightenhill Street besides Bertwistle's Bakery are relics from the days of the British School. These were once used as an infant school and a later additional classroom of the British School. It opened in May 1890, and was erected on top of the warehouse that fronted the main road, and could accommodate 125 infant scholars. It was said to have been semi-octagonal in shape and measured 35 feet by 21 feet, and was built from stone obtained from the Whitegate Quarry and the Pickup Delph Quarry near the bottom of Coal Clough Lane at Burnley.

Attached to the new school was a concrete floored playground reached by the stone steps upwards from the main road and through the arch. The masonry work was done by Mr E. Hope, joinery by Mr James Bertwistle, plumbing and glazing by Mr J. Pollard, painting by Mr Ingham, and the heating by Mr Thomas Blezard. The school was to be under the control of Miss Hilliers. The British School only appears to have survived until around the turn of the 1900s, when it was forced to close down due to financial reasons, however the Sunday School at the chapel continued. [xxviii]

Gawthorpe High School

It was a sad day when Gawthorpe High School closed in July 2006—it must have brought a slight glistening to the eyes of the former pupils who spent their teenage years within its wall learning the secrets of what life was to bring to them. Sure, a brand new school, Shuttleworth College was going to be built to replace the old Gawthorpe High for the newer generations to come—but it was Gawthorpe that held a place in the hearts of all who attended in its 39 year history. Gawthorpe High School came about following suggestions of reorganisation of secondary education within the No., 5 Divisional Education Executive which included Padiham in 1966. To this end a brand new school catering for pupils aged 11 to 16 years was proposed—a school which was officially opened one Friday in June 1967 by a rather special celebrity with local connections. The school was to be opened by Mrs Mary Wilson, the wife of Prime Minister Harold Wilson. Mrs Wilson's parents were born in Padiham, her father was a congregational minister—and at the time she opened the school she still had relations living in the town. Tom Baldwin of Shakespeare Street was one cousin, and an aunt, Mrs Sagar formerly of Padiham but then of Hesketh Bank was able to attend the opening of the new school at a request of Mrs Wilson. Another cousin Vera Ormerod who kept a chip shop on Moor Lane was also invited—but Vera had to leave half way through the opening ceremony to get back to her shop and the teatime rush for fish and chips. The new school was at the time state-of-the-art as far as facilities were concerned. It was built at a cost of £300,000 on land covering 24 acres with the playing fields which was formerly part of the Gawthorpe estate and had panoramic views of Witch Country and old Pendle Hill to the North.

Two pieces of pottery were presented to Mrs Wilson at the opening by head boy Geoffrey Birtwell, the work of Gerald Barker and Geoffrey Farnworth, a three cornered vase—the other piece was an owl made by Allan Robinson. The school which had actually been in use since the previous August and was built to cater for between 520 and 480 pupils, and was phase one of three others phases of building work to be completed at the site. The school buildings were approached through woodlands which provided a natural barrier between the main Burnley/Padiham Road and comprised of four main blocks. 'A' Block contained the assemble hall, gym, dining rooms, and kitchens. 'B' Block contained the library exhibition hall, the library itself and staff rooms. A glazed covered way connected with 'C' Block a three storey building housing classrooms and arts and crafts study areas. These building together with a single storey practical block which housed wood and metal working rooms were grouped around a paved court. A special feature at the school was a vitreous enamel mural on one wall of the library exhibition room, the work of Mr Neville head of workshops at the school. Outside of the school were four football playing fields, cricket pitches, long and high jump practice pitches and eight tarmac courts for tennis and other ball games. [xxix]

Some former pupils might remember Padiham's famous water clock being 'stored' in the reception area of the school in the mid 1990s. Others might remember head-teacher Alan Dean, one of the first heads at the school, or Trevor Nowell who took over from Mr Dean in September 1979 and went on to serve as head for almost 19 years until his retirement in May 1998. Leonard Thomas took over as head from Mr Nowell. Or who might recall the accounts of the Holocaust in the Nazi death camps given in a lecture by one of the teachers on the first Holocaust Memorial Day in January 2001, when many of the year ten students were moved to tears? Gawthorpe High served the teaching needs of Padiham and surrounding area for almost 40 years till the end came in 2006. The new 1,050 place Shuttleworth College took its place when it opened in September 2008—although that too closed just a fortnight later due to a complete power cut at the school. Happily the closure was only temporary. Shuttleworth College has yet to make its own history. Suffice to say that the college was opened by a member of the family from whom it took its name, Lord Shuttleworth, whose family lived at Gawthorpe Hall for 600 years before the property was handed over to the National trust in 1970.

Gawthorpe the seat of the Shuttleworths
(Author)

National School
The National School or what is left of it, was built in 1830-31 and is situated at the bottom end of Mill Street, in the building now used by Prestige Beds. It was built to replace a much older building of the 17th century in or near the back of the churchyard at St Leonard's known as the 'Charity School' or 'Parish School' even the 'Black Hoile'. This 'Charity School' simply consisted of two rooms, one on the ground floor for the quarters of the master, and an upper floor for the pupils. This was hardly adequate for a town growing as fast as Padiham, and so it was decided that a new school should be built to cater for the growing population. The Rev., S.J.C. Adamson, vicar of St Leonard's appears to have been the instigator for this new school who soon took on board Le Gendre Nicholas Starkie of Huntroyde. The pair were able to arouse support from the local gentry and neighbourhood businessmen, and in June 1829 a subscription fund was organised. Amazingly in spite of economic conditions of the time this raised a total of just under £400—a substantial amount for that time.

At a further meeting held in March 1830 at the Starkie Arms it was decided to accept the gift of land off the Huntroyde Estate at the bottom of Mill Street for a new school. With the monies in subscriptions already raised and a grant for the rest from the organisation with the long winded title of the National Society for the Promotion of Education of the Poor in the Principals of the Established Church, the way forward for the new school was set. The foundation stone of the new school was laid by Le Gendre Nicholas Starkie in Masonic fashion on 22 April 1830. Inside the hollowed out foundation stone he placed newspapers of the day and coins of the realm, as a 'time capsule' for future generations. After what must have seemed ages, the pomp and ceremony was over and finished with, and the procession made its way back to the Starkie Arms for dinner followed by a crowd of over two thousand people—probably half the population of town at that time! The first school on the site which was opened in February 1831 was a single storied building with a slate roof, with one large classroom which could be divided by a partition into two rooms measuring 34 feet by 24 feet—one for the boys and one for the girls. In these tiny spaces children of both sexes numbering 250 of each were expected to be taught.

The first schoolmaster, who was a fully trained teacher, was a Mr Henry Robinson, who stayed at the school for over ten years. The second teacher was a Mr Bramley, succeeded by Joseph Bainbridge, who in spite of his surname was not from Yorkshire way but from Workington in what is now Cumbria—he came in 1849. He was the first teacher to occupy the new schoolmaster's house built a little further up at 29 Mill Street in that year. This may have been one of the incentives for the teacher to take on the job of schoolmaster. His unmarried sister Isabella, one of two sisters that were living with him at the schoolhouse was the first female teacher to be employed at Mill Street School in 1850. After the resignation of the successor to Joseph Bainbridge, a William Bertwistle who also resigned 1864—the schoolhouse was no longer used by the teachers by various parish clerks until it was sold off altogether in 1905. In 1855, the school was extended upwards by the addition of another floor, this large room was used by the girls of the school and the infants, separated as always, this time by a large curtain. The boys then used the ground floor, a situation which remained until 1891. After this date both the boys and the girls were taught on the top floor. One of the tiny playgrounds attached to the school can still be seen on Mill Street.

It is hard to imagine now that there were 150 children on the registers in 1850 using this and another small playground close-by. The Education Act of 1902 spelt the end of many Victorian schools, and Mill Street School was no exception, in 1903 the school was condemned as a place for education. The way forward was a completely new school to be built on East Street, to be named St Leonard's School. [xxx] Following the closure of the school at was bought by Padiham Co-operative for use as its drapery department. By all accounts the large hall above was used for dances as late as the 1960s. In 1974 Mr James Dunne opened the place as Prestige Beds, which still trades under that name today although Mr Dunne died in 2008.

Padiham County Primary School
The old Padiham school was on Burnley Road across from the Lodge on Stockbridge Drive of Gawthorpe Hall. It ceased to be a school in June 2010 when the new school across the road opened. The original Padiham Primary School dated from when the school children first took up residence on Monday 22 August 1910 after their annual holidays. The school was built to replace the overcrowding at both Hapton and Cross Bank which the council had rented from the Wesleyans. It is worth noting here that the Council once again had to rent the Cross Bank School in later years to cope with increased demand. The official opening of the school though took place a few weeks previous on 22 July 1910, and was performed by Dr J. Hoyle, of Brierfield and the Rev., J. Robinson the Education Committee who presided over a large crowd in attendance. The land for the new school was purchased off Lord Shuttleworth of Gawthorpe Hall for a sum of £2,789 and contained over 5,000 square yards. The new school was to be built in two separate blocks, one facing Burnley Road which would cater for 370 mixed pupils and one facing Victoria Road to accommodate 259 infants—629 in total. There were separate entrances one for the girls, and one for the boys. The estimated cost of both buildings along with the boundary walls, railings, latrines and paving the playgrounds was around £8,150. Heating at the school appears to have been by coal fires located in a classroom—a former pupil recalls that a teacher used to make Horlicks for the children on the fire. In an old school log book which makes interesting reading there is one entry dated 16 June 1933 when it was recorded that *"The attendance has been very poor, the epidemic of measles still continues"*.

Other contagious illnesses of the time included influenza, mumps, chicken pox, scarlet fever and whooping cough—just one or two such case would spread through the whole school like wildfire. It has been noted elsewhere that in July 1883 there was a serious epidemic of scarlet fever in Padiham and the Local Board decided to close all the schools in town as a precaution as six deaths had occurred. Other entries from the school log included 17 May 1935 *"The weather today has been exceptionally bad for this time of the year. There has been a heavy fall of snow and the attendance has fallen considerably, especially in the infant classes"* And on 21 January 1936 the logbook recorded that *"His Majesty King George V died last night. A service of remembrance was held in the school hall this morning"* One week later the whole school was closed down as a mark of respect on the day of the funeral. It was not all gloom however, there were happier times too. The school, like many others celebrated events such as Empire Day, Jubilee Day and Armistice Day. During the Second World War the school took in a number of evacuees—the logbook recorded that 35 were taken from Manchester who went to live with Padiham families and attended the primary school. In July 1944 another 23 were sent up from London to live for the duration in relative safety at Padiham.

When victory came in 1949 there were two days of holidays and jubilation at the school. The school might have survived two world wars and many other unhappy, and happy time of course, but it very nearly came to an end altogether when a fire tore through the building on 27 June 1995. A classroom caught fire and a section of the roof of the 100 year old school collapsed before the firemen could gain control of the fire. Doubtless there were many days of happiness and celebrations in the school at Padiham County Primary, but it all came to an end in June 2010 when the school and pupils upped and left the old school and its one hundred years of history for a brand new one just across the road. The new school was built at a cost of £2.6m, quite an inflated price on the £8,150 that the old school had cost. The environmentally-friendly new school, on the Burnley Road site however included six extra classrooms, a studio and library suite, also features a ground heat pump, solar and photovoltaic panels and rainwater collection points. The old Padiham County Primary School stood empty for a number of years before being pulled down. The happy days of childrens laughter of long ago are now gone forever.

Mrs Hallam, a teaching assistant at the school summed it all up when she said "Schools are living, breathing places. Down the years the school has had to change to meet the needs of the community as the needs of the community changed" I think we all will agree with that!

Padiham Green School

The National School at Padiham Green was opened in October 1875, followed by a public tea party, which appeared to have been the common event after such occasions. After the tea party various speeches were made under the presidency of the Rev., F.A. Cave-Browne-Cave. The meeting was also addressed by U. J. Kay-Shuttleworth and the Rev., H.A. Starkie, the Rev., C.E. Roberts and others. In 1879 a four day bazaar was held at the Mill Street School to help raise money to pay off the debts at Padiham Green School which amounted at that time to £500, and a total of £314-17s., was raised by the events. It was to be November 1911 before the foundation stone of a Church of England Infant School was laid at Padiham Green. The building was being built at a cost of £1,600, and the foundation stone was laid by Mr A.E. Le Gendre Starkie of Huntroyde. The school was to provide accommodation for 150 infants and consisted of three large classrooms which could be divided or united by sliding partitions, there was a cloak room and a teacher's room as well. Consideration had been given to extending the existing junior school, but it was thought best to build on a new site given by Mr A. Le Gendre Starkie across from the existing mixed departments. When the school was finished it was intended to transfer the infants already at the other school to it, and use the portion taken by them as young men's clubrooms. To perform the ceremony of laying the foundation stone Mr Starkie was presented with a trowel and inscribed upon the stone were the words *"This stone was laid by A.E. Le Gendre Starkie, Esq., J.P. on the 28 October 1911. Arthur E. Mills, Vicar, A. Winfield B.A. curate-in-charge".*

The new C.E. School which had been erected on land adjacent to St Anne and St Elizabeth Church on Padiham Green was dedicated on 23 July 1912 by the Bishop of Manchester. It was stated that the school was furnished in the latest style, with dual desks for the older infants. The baby's room was furnished in accordance with kindergarten principals, each child having a separate arm-chair. Each room was completely furnished with its own cupboards, museum, kindergarten tables etc.

The night of the dedication was wild and wet and the service had to be performed inside the new school by Rev., T. H. Taylor and A. Winfield. In the course of the evening an address was also given by the Bishop of Manchester. There was an interesting reference to Sunday Schools at Padiham in the Blackburn Standard of 10 July 1880, by which all the schools including Padiham Green celebrated the centenary of Sunday Schools in the town—the paper went on to say;

> *The centenary of the founding of Sunday Schools was celebrated at Padiham on Saturday. In the processions that paraded through town there were about 2,000 Church of England scholars representing Mill Street, Higham, Simonstone, Partridge Hill, Padiham Green, Hapton and Clay Bank Schools. There were also 2,000 Wesleyans from Cross Hill, Cross Bank, Giles Street, Hapton Bridge, Higham, Lowerhouse, Sabden, Park and Rosegrove as well as Baptists and Unitarians. At the meeting various addresses were given and hymns sung, the proceedings being concluded by the bands playing Hallelujah Cords. Coffee and buns were afterwards supplied to the scholars"*

Padiham Green Schools prospered until August 1991 when a fierce blaze tore through the school buildings which destroyed more than a third of the structures. The rear section of the school was ravaged by the fire including five classrooms, the hall, the library, teacher staffrooms and offices. There was serious damage to the junior section through fire damaged roof structures and slates. However, the infant section of the school escaped unscathed. In the following days there was a desperate hunt on for alternative premises to teacher the 95 youngsters. There was great relief when parents and teachers were told that they could teach their children at rooms at Gawthorpe High School. In January 1992 Lancashire County Council gave permission to rebuild the school at a cost of one million pounds. A three and a half year wait followed until the new school was finally opened in January 1995. An old stone cross which was a feature of the old school building was salvaged and put on show in the foyer of the new school as a reminder of its historic past. Ten years later in January 2005 the school celebrated it anniversary with a day of fun.

Pupils were allowed to wear casual clothes for the day and a birthday party was arranged. As part of the ongoing fundraising ten penny pieces were laid in a trail around the school, the proceeds going towards extending the playground. Padiham Green School still prospers and is a happy little school its pupils proud to have been part of it and shared just a little of their lives with its teachers and staff.

Partridge Hill School

This school was situated on Partridge Hill in an area now taken by a small children's play area—it started off as an infant school in July 1856. Only the school house still survives today. It was on one Saturday in July 1856 that a public tea meeting was held for the inauguration of a new infant school at Partridge Hill. Here upwards of 200 sat down to an excellent tea, served in the open air on a grass plot in front of the school which 'was beautifully situated upon the top of Partridge Hill'. After the tea the public meeting adjourned to the National School in Mill Lane, where Sir J.P. Kay-Shuttleworth occupied the chair, around him were several eminent people including Le Gendre N. Starkie and Henry Starkie of Huntroyde, the Rev., J.S. Adamson, T. T. Berger B.A., and a number of others connected with the Church. The Chairman addressed the meeting and spoke of the necessity there was in Padiham for such a school as the one they were there to inaugurate. It had been in his opinion for many years that there ought to be an infant school in Padiham, and that the town might enjoy the same privileges as Burnley. The chairman spoke of the school being spacious and well ventilated, so much better for the health of the children would be if they were sent to it instead of being permitted to run loose in the streets, being as he put it "Companions to the kennel". He spoke of the Sabbath School and told how he himself had been a Sabbath teacher from the age of 13 to the age of 18. After this and say that the inhabitants of Padiham could not be too grateful to their pastor, the Rev., Adamson he sat down to loud applause and the voice of the choir "Blessed be the Lord God of Israel". Later Sir J.P. Kay-Shuttleworth went on to provide a schoolhouse which still bears the date '1870'. The cornerstone of a girl's school was laid in September 1871 by the Rev., S.J.C. Adamson and later a boy's school was added. The school soon became known as St Matthew's School and was closely associated with the church of that name not far away at the back of Garden Street.

Although it was built as an off-shoot school belonging to St Leonard's Church it did accept children of all denominations. Two of the schoolmistresses, Sarah Brown and Elizabeth Holmes were listed as living at the schoolhouse in the 1871 census returns. Edward Coward was the schoolmaster in 1880, although it was Edward Riley who was the schoolmaster in 1883, these two probably taught at the boy's school. Two unmarried 28 year olds, Miss Fanella Ross, and Amelia Brooks were the schoolteachers at the girl's school in 1881. The school was closed down in later years and by the mid 20th century the site had been cleared save for the old schoolhouse and a stone perimeter wall surrounding the old school playground and a more modern children's play area.

Private Schools

There were a number of private schools being run in Padiham at various times, mainly to give tuition on a one to one basis, or perhaps more, for the better off in society. Agnes Hartley ran a girls day school in Burnley Road in 1834 and Christopher Hudson a boy's day school in the same year. A John H. Hudson of Grove Lane described himself as a schoolmaster in 1883. In 1887 there was a private school being run at 17 Grove Place by John Cocks teaching shorthand and bookkeeping. He actually lived next door at 19 Grove Place, and in 1891 he said that he was a schoolteacher and mathematician, although in the following census of 1901 he was listed as being a joiners bookkeeper aged 66 years. An infant school was being run in 1868 in one of the terraced houses in 'Mitton Street' by Isobella Taylor, but appears to have been short-lived. Doubtless there were other private schools which catered for just one or two pupils around the town, but of which we now have little knowledge.

St John the Baptist School

This little Catholic School on St John's Road is the oldest school in Padiham to still be in used as it was originally intended for education. The memorial stone for this school was laid in October 1888, and the new school was brought about by the increased numbers of scholars at the old school. It was built to accommodate 400 pupils at a cost of around £600 and built under the superintendence of Father Mussley of Rochdale, who was also the architect.

The new building was intended to be used for the higher classes, while the old school in part of the chapel was to be used for the infants which numbered around 250. The laying of the memorial stone was a grand affair as a procession 300 strong headed by the Padiham Brass band and a large double polled banner with Father Jones at the front walked along Hapton Road, Green Lane, Burnley Road and returned via Station Road to the site of the new school. Father Aidan supported by Father Jones and Father Morrisey then proceeded to perform the important ceremony. The prayers were read and the incense burned over the stone which was then placed into position. The new school was officially opened on 26 May 1889 after 'Being approved by Her Majesties Education Department as a place suitable for day school teaching' The school was built from stone got from Read quarries, with corner stone from Yorkshire quarries. [xxxi]A number of additions have been built over the years but the school still retains its quaint village school atmosphere, and is still held in great affection by pupils past and present—they are proud of being educated at St John's School.

St Leonard's School
This school came about with the condemning of the old National School on Mill Street in 1902 by the Board of Education. Towards the end of that year Captain Starkie J.P. of Huntroyde gave land for the new school to be built on. A committee was formed and plans were prepared and adopted. A new school larger than anything that Padiham had ever seen before was about to come into fruition. It was to be built to accommodate 540 children, 340 in the mixed department and 200 in the infant's side of the building. The site had an open aspect looking south with ample room for playgrounds and would be built to a design of Mr Bell of Burnley. The mixed department was to have a central hall and five classrooms with separate cloakrooms and entrances for the girls and boys. The infants department would also have a central hall two classrooms and a baby's room. The estimated cost would be around £5,400, but private subscriptions poured in. For instance in December a bazaar and over £3,000 was raised. The foundation stone was laid on 23 January 1904 and it opened for teachers and children the first time in March 1905. At the opening ceremony which took place at nine o'clock in the morning on 3 April 1905, there were the usual large crowds, and the Rev., Coverdale led the children in a dedication service.

Inside the large hall was a fine portrait of the late Vicar, with a brass plaque bearing the inscription *"The Rev., Henry Haworth, M.A., born 1856 died 1904, Vicar of Padiham 1896 to 1905. By whose indomitable energy these day and Sunday Schools of St Leonard's were erected 1904"* Across the other side of the hall were portraits of two worthies, Mr J. Whittaker, J.P., and Mr R. Thompson J.P. There were also pictures of the King and Queen, and one bearing *"Charity Begins at Home"*. A splendid engraving bore the inscription *"Presented by Ernest and Kathleen Granger on the occasion of the opening of the new schools, April 3rd 1905"*.

It was in this room that the scholars assembled, the arrangement of the sliding partitions allowed seating for a large number of people. Close to the headmaster's desk was a switch which activated an electric bell which communicated with all of the building. The teachers at the new school included Mr Butterworth in charge of class IV, Miss Holden in charge of class III and Miss Gregson in charge of class II who was assisted by Miss Siddell. The infants department was controlled by Miss Hudson as headmistress, assisted by Miss Riley. One hundred years hence the school was able to celebrate its anniversary beginning in January 2004. A special service of celebration was held at St Leonard's with guest speaker Canon Peter Ballard. This was followed by a gathering at the school where a special exhibition was on display showing photographs of past events at the school—many of these had been donated by past pupils at the school. One of the exhibitions was a school report and exam results belonging to head girl Jennie Crossley in 1928. The present day pupils found it fascinating to view pupils of the Victorian era which were previously taught in the very classrooms that they were now being taught in. The anniversary celebrations came just weeks after the school was named as the Most Improved School in Lancashire, and 35th in the country of schools which have improved the most and at a time when the school was in the charge of headmistress, Mrs Julie Bradley. The celebrations did not stop there they went on and on. In November 2007, they were celebrating as they received a glowing report from Ofsted. In December 2009 the school became the first in the U.K., to have 'free running facilities' installed. In March 2010 the primary section of the school was named as Spar School of the year and also reached the Lancashire Youth Games gymnastic finals—and long may they continue their awards and celebrations.

Technical Institute

The Padiham Technical Institution used to be located on the corner of Institute Street and Burnley Road almost opposite the Burnley Road end to Victoria Road until it was demolished in October 2001. The land for the 'Tech' as it was known locally was given by Sir Ughtred Kay-Shuttleworth M.P. of Gawthorpe Hall, who also donated £1,000 towards the building fund. Advance education in Padiham had always been an uphill struggle. From 1857 to 1862 science classes were held in a small room over a shop in Burnley Road under the direction of Leonard Clement J.P. of Nelson assisted by J.R. Smith, along with Mr T. Langstaff. During the Cotton Famine the classes were transferred to the Trade Hall, which in effect was a room over the old Liberal Club, part of the old Padiham corn mill in Burnley Road. For a few years after this classes in drawing were held in the National School on Mill Street, and classes in physiology and physical geography were held at the Wesley School. In the year 1875 classes in science were taught by Mr J.T. Smith in the Wesley and Unitarian Schools—and these continued for many years. After this came a quite time when no classes at all were held at any of the schools, that is until 1883 when classes in science were resumed at the Wesley Schools and also at Partridge Hill School. A further break came when the committee of the Mechanic's Institute at Burnley decided to hold branch classes at Padiham at the Salvation Army Barracks in Guy Street.

In 1886-87 a new committee was formed consisting of, amongst others, the Rev., J. Tylas as chairman and William Stephenson as secretary. A room was rented over what was then the Manchester and County Bank at 69 Burnley Road, now the site of the NatWest Bank, or the 'Bottom Bank'. This was soon given up, and a new place was sought, and to this end a room was secured at the Partridge Hill Schools in 1887. A place was found here for the teaching of technical instruction in cotton manufacture, shorthand and book-keeping were also added. Also, an 'evening continuation' school was established for boys and girls. During the summer of 1889 a natural history class was added, and in 1890 the assembly rooms in Guy Street were secured—although it was true to say that the rooms were not well adapted for the purposes of teaching. The title of Padiham Technical School was applied to this building—the number of student rose to 280, there being a great increase in students in art.

In order to make proper instruction in cotton manufacture, the town's staple trade a cottage next to the assembly hall was also secured, and the basement fitted out with a loom and dobby, a handloom and a loom adapted for jacquard weaving.

The Technical Institute
(Author)

To complete the outfit a grant from the County Council enabled them to install a gas engine. It was in the year 1897 that Sir U. Kay-Shuttleworth made his generous donation of 4,000 square yards of land off Burnley Road for a new Technical Institution as well as a sum of money to the total of £1,000. Its full name was to be the Padiham Victoria Memorial Technical Institute, little wonder that the locals called it *'T'Tech'* and it was opened on 31 October 1901. It was an impressive building with a frontage 88 feet long, and comprised of a basement, ground and first floors. The basement was to be used as laboratories, storeroom lecture theatre and preparation rooms. On the ground floor there were two classrooms, a library, a museum and the secretary's office. The first floors contained the art rooms, a large elementary drawing room, antique and painting room, and a room for cookery.

The new building was constructed to cater for 400 students. The work was carried out by the following contractors; Masonry work, Mr B. Smith, joinery, Mr J. Bertwistle, plumbing Mr R. Roberts, plastering, slating and painting by W. Foster and sons, and the heating by Mr J. W. Todd. The opening ceremony was a lavish affair, and started off with a long procession led by the Volunteer Band beginning at the top of Mill Street, thence along the main Burnley Road to the Institute. Crowds lined the streets throughout and the school children were all given the day off. The workpeople were allowed to celebrate the event by working until one o'clock and having their dinner an hour late.

The town officials were met at the Institute by members of the Burnley representatives such as Lady O'Hagan and the Mayor, soon to be joined by Sir Ughtred Kay-Shuttleworth and Lady Kay-Shuttleworth and Lord Derby who was to perform the opening ceremony. After the pomp and ceremony of the opening was over there was tea and biscuits upstairs in the new school and an exhibition of Padiham made goods were on show. The new institute was to be put to good use for the folks of Padiham, in November 1928 a branch library was opened on the ground floor—the following year a juvenile section of the library was opened. The branch of the County Library remained at the Padiham Tech until it was transferred to the new town hall in March 1938, a place where it remains to this day. In October 2001, the Burnley Express showed a picture of the Padiham Tech in the process of being demolished, almost one hundred years to the day after its opening. New housing now takes the place of the old *'T'Tech'* at Padiham. The demolition of such a fine building still leaves a bitter taste in the mouth of many a Padihamer, and its destruction was looked at as an act of municipal vandalism even to this day. [xxxii]

CHAPTER FOUR

Industry at Padiham.

Because the Padiham we see today is basically the product of the Industrial Revolution, this chapter will study the industries that made Padiham. The principal industry was of course cotton spinning and weaving and its allied trades. In Chapter One we mentioned that there was an early mill at Padiham attached to the old corn mill and the fire there in December 1815 with loss of life.

This may have been Peels and Yates' mill dating from circa 1790, or even James Fishwick's mill, but we have little information about these really early mills. In any case, most of these were essentially just large buildings probably erected initially as warehouses and later converted to hold a number of looms. Here the operatives would come to do a day's work, and get paid by the pieces of cloth they wove. Piece work is a term we still use even today. Thus begun the Factory System. At one time Padiham and its near neighbour Burnley were almost the same size, Burnley prospered into a much larger cotton spinning and manufacturing centre because of the railway and canal. Padiham was bypassed by the canal, its nearest point being at Hapton, and the railway was much later in coming to the town. Nevertheless, for a town of around 10,000 people it has a remarkable collection of old mills as a legacy to its great industrial past. The mills were generally centred on the River Calder, or Green Brook for obvious reasons—a plentiful supply of water for the steam raising boilers for the engines. We begin then with the history of the textile trade at Padiham with the known Padiham mills, and to make things a little easier these are listed in alphabetical order.

THE COTTON INDUSTRY

Albert Mill
This mill was named after Prince Albert (1819-1861) husband of Queen Victoria. The mill is situated between Wyre Street and the River Calder and almost opposite the bottom end of Cobden Street, which is named after Richard Cobden (1804-1865) the British manufacturer, Radical and Liberal Statesman. The Padiham folk were great Liberal supporters in times past, and this reflects in the fact that many other street names in the town are named after prominent Liberals of the day—Melbourne, Palmerston, Cobden, Morley, Peel, Cardwell, and Bright Streets are examples of others. If Burnley has its *'Weavers Triangle'* then Padiham should have its own *'Weavers Square'* centred all round the complex of mills between Ribble Street, Wyre Street, Lune Street and Holmes Street. Albert Mill was begun around the mid 1850s by William Ingham—he, his sons and grandsons and great grandsons ran the mill for most of its life. These were from small beginnings, but by the early 1860s, William Ingham was employing 19 men, 16 women, 7 boys and 7 girls.

The first building at Albert Mill was the three storey spinning mill which still survives, this housed 866 looms and 15,000 spindles. This was followed in 1870 by a weaving shed, additional extensions to the sheds took place in 1877 and in 1881—in the latter year the firm was then employing 240 operatives both at Albert Mill and Riverside Mill. By the time of the 1881 extension the weaving sheds were being compared to the massive new Jubilee Mill being erected at the same time. When the structure at Albert Mill was completed, it gave employment to 400 local weavers and housed 1,200 looms. This new shed was built to a design of Peter Pickup, the Burnley architect. The engines to drive all the weaving machinery were a pair of horizontal ones made by William and John Yates of Blackburn, having a five feet stroke and a speed of 45 r.p.m., and were calculated to indicate a power of 460 h.p. During the erection of the engine-house a crane was installed which greatly increased installation of the engines and engine beds. The ten ton stones used for the engine beds were *'lifted into position with ease'*. The crane remained in position even after the installation of the boilers and engines, in case of repairs to either. There were three boilers, two of which were removed from the older boiler house, and placed side by side with the third. The new boiler, which did the work of the older two boilers while they were being transplanted was 30 feet long and 8 feet wide and was built by Thomas Beeley of Hyde Junction near Manchester. The engines were named *'William'* and *'Alice'* in memory of the founder of the firm and his wife, and they were 'christened' by the oldest surviving member of the firm at that time Mr John Ingham. After this event, a large crowd of some forty people retired to the warehouse to celebrate the occasion with a dinner and toasts to the new project. [xxxiii]

In 1884, the firm became a limited company under the title of 'William Ingham and Sons Ltd' and by this time the firm was running 15,000 mule spindles and 860 looms. Ring spinning replaced the mules in 1902, and spinning ended altogether during the year of the General Strike of 1926. One of William's sons James, married his wife Ann, and they lived at 106 Burnley Road—another son Henry, wed Czarina Dixon in 1860, this family lived at 81 Windsor Terrace on Church Street, Padiham. By 1932 the firm was operating 1,544 looms, but there soon followed a decline in the cotton industry—Riverside Mill was sold off, and the number of looms at Albert Mill was reduced to 374 manufacturing Twills, Plains and Jeanette's etc.

In 1955, the firm was running 470 looms, but by the end of this decade William Ingham and Sons Limited (1854) as they were then named, after over one hundred years ceased trading. The firm of Nelson Jute Manufacturers took over the weaving shed part of the mill soon afterwards—it was while this firm was there that there was a huge fire which destroyed all that section of the mill in November 1968. The fire was discovered by Colin Dower, the son of Fred Dower the owner of Nelson Jute Manufacturers. It was soon after the 15 people employed at the mill came into work about eight o'clock in the morning, and about an hour later when they were having their nine o'clock brew in the canteen. Colin was working on his own when he noticed flames licking round the back door. He raced into the office to call the fire brigade then started to tackle the blaze with the factories own fire fighting equipment. Soon men from eight fire brigades were on the scene, but soon the roof of the weaving shed collapsed causing thousands of pounds worth of damage. There was more drama added to the day when a gas mains exploded not far away at United Abrasives. One man named Gerald Jerome was blown across the factory floor by the blast, but happily not seriously injured. Albert Mill was left gutted after the blaze and under two feet of water pumped from the nearby River Calder to fight the blaze. Today, the three storey stone built spinning mill remains almost intact if somewhat derelict on Wyre Street just beyond Fleetwood Road, but most of the weaving sheds between Holmes Street and Fleetwood Road have been destroyed following the fire and only the outer walls survive, one of these spaces has been converted into a 'yard' for a local scaffolding company. The nearby Ingham Street is named after the family that ran the mill. There was a rather amusing incident in March 1965 when smoke was seen coming through the roof at Albert mill, and fire engines from three brigades were rushed to the scene. It turned out that there was a demonstration in progress by a Huddersfield fire fighting firm who had deliberately started a fire to show off their new chemical flame killer. The director of Reeve Brothers, Mr J. Worthy, hospital clothing manufacturers who also occupied part of the Albert mill gave the alarm. Happily, the chemical flame killer did its job!

Albion Mill
A full report of the starting of Albion Mill on land between Albion Street, back Shakespeare Street and Abingdon Road, was given in the Burnley Express 4 April 1906.

"The present boom in the staple industry is probably unprecedented in the number of new mills it has called into being in Burnley and district. About 12 months ago the formation of a new weaving concern was decided upon in Padiham, the first sod cut last May, and on Saturday the 880 horse power engine to operate the 1,600 wide looms in Albion Mill was christened and formally started in the presence of an enthusiastic little company. The new mill is situated on land at the end of Shakespeare Street, and the company concerned—the Albion Room and Power Company Limited consists of Alfred Blezard, Walter W. Helm, Herbert Noble, Thomas Riding, James Thompson, Andrew Wilkinson, Harold Worswick, and J. C. Waddington, directors and about 66 shareholders in addition. At present about 300 looms have been installed, and the actual weaving operations will commence tomorrow. Excellent tenants have been secured in the Church Street Manufacturing Company, and the Perseverance Mill Company, and the new shed will be divided between them. Thomas and Herbert Noble are prominently identified with the two concerns named, and the high pressure side of the new engine was christened 'Isabel' by Mrs T Noble, Mrs Herbert Noble giving the name 'Martha' to the immediate opposite cylinder side. The engines built by the Burnley Iron Works Company are of the horizontal triple condensing type arranged with four cylinders, one high pressure, one intermediate, and two low pressure. A compact arrangement which not only gives the best results for regular turning but an economy in steam and a symmetry which cannot be arrived at by any other type of triple engine. Looking towards the flywheel end of the engine house, the left hand engine consists of the high pressure, and one low pressure cylinder, and the right hand one of the intermediate and the other low pressure cylinder. The respective diameters of the cylinders are, high pressure 18 inches, intermediate 28 inches, and the two low pressure 31 inches. The stroke of both engines is one of five feet, and the machinery makes 60 revolutions per minute under a boiler pressure of 180 lbs, this gives a piston speed of 600 feet per minute. Each engine has a separate pump and condenser 24 inches diameter by 13 inches stroke, worked from the crosshead by lings and steel rocking levers. Each cylinder is fitted with Corliss valves, those on the high pressure being automatically actuated by the governor. The driving pulley which weighs about 35 tons is grooved for 24 ropes of 1 ¾ inch diameter. The diameter of the pulley is 22 feet and it drives on two second motion pulleys of 11 feet in diameter, the sped of the ropes being 4,147 feet per minute.

The driving pulley is built up in the usual way, and has an internal rack rim for use with the barring engine, which is of the double cylinder type with effective disengaging gear. The whole engine is of a strong and massive character and capable of yielding 880 horse power under the steam pressure named. The engine house is also equipped with a travelling crane to lift ten tons. The mill has been erected to a design of Messrs G. and S. Keighley of Burnley and contains 1,600 50 inch reed space looms, a three storey warehouse, with engine house, boiler house, chimney etc. The premises are built of local stone and are of a very pleasing design. The motive power is obtained from three Lancashire boilers 30 ft x 8ft diameter, and one pair of horizontal triple expansion engines. The engines are an exact duplicate of the engines at Peel Mill Burnley and built by the same engineers to a design of the later Samuel Keighley. The names of the contractors are as follows; Mason work, Messrs Smith Brothers of Burnley, joinery work, Messrs W. Boothman of Nelson, slater and plasterer, Thomas Foster and Sons, Padiham, ironfounder and millwright, W. Roberts and Sons Nelson, plumber and glazer J. Pollard and Son, Padiham, steam and gas pipes, by Mr H. South of Burnley, and the driving ropes by Healey Brothers of Heywood..."

What the report did not include is the fact that a large section of Green Brook had to be culverted in order to accommodate the new shed. By the time a second shed was added in 1912, the mill had become the largest weaving shed ever to be built in Padiham. The Church Street Manufacturing Company ceased operations at Albion Mill in 1932, and the lease of their section of the sheds was passed on to Dean Brothers Limited. This company failed to restart weaving after the Second World War, and in 1946 the whole mill was taken over by the Perseverance Mill Company. In 1959 this company merged with R.F.D. and soon afterwards changed the name to the Perseverance Mill Company Limited, of which Alan Noble became chairman. By this time 600 workers were employed at the mill, and in 1986 the business was bought out by Scapa Group P.L.C. of Blackburn, and the company was renamed Perseverance Mill Limited. A further change in ownership took place in 1997 with a management buyout who also took over Moorgate Mill at Blackburn and Scapa Mouldings of Rishton. However in April 2005 the firm went into administration with a loss of 200 jobs, soon afterwards the whole mill was demolished after just short of one hundred years production.

Alma Mill
Is situated on Wyre Street, and was built in 1854 to house 350 looms by Bowers Bertwistle, who then leased the shed to James Knowles and Company. Bowers Bertwistle went on to become a stock broker at Burnley, married Mary Bertwistle in 1845 at Burnley and died in 1883. James Knowles and Company soon failed, and the lease was taken over by the Burnley firm of temple and spring manufacturers, Cooper and Baldwin—who unfortunately were also declared bankrupt in 1864. Soon afterwards, the mill was taken over by Richard Thompson and Sons who occupied the neighbouring Britannia Mill, and in 1870-71 purchased Alma Mill outright. [xxxiv] Richard Thompson (1831-1913) went on to become the first Chairman of Padiham and District Local Board, a leading industrialist in Padiham, and a well-known figure at the Liverpool Cotton Exchange—Thompson Street in Padiham is in fact named after him. He was also a lifelong Conservative, a J.P., one of the founders of Padiham Conservative Club on Mill Street, and Chairman of Burnley County Magistrates Court. [xxxv] In 1899, Alma Mill was enlarged and a new engine and boilers were installed and mill chimney erected. In 1928 the Alma Mill was taken over by J. H. Bertwistle, and in 1932 this firm who were also running the Britannia Mill had 40,000 spindles and 1,047 looms in operation. The firm was also running the Grane Road Mill at Haslingden, the Park Mill at Helmshore, and later the Albion Mill at Littleborough. Although the firm closed down the Alma Shed at Padiham in 1956, the Grane Road Mill continued to be run by them until April 2009 when it went into liquidation, being taken over by former manager Peter Heaton. In 1957, Alma Mill at Padiham was taken on by Raymakers and Sons Limited, specialist weavers of cotton pile velvets, curtain, soft furnishings and upholstery cloth. A relatively new company, British Velvets, founded in Accrington in 1932, moved into Alma Mill in 1955. The naming of the mill is after a battle, often considered to be the first battle in the Crimean War and which took place on 20 September 1854.

Bridge End Mill
'Wonder Mill' as every Padihamer will know, is the local name for Bridge End Mill which used to stand on the site of that now taken by Padiham town hall. It started out as a four storey mule spinning mill erected by the Roughlee spinner John Roberts, along with Padiham men Paul Tickle and James Whittaker in 1836.

It was eleven windows long, with a large mill chimney on the corner on the Inskip end of the building. Almost 300 people were employed here in the early 1850s, when the mill was being run by William Wilding—by the end of that decade there were 18,500 mule spindles and 274 looms all powered by a 50hp beam engine. The mill at that time being run by Temple and Sutcliffe Company who later moved to Rosegrove. There was a minor fire at the mill in January 1856 brought about by a piece of cotton fluff catching fire at a globe of a gas lamp at the mill, there were no injuries, but damage was caused to the value of around £30. Another fire in the following year when the mill was owned by William Bear was caused by some cloth being placed upon the flues in the boilerhouse to dry. They caught fire and the place was soon in flames. The boilerhouse roof was burnt off and some other parts of the building were damaged. The fire was put out by the jets of Padiham Waterworks being brought into use. Temple and Sutcliffe's lease expired in 1864, and the mill remained empty for a number of years before being sold to the owner of Orchard Mill, Charles Waddington in May 1871for the sum of £4,700.

Waddington invested heavily in the mill installing 32,000 weft mule spindles, a new boiler and a new engine, but the investment crippled him financially, and he went bankrupt.[xxxvi] By the 1880s Charles Waddington was living in some style however at Stocks Hill at Whalley and described himself as being a 'retired manufacturer' with his wife Alice and son James Charles, a solicitor. In 1902, one of the shareholders of the firm Lancashire Property and Investment Company, Richard Ryden, along with Mark Noble and John Walker, a Blackburn spinner formed the Bridge End Company Limited to run Bridge End Mill. Spinning ended fourteen years later, and apart from a brief attempt by the Wonder Cotton Mill Company Limited in 1924, little attempts were made to get the mill up and running again. Local sarcasm dictated that the Wonder Mill Company was so named because it was a 'wonder' that it made any money. The Bridge End Mill had been acquired by the Council in 1920 and leased out to a number of small firms, including the Wonder Cotton Mill Company, and in June 1933, the tenants that remained were given three months notice. By the end of 1934, Bridge End Mill had been demolished for the site of the new town hall which was officially opened in February 1938. There was an alarming incident at Bridge End Mill back in February 1906 when a fire was discovered on the second floor of the premises.

'*A stampede of terrified workers was seen dashing into the street and out of the blazing mill*' said a report in the local newspapers. Luckily the fire station was just around the corner and the firemen were soon on the scene. Literally within a few minutes the brigade had three jets of water pointed at the conflagration, and another four jets from the street hydrants were also soon in place. Smoke coming from the building was a major hazard, and at one time it was thought that the firemen might lose control of the blaze and the building might have been gutted. Happily this was not the case, and with the jets of water being pointed in the right direction the smoke began to clear and the firemen won the day. Naturally, the weavers caught out on the floor where the fire originated were terrified and scared, as the flames and smoke spread in seconds. There was considerable excitement, as workers clambered down the escape ladders or rushed down the internal stairs. One man threw his jacket into the street before making his escape, forgetting that his jacket contained six shillings—but only four shillings were later recovered! Happily, no-one was seriously injured in the fire, but there was considerable damage done to the mill, most of it water damage from the fire hoses.

Britannia Mill

The Britannia Mill on Ribble Street and Lune Street, housed '*Padiham Carpets*' and a number of other small companies. The mill was begun as a co-operative mill in 1854, and constructed by the Padiham Cotton League Company, consisting of a weaving shed containing 480 looms powered by a 45 hp steam engine manufactured by Marsland's of Burnley. It was however an ill-fated venture, and two years later was in financial difficulties, production ended around 1857, and the mill was taken over by Richard Thompson and Sons of Blackburn. Major extensions were undertaken by the Thompsons, in 1860-61, a multi-storey spinning mill was constructed besides the existing shed. It was also in 1860, that Richard Thompson married Eliza Robinson, the daughter of Thomas Robinson of Lowerhouse at St Leonard's church. The 1881 census returns shows the family living at Vale House, at Whalley, and although he lived outside of Padiham he still took a great interest in the running of the town. However, these were difficult times for the cotton industry aggravated by the Cotton Famine of the early 1860s brought about by the American Civil War.

Richard Thompson got round this by importing Indian cotton, which whilst difficult to work ensured that his mill was one of the few to keep running during the crisis, and kept his 200 operatives in employment. Thompson prospered, and a pair of compound beam engines was installed at Britannia Mill in 1868, in the 1870s he was able to purchase the weaving sheds at Alma Mill in Wyre Street and the Perseverance Mill on the corner of Green Lane and Burnley Road, besides Padiham Bridge. Richard Thompson and his firm were forward looking employers, and were the first to experiment with the new electric lighting in Padiham by installing 50 incandescent lamps in the two carding rooms at Britannia Mill run by a generator coupled to the mill engine. There was a fatal accident to a lad named George Alston employed as a weft carrier at the mill in December 1884. George had entered the lift hoist at the mill on one of the upper floors, and while it was still descending tried to get out before the hoist had stopped. He was caught between the top of the lift cage and his back was broken—he died almost immediately. A new company was formed in 1890, Richard Thompson and Company Limited, and as such purchased the Green Lane Mill in that year.

Another new company was formed yet again, this time named Richard Thompson and Sons (1916) Limited, which traded throughout the First World War, but by the late 1920s trading conditions deteriorated and in 1928 the business was sold off as a going concern to J.H. Bertwistle and Company Limited, the Haslingden manufacturers. Four years later this company was running 40,000 spindles and 1,047 looms at the Britannia and Alma Mills. Bertwistle had 40,000 spindles running and 1,301 looms in 1950 at the Britannia, Alma and Riverside Mills. The spinning section of the mills ceased around the first half of the 1950s, and for a short period the spinning mill was leased to Mullards for storage and assembly work. Bertwistle's finally closed all their Padiham mills down in 1956 and concentrated their production at the Grane Road Mills at Haslingden. By 1965 Britannia mill had been acquired by the Padiham Cotton and Cotton Waste Company Limited, who also ran the Green Bridge Mill, manufacturers of oil rags and engine cleaning cloths, also cotton waste for re-spinning. Among the directors were Albert Hargreaves (manager) R.D. Wood (also secretary) Harold Hargreaves, and John L. Hargreaves.

Clay Bank Mill

Unfortunately, the old Clay Bank Mill was demolished in 1996, and the site today is taken by a block of modern housing off Moor Lane. This small factory probably started off as a warehouse in the early years of the Industrial Revolution, being built in 1790, before then being converted into a loom shop containing a number of looms which were operated by the local handlooms weavers. Power loom weaving, that is looms powered by steam engines was introduced at the mill about 1848 by George Hargreaves, a local grocer and draper, who later moved to Industry Mill. By 1854, Clay Bank Mill was in the occupancy of Thomas Bibby, and in the same year was advertised to be let, and had seventy eight looms at that time. When it was advertised again in 1865, it boasted eighty five looms—however by the early 1880 Clay Bank Mill ceased to be associated with the staple trade of the town and took on several other occupancies over the following years. It became a marine store, run by George Hargreaves, and then a brass foundry, and from around 1910 it became an institution known locally as *"T' Ragged School"* which closed down in 1952. From around the 1952-53 it was associated with the print trade, by way of the *'Padiham Advertiser'* and today a new row of houses, appropriately named Clay Bank Fold now occupies the site of the old Clay Bank Mill.

Commercial Mill

This mill was the first of two co-operative mills to be built in Padiham, and was erected in 1851 by the Padiham Commercial Company with the support of many of the local mill operatives. Interestingly, a co-operative to run mills was formed as early as 1848 at Padiham, this was known as the "Padiham Co-operative Cotton Society" and it was to be another 15 years before Burnley had anything similar. The Commercial shed held around 300 looms powered by an engine of 25 horse power built by J. & J. Landless of Marsden (Nelson) The venture lasted just four years by which time the mill was being run by its former manager, James Knowles, and in 1858 the property was bought out by him, Thomas Duckworth, James Sagar, Wilkinson Wilkinson and Henry Edmundson. Wilkinson who described himself as a retired manufacturer and his wife Ann were living on Albert Street in the early 1880s. A second shed was built in 1862 adjoining the old mill which increased the number of looms to 582. The firm, now named James Knowles and Company went bankrupt in the following year. In 1867 John Brooks and William Waddington took over the running of the mill.

Brooks withdrew from the partnership in 1872, his place being taken by John Hargreaves. Further extensions were constructed bring the number of looms to 806 during 1886, the mill at that time employing a labour force of some 280 operatives. The Blackburn Standard reported that the mill had recently started work and has nearly all the looms working.. " *and on the whole the town is in a much better position than it has been for a considerable time "*. [xxxvii] After the 1914-18 war Commercial Mill became part of Thomas Catlow Limited, they of Orchard Mill at Padiham. Weaving ended at the Commercial Mill by 1927, and the numerous attempts to sell the business failed, and eventually the looms were broken up for scrap. The mill buildings themselves survived for a time before being demolished, and in 1980, K. Raymakers and Sons Limited of Alma Mill across the way on Wyre Street erected a warehouse on the site. [xxxviii]

The William Waddington mentioned above lived in fine style at 46 Osbourne Terrace Padiham with his wife Annie and their two children Francis and John and two domestic servants. A popular manager at Commercial mill was Henry Robinson of Partridge Hill Street—said to be one of the best known managers in Padiham. He started work at Commercial Mill in 1866 as a tackler, and afterwards became manager at the firm, a position he held for a remarkable 51 years up to the time of his death at the grand age of 80 years in 1921. He had worked under four different employers during that time. Henry was born in Adamson Street, and lived in Padiham all his life, his only son, Harry was one of the many thousand who perished in the war of 1914-18. At the very far end of the site of the former Commercial Mill is an area of open space—here can be seen some large stone engine beds, relicts from the old mill.

Enterprise & Industry Mill

These mills on Wyre Street, the first, Industry Mill was begun in 1851 by William Monk, Thomas Bibby and Wilkinson Wilkinson. Enterprise Mill adjoining was started two years later by George Hargreaves. Thomas Bibby went on to run the Clay Bank Mill in 1852, whilst William Monk went on to built Daisyfield Mill in 1854. Wilkinson Wilkinson entered into a partnership with Christopher Laycock, but it was ill-fated and failed in 1855. Soon after this George Hargreaves came back on the scene and purchased the mills leasing them out to various tenants, such as Richard Mercer and Hull and Ingham. It was while Hull and Ingham were at the mill that there was a prolonged strike in June 1859.

Tempers flared, and there were courts cases with charges of alleged intimidation. Edward Wilkinson was brought before the courts on such a charge and using threatening language towards a weaver John Whittaker employed at Hull and Inghams' mills. Whittaker stated that while he was returning from work about six in the evening he saw a crowd of about 200 persons assembled a hundred yards away from the mill—Wilkinson was one of these men. He approached Wilkinson and said *"Damn thee, devil as thou art, when it comes dark we'll pay thee for working, and we would do it now if it were dark"* Wilkinson also held his finger up to within a few inches of his face and followed him to his doorstep 300 or 400 yards away, using foul language all the way. The rest of the crowd followed and hooted. A witness who worked at the same mill named William Hargreaves confirmed what Whittaker had said. After some consideration the courts found Wilkinson guilty and ordered him to keep the peace for twelve months or risk a fine of £20 or be imprisoned for three months in default.

The rules of the Padiham Power Loom Weavers Association some time later in 1897 makes interesting reading;

Payment for Surgical Certificates.
If you are ever charged more than 3d. For your own or any other child being examined by the Certifying Surgeon, report the same at once to the Committee.

Abatement or Ill-treatment.
Whenever you think you are being unjustly abated, or otherwise ill-treated, do not use in retaliation, any abusive, insulting, or improper language. And if there be any Rule or Rules in the establishment requiring notice, do not leave your work without serving such notice, as some do—saying they will leave before they will be bated—but instead protest against such abatement or ill-treatment, and if you obtain no redress, report your grievance to the Committee at their next meeting.

Going off Work.
Whenever you wish to get off your work, whether for a long or short period, do not go away from your work without first getting proper leave of absence, nor stay away for a longer period than that for which you have got leave.

Sickness and Asking Off,
Should you be taken sick at the mill so as to prevent you following your employment, ask off, and, if possible, get permission before leaving your work; and if taken sick at home, go yourself at once to the mill if you are able and ask off, if not, send word immediately the engine commences, or before, stating the cause of your absence by someone you can rely upon delivering the message properly to the person in authority.

Finding Sick Weavers.
It is always very unwise for you to find a weaver to supply your place while you are away, for by so doing, you make yourself responsible for the action or work of such weaver. It is the duty of the employer or person in authority to find weavers, not you, and if you do so it must be with his consent.

Payment for Property belonging to the Employer.
Never pay, or agree to pay, for any shuttles, forks, brushes, or any piece of machinery, matter, or thing belonging to the employer, or used in his business in any way whatsoever, except what you may have by gross negligence wilfully or maliciously broken or destroyed; and if they stop it from your wages, bring it before the Committee at their next meeting.

Neglecting Work through Drinking,
Under no circumstances leave your work to go off drinking, because you not only get punished and bring yourself into disrepute, but other weavers get to suffer in consequence, as the employer cannot always distinguish (if he is inclined) between persons who stop off drinking and persons who stop off on fair and reasonable grounds, therefore they are treated alike, and the innocent often get punished equally with the guilty.

Fresh Looms or New Class of Work.
Whenever fresh looms are imposed upon you, of which you do not approve, or from which you cannot earn as much money, you should protest against it; but if there are Rules requiring notice, do not leave, but lay your case before the Committee and at the expiration of the term of notice you may bring an action for the loss, if any, that you may have sustained in consequence.

Orders of the Employer.
Never disobey any reasonable order of your employer in anything pertaining to the proper performance of your duty; but if he orders you to do something which does not belong to your occupation, or is dangerous to life or limb, or is exacting in its nature, you have a right to object.

Attendance at Work. Stoppage through Accident, &c.
Endeavour always to attend at the time stated on the time board, and when there has been a stoppage through a breakdown or any other accident, you should always return to your work at the time stated by the employer, manager, or other person in authority, for re-starting the engine, or if Notice of such re-starting to be short, as soon after as possible, whether such notice be given verbally or otherwise.

Disputes and Strikes.
Whenever there is any dispute at the mill at which you work, never turn out or stop at your looms and refuse to work, but at once see the employer to see if the complaint cannot be rectified, or otherwise see the Committee so that such complaint can be redressed if possible, as by turning out you make yourself amenable to the law.

Sick Weavers and Notice.
Sick weavers may at any time leave without notice and without any action being brought against them or the wages detained, whether there are Rules or not, except when they have contracted to work for a stated period, or until a certain person returns to work, or is able to return. This would amount to a special contract, and should be fulfilled.

Discharges.
Never leave your work unless positively discharged, and told that you must not work there any longer, or in some such positive language ordered to leave the place. Sometimes a manager, overlooker, or tackler, will say that "you had better give over," or, " if you don't like, you can give over," or, "if you cannot do better, give over j" take no notice whatever of this, but go on working, as it is not a discharge in the eyes of the law.
Getting Work after Illegal Discharge.

When you have been discharged without just cause, always endeavour to get work at some other place as soon afterwards as possible, if not, it may damage any action for wrongful dismissal you may afterwards bring.

James Bear and Henry Dean had taken over both mills by 1868, but this partnership was dissolved just two years later in March 1870.[xxxix] George Green and John Robert Sagar took over the lease after this. This partnerships last until the very early years of the 1880s when it too was dissolved, partners named Walmsley and Cooper were then able to lease the mills for a period of six years. There were various other unsuccessful tenants over the next few years towards the end of the nineteenth century, until 1900 when a new room and power company to be named the Enterprise Mill Company was established. This company leased the sheds out to various tenants, and in 1907 the premises were purchased outright by James Ingham Company Limited, which was soon followed in 1910 by the Crescent Manufacturing Company—the last manufacturing business to occupy the mills who went bankrupt in 1930. At the time of occupation by the Crescent Manufacturing Company the mill employed 150 workpeople and ran 450 looms. During the second week of the annual summer holidays in 1927, Edward Proctor of Hambledon Street Padiham was walking past the mill when he noticed a fire had broken out in the engine house of 'Crescent Mill' on Wyre Street. He ran to the mill offices and informed the mill owner Fred Bardshaw of Nether Leigh, Wilpshire of the fire before running off to the fire station to get help. Because it was the summer holidays most of the firemen were out inspecting the fire hydrants and taking an advantage of the slack time at the mills to test them. Three firemen were on standby at the fire station and they turned out with the large engine. The other firemen were going up towards Higham when they spotted flames and smoke coming from the mill—they returned to Padiham as quick was possible. Two hose pipes were brought into play taking water from the street hydrants and from the 'Goit'. An hour later the fire had been brought under control. The boiler-house, the engine room and the preparation plant at the mill were completely gutted, damage was estimated at being over £10,000, but covered by insurance. Soon after bankruptcy of the Crescent Manufacturing Company the mills were sold to Eddlestone Company Limited, mill wrights and textile engineers, and aluminium founders, who later concentrated on business as plumbers merchants.

This firm in 1930 purchased the massive Victoria Mill and moved their business and that of James Blezard to that mill. By the late 1980s when trading as James Blezard and Sons Limited the business was sold out to its manager, trading stopped soon afterwards and the mill buildings at Enterprise and Industry mills was sold off. A van hire centre now occupies the premises of the former Enterprise and Industry Mills.

Green Bridge Mill

This mill is located on Station Road and besides Green Bridge on Green Lane on the right hand side going up towards Station Road. The mill, a former sawmill and bobbin works was built in the mid 1850s by Richard Kay, powered by two small steam engines. The Bobbin Mill was that section nearest the railway embankment of the former railway, now part of the linier park. Kay later added the weaving shed in 1865 which then containing 130 odd looms. The weaving shed was leased out to James Thornber of Church near Accrington, but he was declared bankrupt within a few months. It was several years before the next tenant, Elijah Helm junior of Padiham took over the shed in 1870. Other tenants included the partnership of Frankland, Pilling and Wilkinson who failed in 1885. John Pollard and Company who took over also failed in 1889—they were running 180 looms at that time. The mill was then unoccupied for five years until 1894 when William Slater and Hezekiah Slater of St Anne's Terrace, Padiham took on the lease—but they failed after a lengthy dispute amongst the workers and were declared bankrupt in May 1898 at Burnley bankrupt court. A Blackburn machinery manufacturer Richard Ryden bought out the entire site in 1905, which also included the bobbin works. Following this the shed was reorganised with the bobbin works being included into the weaving shed, which was increased in capacity with 350 looms. Ryden did not however put the mill to his own use but leased it out to, amongst others such as The Greenbridge Manufacturing Company and Messrs Blackburn and Derbyshire. It was while the latter firm was at the mill that there might have been a serious fire there in 1908 had it not been for the prompt action of a passerby. In late January 1908, a weaver, named Albert Wilkinson of Cotton Street in Padiham was walking along Green Lane around half past seven when he noticed smoke coming out of the windows at Green Bridge Mill.

Green Bridge Mill
(Author)

Rather bravely, or perhaps rather recklessly he broke a window and got into the shed. Here he found in that portion of the shed dividing the store-room from the warehouse a number of bales of cotton on fire. Wilkinson threw a number of the blazing bales out into the street, and then the fire brigade was sent for. The engine and horse tender were soon on the spot under the command of Superintendant Gregson and his men. Several jets were got to work from the street hydrants, the fire by this time having got a good hold on the storeroom. After half an hour the fire was under control, but damage had been done to the amount of £600—this being covered by insurance. The cause of the outbreak was unknown. A decline in trade between 1915-16 and the effects of WW1 caused the end of weaving at the Green Bridge Mill. Just after the end of WW1 the Padiham Cotton and Cotton Waste Company Limited was formed by Thomas L. Hargreaves of Shuttleworth House, Hapton who occupied the mill for many years after this date. There was a terrific blaze at the mill while the Padiham Cotton and Cotton Waste Company were at the place in March 1965 by which three firemen and a woman bystander were injured. Padiham fire brigade were alerted just before 10.00 on the Sunday morning, and were the first brigade to arrive at the scene.

Soon there were forty odd firemen at the site with men from Burnley, Accrington, Nelson, Oswaldtwistle and it was over two hours later that the blaze was brought under control. The three firemen who were injured were playing their hoses on a section of the mill besides Green Brook and the footbridge over the stream there when a wall and part of the roof caved in. About sixty feet of walling fell and some of it caught the brigades' appliances in Green Lane. Twenty one year old Anne Latham of Stockbridge Road was also caught by one of the falling stones—she had stepped in front of her mother, Alice Latham in a bid to protect her from the falling masonry. The 21 year was taken to hospital where she had six stitches on the wound. The three firemen were taken to Accrington hospital, but were not detained, although one of them, Jim Foley of Padiham had to have an x-ray on his foot. [xl] Today (2010) most of Green Bridge Mill is taken by a car breaking firm.

Green Lane Mill

The three storied Green Lane Mill stands on the corner of Stockbridge Road and Green Lane. The weaving shed, which is scheduled for demolition at the time of writing, was further up Stockbridge Road. This 'mill' actually started out as an iron foundry being built by Thomas Dewhurst. He had previously operated from premises on Adamson Street. It was Dewhurst who also constructed the three storied spinning mill on Green Lane around 1865, which was powered by a beam engine built by the millwrights, J. And C. Thompson who were also using another part of the site. It seems that the weaving shed with Northern Lights had been in existence from about 1856. Once the spinning mill was completed, cotton spinning began almost immediately by the firm of Shaw and Whittaker who took a lease out on the mill from Dewhurst. However, three years later in 1869 they were declared bankrupt—the machinery at that time included almost 130 looms. Towards the end of the 1870s, the mill was purchased by Thomas Stephenson, a former manager with the extensive Lowerhouse Mills—he however only used the spinning mill initially. The weaving shed was worked by a partnership consisting of Sagar, Butterworth, Green and Dean who took over the premises circa 1875. The partnership was dissolved in 1881, although Henry Dean ran the weaving section on his own account for a short period before moving onto the Levant Mill later that same year. After Dean moved out Thomas Stephenson and Company began to operate the mill as a whole on their own.

The spinning mill was worked by the Stephenson Family until around 1895 when it was closed down. There was a serious fire in 1903 which gutted the building, later the surviving walls were reduced in height to single story and then re-roofed creating a second weaving shed containing around 120 looms. This weaving shed was leased out to Green and Company. Later, as part of improvements at the mill a horizontal cross compound steam engine, originally built for Burnley Corporation Electricity Works was installed. The George Green and Company (Padiham) Limited was to run successfully until the second part of the 1960s when closure was brought about by bad trading conditions. The closure was announced in January 1967. A meeting followed of directors and representatives of the Textile Trades Federation, before notices signed by the chairman of the company, Sir Harold Parkinson posted notices that the mill was to shut. The notice read;

"It is a matter of great concern and deep regret to Lady Parkinson (whose grandfather founded the mill over one hundred years ago) and myself and indeed to all concerned that we are forced to weave out owing to foreign competition. Up to recent years this foreign competition was not felt, but now our customers can buy imported cloth at about two thirds of the price that it costs us to make. We therefore cannot continue to trade under such conditions, and this is to give notice that operatives will become redundant at stages from 13 January"

It was hoped that the twenty or so operatives left at the mill might find work at the subsidiary company at Stockbridge Mill which packed the woven articles. A few other firms tried unsuccessfully to operate on the site but to no avail, and weaving finally ended in the year 2000. The firm of Sherry's did continue for some years operating a mill-shop on the site after this, but they too succumbed to trading conditions around 2005.

Grove Mill
Is situated between Higham Street, Partridge Hill and Grove Lane at Padiham, and today what is left of it is mainly occupied by small industrial units. The mill was started by Elijah and Henry Helm, who also ran the Padiham Old Mill, and various extensions were added to Grove Mill over the years. After the Cotton Famine of the early 1860s, the company traded as Helm and Company Limited.

Originally, the mill consisted of two separate spinning mills, and a fierce fire in 1879 at the smaller spinning mill greatly reduced its capacity. A second fire in November 1883 caused damage to the premises amounting to £12,000, although the buildings were fully insured. At that time the mill consisted of the two spinning mills, each containing eight pairs and four pairs of mules, and the weaving shed contained 180 looms together with the necessary warehousing and other accommodation. The larger spinning mill started in 1838 was composed of three storeys and an attic, and contained 12,000 spindles. Elijah Helm went on to build the large walled garden house almost inside the Grove Mill itself known as Grove House in 1845—he died on 5 June 1859 and is buried at St Leonards Churchyard. His gravestone can still be seen there, it is one of the very few that remain in the old churchyard. The firm Helm and Company Limited was wound up in 1889, and the mill was sold off to James Blezard of Guy Foundry who moved their engineering operations to the site. Some additions were made to the weaving sheds, and leased out to Graham and Walmsley in 1890, they who worked the Fir Trees Mill at Higham village, and five or six years later they were running 320 looms at the Grove Mills. Jeremiah Graham was a prominent industrialist, and although a native of Blackburn spent most of his life at Padiham, having left Blackburn in 1889 to take over the Fir Trees Mill. He remained at Higham for three years before becoming the head of the firm that controlled Grove Mill. He was concerned with Grove Mill for twenty years, before moving to the Levant Mill where he was associated with management there for twenty two years. Blezard's went bankrupt in 1910, and in the same year Grahams moved to the Levant Mill. Jeremiah Graham retired from his duties in September 1932, and passed away in April 1934 aged 76 years of age, he was buried in Padiham Public Cemetery on St John's Road. Major extensions were undertaken at Grove Mill in 1914 increasing the number of looms to 743 by the Grove Mill Company who had taken over the mill in 1911. Cotton manufacturing ceased in the early 1920s, and since around the 1930s the site has been used for various small industries such as storage units, plastic firms, garages and engineering—it remains as such today.

Holme Mill
A small compact weaving mill constructed in 1881 which was situated off Thompson Street in an area now taken by Inglewhite Fold.

The mill which contained just over 300 looms was built by John Robert Sagar, who used to be a partner in the running of Green Lane Mill, he describes himself as being a 'gentleman' in the 1881 census returns when he lived at 21 St Leonards Street in town—he married Agnes Heap at St Leonards Church in 1852. The completion of the new shed was reported in the local newspaper as follows: *"The shed built by J. Robert Sagar which will hold 308 looms is now nearly completed and on Saturday last the ceremony of christening the engines took place. The ceremony was performed by Mr Ormerod Butterworth who took a bottle of wine and broke it on the engine and wished success to 'Agnes and Mary Jane'. The roof of the new shed is in a new style as well as the shafting, and all the machinery is on the ground. The shed has been visited by a number of manufacturers and are much admired. There is land taken for 600 looms".*
[xli]

The looms at Holme Mill were run by a horizontal compound steam engines named *'Agnes and Mary Jane'* named after Agnes his wife, and his daughter. The 'land taken for 600 looms' mentioned above was taken by Butterworth and Bridge *'and the necessary preparations for the buildings are in progress'*. Said the report in the same newspaper. Following the death of Sagar in 1883, the former manager and a principal shareholder Thomas Noble bought the mill outright from Sagar's Executors. It was while Holme Mill was under the ownership of the Nobles' that a further extension was added as noted above, this was driven by the same engine in the adjoining Levant Mill. The Noble family continued its interest in Holme Mill until just after WW2, when they sold out to the Church Street Manufacturing Company, who ceased trading in the mid 1950s. Weaving ceased altogether at the mill in 1956 after a brief period of being worked by a firm of handkerchief manufacturers named the Burmah Company. What followed was a short period of making of nylon shirting and knitted fabrics by the Calderbrook Knitting Company Limited, these types of operations too had ceased by the 1970s. After being in a ruined condition for a number of years, the site of Holme Mill was cleared and in 1996 the modern housing named Inglewhite Fold was constructed.

Jubilee Mill
The fine engine-house, which survives on Shakespeare Street, tells us that the Padiham Room and Power Company constructed Jubilee Mill in 1887. The Blackburn Standard of 26 March 1887 told that;

"The contract for the mill of the Padiham Building Company, to be known as Jubilee Mill has been let and the operations commenced" 'Room and power' was in its simplest form a group of businessmen who got together funding their resources and built new mills, which they then leased out, to various tenants. There was always some would-be cotton manufacturer willing to take on these premises in order to seek out his riches. Many however were destined for bankruptcy; the Room and Power Company still had their premises though, and simply leased them out to the next tenants. The Padiham Room and Power Company consisted of John Charles Waddington, Norman Blezard, George Green. Ormerod Butterworth, J. Bertwistle and J. Haworth, most of who were well established manufacturers. John Charles Waddington was a solicitor, and the son of Charles Waddington of Orchard and Bridge End Mills—this family had a great influence n the development of the textile trade in Padiham. The original Jubilee Mill built to a design by Sam Keighley of Burnley had space for 1,200 looms. To power these looms a massive cross compound engine built by W. And J. Yates was installed in the engine room we see today. Eight hundred looms were soon being run by the Greenbrook Manufacturing Company Limited, taking its name from Green Brook which runs beside the mill. This company was formed by George and James Moorhouse of Sabden and others. The other 400 looms were being worked by the Church Street manufacturing Company Limited based at Great Harwood. The Greenbrook Company went into liquidation in 1897, and were replaced by George Green and Company of Green Lane Mill.

In the latter year a new tape sizing department was added to the mill, and an extension for a further 400 looms was added in 1903. Both these new additions were leased out to the Church Street Manufacturing Company, who were soon employing around 600 operatives. A depression in the cotton trade of the 1920s led to Green and Co., giving up their lease in 1926,and the Church Street Manufacturing Company during the early 1930s. New tenants were soon found by way of Dean Brothers (Padiham) Limited who in 1926 took on over 800 looms at Jubilee Mill. In 1930, a new company, the Progress Mills Limited was formed by John Charles Waddington and his sons, and L. Woods, a former manager of the Church Street Manufacturing Company, five years later this firm was running 800 looms at Jubilee Mill.

In 1933 J. And J. Roberts, formerly of Levant Mill moved into Jubilee Mill. By the 1950s the latter company, along with Progress Mills and the Padiham Room and Power Companies were all closely associated with the Waddington family. A decade later, the grandsons of John Charles Waddington, John Waddington and his cousin David were the only directors of the three companies. David Waddington is perhaps best remembered as being the Home Secretary in the Conservative government of the 1980s and the Thatcher years. In that same decade, steam power for the looms at Jubilee Mill was abandoned, although the engine remained and was used a couple of times a week to power the lifts at the mill. After this 25-horse power electric motors attached to line shafting drove the looms. The hey-days of Jubilee Mill were numbered, and in July 1984 trading conditions forced closure of the sheds, two years later the mill was sold off and demolition followed. Only the fine engine house survived and parts of the lower walls of the weaving shed serve as a boundary wall to a modern house development. The grand horizontal engine after serving the mill for almost one hundred years was removed to Matlock in Derbyshire for preservation in 1999. For this we have to thank historian Robert Mountford-Aram of Old Cossell near Nottingham—it was he who snapped up the old engine, and the engine house just before both were about to fall under the demolition hammers in April 1986. Mr Mountford-Aram was something of a collector of old engines and engine-house chimneys, at a last count he had no less than 18 engines and 18 mill chimneys. He was however too late to save the Jubilee Mill chimney and a few days later it came crashing down, demolished by well-known chimney toppling expert Ronnie Goggins of Bacup. Jubilee Mill itself was being demolished by N. And R. Demolitions (Todmorden) Limited, the cleared site was proposed to be utilised as old persons' homes—now named Hathaway Fold.[xlii]

Levant Mill
This mill behind numbers 59-79 Thompson Street in the town was built in 1881 by William Bridge and Ormerod Butterworth for use as a room and power shed with space for 336 looms. The first person to take on the lease of the mill was Henry Dean and Son in 1882, Henry had previously been a partner in the Green Lane Mill enterprise. Henry Dean and Son went on to employ over 100 mill workers, the output mainly going to the India market.

George Dean, a member of Henry Dean and Son was declared bankrupt in 1892, and the business had to be reorganised taking on the name of the Levant Manufacturing Company Limited—after which the workforce was increased to 150 operatives running 446 looms. However, this company only lasted three years when it too went into liquidation in 1909. J. And J. Graham of Grove mill took over the Levant the following year, and with the death of Ormerod Butterworth in 1912 the business was purchased by The Padiham Room and Power Company. Later J. And J. Roberts Limited worked the Levant Mill until they removed to Jubilee Mill in 1933—this marked the end of weaving at the Levant Mill. Since that time the old mill has been used for other purposes unconnected with the textile trade.

Lily of the Valley Mill (Vale Mill)
This mill sometimes known also as Vale Mill, or simply Lily Mill is situated on Wyre Street and was begun in 1854 by William Horne and James Horne and Henry Taylor. It was built as a weaving shed for 252 looms. After completion the mill was bought out in 1856 by Henry Helm of Grove Mills, who later traded as Helm and Company limited, a firm which got into difficulties and which was forced into liquidation in 1890. After this the mill lay empty for a period until it was bought by the Padiham Co-operative Society for use as stabling, a slaughterhouse and stores. The Co-op continued to own the mill until well into the 20th century. The high esteem of a former mill manager was shown at Vale Mil in 1876, when the workpeople clubbed together to buy a watch and a copper kettle on the leaving of Mr Eli Sagar. Mr Sagar who was leaving for a similar post with the Sabden Weaving Company was very touched by the tokens and expressed his sincere thanks. About the mid 1950s weaving was once again started at the mill by the Manchester firm of the Eastwood Mill Company who installed 220 looms. In the early 1960s the firm of J.P and P. Brierley took over the Lily of the Valley Mill, and this firm merged with James Stuttard in 1965 when operations were transferred to Sabden. There were a few spasmodic attempts to operate the mill by various firms until 1979 when K. Raymakers took on the mill. The old mill was demolished and a new one erected on the same site in 1983 housing 21 velvet looms. [xliii] Raymakers are specialist weavers of cotton pile velvets.

Orchard Mill

This mill occupied the site now taken by the former Co-operative supermarket besides Padiham Bridge. The factory was constructed as a weaving and spinning shed in 1853 by the Waddington Family, namely Charles and John, who for a short time had previously worked the Clay Bank Mill around 1850. In August 1866 a man named Thomas Thistlethwaite a self acting mule minder at Orchard Mill was summoned for allowing a creeler named Thomas Stevenson aged just nine years old to be in a situation whereby he was injured on the head between the travelling parts of the mule. The Bench did not hold the accused responsible and dismissed the case saying that it was improper to employ a boy aged nine years old at such dangerous work. The last member of the Waddington family to occupy the mill was William Waddington in 1882, the year he was declared bankrupt. This must have caused quite a shock to his lifestyle, for he was living, with his family and two domestic servants at Osbourne Terrace a grand house on Church Street. The above-mentioned Charles Waddington had left the partnership to take over Bridge End Mill in 1872. Soon after William Waddington's failure, Orchard Mill was purchased by James Hitchon Whittaker a Burnley cotton manufacturer for £7,600.

The mill at this time consisted of a weaving shed containing 600 looms and a spinning mill separated by a stone partition which contained 25,000 spindles, together with mixing, blowing rooms and offices. It was at the spinning mill which was three stories high and twelve windows long that a fire broke out in June 1885. The engine was stopped as usual at half past five in the afternoon, and the place was cleared by six o'clock. About half past seven later that evening smoke was seen issuing from the top story of the main spinning mill. The fire station which was close at hand was alerted and the firemen were soon on the scene with the 'manual engine'. This was taken down to the river while the hydrants in the mill yard were put to use. A message was sent out for the Burnley Fire Brigade who arrived just before eight o'clock. *'They were under Superintendant Slater and a full complement of men and the steamer was set to work at once'* said the newspaper report. The firemen played their hoses on the flames until a quarter past ten—by this time the roof had gone and the upper floor was burnt out. A good portion of the carding room and preparations rooms were also burnt out.

Like the Phoenix the mill must have risen from the ashes, for a Mr David Stuttard leased the mill off Whittaker in 1887, taking over the lease to the spinning section of the factory in that year. The business was short lived however and he failed in 1890—Whittaker again took over the running of the mill but he too was declared bankrupt in 1891. James Hitchon Whittaker was a bit of a controversial character to say the least. Whittaker knew full well he was heading for bankruptcy in 1891, and he decided to take precautions to make sure he had some money stacked away and out of sight of his creditors before he was declared bankrupt. In March he began to order large quantities of yarn, both at the Manchester Exchange and at Burnley. He even began to order from firms which he had no business with for many months—and when he started to urge for immediate delivery suspicions were aroused. Whittaker was arrested and charged with fraud, he was also charged with having obtained under false pretences a travelling bag, a trunk and other property from Messrs Freeborn of Manchester. It seems that Mr Whittaker was calmly making plans to travel! It's not too clear whether James Hitchon Whittaker was taken to court, or if he was found guilty or not—but in June 1891 the weavers at Orchard Mill and at Whittaker's' other Mill, Ashfield Shed at Burnley were told to weave out their warps.

Three years later he was living in Sale, Cheshire, where he again found himself in trouble with the law. Dr W. A. Stewart of Oldham had advertised for sale a pony and trap, and it was Whittaker who answered the advertisement. Whittaker talked his way into having the pony and trap on trial, but then sold them both in a public house. He was soon found and taken to court where he was given three months imprisonment. On another occasion while Whittaker was still in Padiham and at Orchard Mill there was a prolonged strike at the factory which lasted almost twelve months. There was a great deal of distress amongst the mill workers, and many a bad temper. One day as Whittaker was riding his horse towards the mill he was confronted by a large and very angry crowd. They jeered and shouted at Whittaker, but he was determined to get through to the works. He reared up his horse and dashed forward firing a pistol into the air, and reached his goal without injury. In later years James Hitchon Whittaker moved to Germany, where he married a German lady, his second wife, the first had died some years previous—it was here that he passed away in December 1898.

Just after David Stuttard took over the mill there was another strike by the operatives on account of the manager's behaviour towards the mill workers, who they said was constantly intimidating them. The workers called a meeting and assembled on the recreation ground before removing to the Oddfellow's Hall. Here, Bill Dean occupied the chair and listened to the grievances of the weavers. It was decided to send six of their number to go and see the mill master David Stuttard, who agreed to meet them at the factory. The deputation by the weavers was received by Mr Stuttard, who stated that this was the first he had ever heard of the intimidation—the weavers demanded that the manager be removed or dismissed. An agreement was eventually reached whereby the manager should not be removed from his position for at least a fortnight—with that the operatives returned to work the following Tuesday. David Stuttard of Windsor Terrace Padiham along with John Stuttard of Sabden and Tom Stuttard of Hargrove, Padiham trading as D. Stuttard and Sons, Orchard Mill, Padiham and Cobden Mills Sabden cotton manufacturers and spinners were declared bankrupt in March 1890. Many manufacturers saw Orchard Mill as a bad investment, and despite a number of attempts to sell the mill at auction, each one failing until it was finally sold to Burnley businessman Robert Simpson in 1893—he leased it out to another Burnley man Robert Catlow and Co., who took over the entire mill in 1906. In late October 1899 there was another fire at the Orchard Mill belonging then to the Vine Spinning Company. The fire broke out on the third story of the four story factory catching the mill operatives unexpectedly, amid panic and mayhem scores of mill workers rushed out of the building. Padiham fire brigade were soon on the scene, but the fire spread rapidly to the top floor—an hour after the alarm was given the roof gave way. Two and a half hours later the fire was brought under control, but at a loss of the top two floors, and extensive water damage to the other floors. Several thousands of pounds worth of damage was done to the mill. As a direct result of a general decline in the trade both spinning and weaving ceased forever Orchard Mill in 1927, and early in the following decade the whole machinery was broken up for scrap. Twenty years later the site of the old Orchard Mill had been cleared and later the present building was constructed.

Padiham Old Mill
This mill on Factory Lane, between Ightenhill Street and Guy Street is Padiham's oldest surviving industrial building.

It was built as a mule spinning mill by Henry Helm in 1807. A datestone bearing this date can still be seen above the projecting window at the bottom end of the mill. The Helms' had been associated with the towns staple trade for generations and had run various mills throughout Padiham over the decades—they probably started out as simple handloom weavers. The mill was also known as 'Guy Yate Mill' the mill besides the way, or gate, 'gate' means 'street' to Guy Street, and in the 1840s it even had its own gasometer. There were other buildings associated with the Padiham Old Mill to the rear, but it seems that some of these had to be demolished to make way for the extension of the massive Victoria Mill. The Cotton Famine of the early 1860s forced the closure of Padiham Old Mill, and from around the early 1890s the mill was used by a furniture dealer until the late 1920s. Some local might still remember the old mill being occupied by Fred Pollard Textiles Limited, who dealt in carpet off-cuts and fent ends. This firm closed down comparatively recently in April 2004, and soon after this date the mill was converted into flats—an excellent example of how old industrial buildings can be put to other uses and saved for future generations. For a time the top floor of the mill was used as a billiard hall just after WW2. Padiham Old Mill is a statutorily listed building, Grade II for its historical and architectural interest.

Peel's Mill
A small and early carding shop and spinning mill possibly next to the eastern end of the site of the old Padiham Corn Mill—little else is known about this factory, although it probably dated from around the late 1790s. Mike Rothwell says that the premises consisted of two rooms and an attic, 20 yards by 12 ½ yards, was water powered and contained 1080 throstle spindles in 1811. After this date it may have become part of Padiham Corn Mill.

Perseverance Mill
Much of the site of the old Perseverance Mill is now taken by the housing complex of Waterside Mews. The mill was next to Padiham Bridge on the corner of Green Lane. There was a great deal of rejoicing when William Bear a Padiham sizer opened his Perseverance Mill—and a celebration dinner was held at the Bridge Inn on 30 August 1861. The new mill was capable of holding 800 looms with a large steam engine to power the same.

At the dinner were Humphrey Waddington of Stockbridge House who acted as chairman, and Richard Thompson of Britannia Mill acted as vice-chairman. The first toast of the evening was *'The Queen'* followed by *'The Prince Consort and all the Royal Family'* and finally the toast to the *'Success of Perseverance Mill, the engine and its owner, Mr William Bear'*.
xliv

This was not the best time to be constructing a new factory, it was the start of the American Civil War and the severe cotton shortage that followed after the American ports were blocked. This became known as 'Dole Time' or the 'Cotton Famine' and caused great distress in the manufacturing districts of Lancashire such as Burnley and Padiham as the mills and factories were starved of cotton. However William Bear, whose family originated in the Lowerhouse district, at Habergham Eaves, Bear Street there is named after them, appeared to have survived the Cotton Famine. The firm was employing 350 hands in 1871, but the following year in 1872 he was declared bankrupt. The Perseverance Mill was then sold off to Richard Thompson and Sons, of the Britannia Mills. The Thompsons did not take over the running of the mill themselves however, but leased it out to, and later sold it to the Blackburn cotton manufacturers Briggs and Company. A new company, The Perseverance Mill Company was founded in the dawn of a new century in 1900, instigated by Herbert Noble, and soon they were employing 250 operatives at the shed. Herbert Noble was born in 1869 at Great Harwood, the son of cotton manufacturer Allan Noble and Elizabeth, nee' Wensley who were married at St Bartholomew's Great Harwood in 1867. He came to Padiham in 1900 and formed the Perseverance Mill Company in October that year. Herbert lived at Higher Trapp, Simonstone and went on to become a director of Albion Room and Power Company, Padiham, Prospect Manufacturing Company Limited, Blackburn, and Barnes and Rothwell of Church. He became a county magistrate, a position he held for more than 30 years, and at one time was chairman of the Bench. He also had a long association with Padiham Urban District Council, both during and after the First World War, when he was chairman. He was on the Education Committee, chairman of the School Attendance Committee, he was on the Burnley Hospital Board, he was a member of the Cotton Spinners and Manufacturers Association and many other local organisations and boards. Herbert moved to Higher Trapp in 1914, where, he like his grandfather and father before him took a great deal of interest in agriculture, being a member of the Great Harwood

Agriculture Society. When he died in 1948, Albion Mills were closed down for the day as a mark of respect to this great man. He left two daughters and four sons and ten grandchildren. His wife Martha, formerly Sharples whom he married at Blackburn Cathedral in 1896 predeceased him by a few years. Soon after the Second World War in 1946 it was decided to concentrate and centralise all future production at the Albion Mill, and Perseverance Mill was leased out to Robert Pickles who also had a number of mills in the Whittlefield area of Burnley. There was a serious fire at the boiler house at the mill in 1958 which gutted the place and the first floor section of the mill, then occupied by Billington and Bridge who employed about 30 women making leather cloth and piping. The firemen managed to stop the blaze spreading to that section of the mill occupied by Robert Pickles and Northern Handicrafts. On Monday 30 August 1965 another huge fire ripped through the Perseverance mill causing thousands of pounds worth of damage to machinery and stock. Hundreds of people gathered to watch as firemen from Burnley, Padiham, Nelson, Accrington and Oswaldtwistle battled to keep the blaze under control, all the traffic on Burnley Road was diverted save for the buses. The mill at this time employed around 60 people, the main businesses being Northern Handicrafts, Billington and Bridge, and Robert Pickles Ltd. The blaze effectively spelt the end for the building then over one hundred years old. It was reduced in height and used for a short time by various firms until around the end of the 1980s when the rest of the factory was demolished. Today, only fragments of the outside walls are visible, the rest was taken up by new houses named Waterside Mews built in the 1980s.

Riverside Mill
This mill located to the rear of the Britannia Mill was constructed as a weaving shed in 1888 by William Ingham of Albert Mills. In 1900 Inghams' leased parts of the mill to Gawthorpe and Jackson of Industry Mills who ran 420 looms, and J. And R. Nuttall of Burnley who installed 120 looms. Both these firms had given up their leases by 1907, Inghams then ran the mill themselves until they closed it in 1933. For a brief period the mill was operated by a firm of waste spinners, until textile manufacturing was again introduced in the 1960s by way of Walter Crane Limited weaving furnishing and dress fabrics—this finished circa 1974. The head office of Walter Crane and Company was at 39 High Street, Deansgate Manchester.

The directors of the Cloverbrook Mill at Higham formed the Riverside Knitting Company Limited in 1977 and operated from the mill until manufacturing was transferred to Gannow Lane in 2002. The mill still survives and consists mainly of non-textile companies.

Smithy Gate Mill
This mill was demolished during the mid 1960s and stood on the site of Padiham Clinic and to the rear of the Post Office on Burnley Road. The mill was built by a partnership which included corn dealer, and grocer William Heap, Paul Tickle, an agent for the Shuttleworth's of Gawthorpe and John Dewhurst during the mid 1830s. It was four stories high and built as a mule and throstle spinning mill housing 10,000 spindles and equipped with an additional weaving shed capable of holding 86 looms—a 35 horse power beam engine provided the power for the machines. The first lease on the building was taken up by Padiham manufacturers Henry and Elijah Helm who ran the mill until 1853. Other tenants followed including Richard Hindle of Clayton-le-Moors and on his removal in 1871 spinning at Smithy Gate Mill ceased. It was advertised for sale by auction in May that year when most of the weaving looms were sold off. Once again the mill was put up for sale in 1877, tenants at this time included John Whittam and Thomas Holland. The number of looms in the weaving shed increased slightly to 108 in 1880, and the weaving section was leased out to various tenants, most of whom failed. The Church Street Manufacturing Company, a Great Harwood firm took over in 1885, and when their lease expired in 1897 so did weaving at the mill. A longstanding tenant at the mill was James Bertwistle who occupied a section of the mill from around the start of WW1 to the early 1940s at what was termed 'Central Garage'. The looms were taken out on the expiration of the lease of The Church Street Manufacturing Company and the Padiham Soap and Chemical Company converted the premises to that of soap-making. Other firms made use of the former spinning mill, the most notable being the Padiham Aerated Water Company Limited—a business founded by Josiah Monk of Brookfoot Farm. He moved to Smithy Gate Mill around 1900. Josiah Monk passed away in 1907, and just over twenty years later the brewery firm of Grimshaws' took over the aerated water concern—this firm Grimshaws' was later taken over by Massey's Burnley Brewery.

In June 1965 it was announced that Massey Burnley Brewery had agreed to purchase all the shares of Padiham Aerated Water Company Limited not already owned by them. *"The company were confident that the fact that Padiham Aerated Water Company would in future be supported by the full organisation of Massey's Brewery and its subsidiary companies and will enable the services given to customers of Padiham Aerated Water Company to be maintained and extended"* continued the report. It was not to be—production ended the following year when the mill was sold off to Padiham District Council. Demolition soon followed at a cost of £1,765 and the area where the old Smithy Gate Mill had stood was landscaped.

Spa Mill
This mill was begun very near the start of the Cotton Famine by partners named William Foster, George Hitchon and Thomas and William Whittaker in 1860-61. It was built as a four story spinning mill capable of housing over eight and a half thousand mule spindles. Two or three years later a weaving shed was added, and leased out to the first tenants Gregson and Walsh. Following the failure of the Foster, Whittaker Company in 1869, the Spa Mill was taken over by William Bear, who was also running the Perseverance Mill besides Padiham Bridge. However, Bear too went bankrupt in 1872, although by some arrangement was able to continue running the mill until 1879 when the premises went into the hands of the Burnley Building Society. Bear survived as their tenant until he ceased business in 1884. For a good number of years the mill remained vacant, and in 1894 a local iron monger named Francis Helm was able to purchase the mill. Helm was able to convert the spinning section of the mill into his foundry, and the weaving shed was continued on a room and power basis, and two years later in 1896 it was leased to William Bradshaw and Co. In September 1906 there was a fire at the weaving section of the mill, which at that time contained 300 looms. The blaze was quickly brought under control however and damage was limited to about £300 worth. At the end of WW2 Richard Haworth and Company Limited cotton manufacturers were working Spa Mill, they had 224 looms running manufacturing high class plains, drills, rayon dress and gabardine fabrics. The registered office of the firm was at 35 Dale Street, Manchester. Various tenants took on the mill over the decades and weaving ceased altogether in 1959-60. Most of the factory was demolished during 1993, and in 2005 an application was put in to erect 55 dwelling houses on the site which was approved.

Spa Mill was probably so named on account of a feeder spring running into the River Calder close-by which might have had medicinal qualities. There was a Spa Mill at Burnley so named on this account.

Victoria Mill

The massive Victoria Mill, now Victoria Apartments was built between 1852-53 by Henry and James Helm as a mule spinning factory. A 25 horse power beam engine here in an integral engine house at the western end of the building drove 7,400 mule spindles and 126 power looms. This engine house today is marked by two slender arched headed widows facing Ightenhill Street. The Cotton Famine of the early 1860s forced the closure of Helms Victoria Mill, and it remained closed, despite a number of attempts to sell until the Padiham Spinning Company purchased the mill in 1873. This Company was supported by mill manager John Shackleton, a carding—master named E. Greenwood, W. H. Woods, a spinning manufacturer and Thomas Broughton, a shoemaker of all things. The Company soon extended the mill in length on one side of the building which doubled the size of the factory—it is still possible to see where this extension was built in the middle of the block on Ightenhill side. Soon after this the mill was employing a workforce of around 75 operatives and contained 30,000 mule spindles, and became known locally as the 'Co-op Mill'. Under this situation the Victoria Mill ran until around 1927 when the Padiham Spinning Company went into voluntary liquidation. After this Victoria Mill became known as 'Guy Works' producing cast-iron school furniture by the firm Eddleston and Company who had purchased the former mill in 1930. Then and along with Blezard and Sons who manufactured cast greenhouse boilers moved their production to the factory. Eddleston and Company sold the firm in 1989 and moved their production to Industry Mill. James Blezard and Sons continued at the mill as plumbers merchants, and lasted until the early 1990s before finally closing. Planning was submitted for the conversion of the mill into 25 apartments along with sympathetic upgrading of some adjoining cottages, and in 1995 this application was approved. Another excellent example of compassionate restoration of an old industrial mill which still retains some of the heritage of the area.

Wellington Mill
This mill on the corner of Ribble Street and Wyre Street was begun in 1852-53 by Henry Watson, and a local corn miller of Church Street, Thomas Sherburn. The datestone was on the keystone above the former engine house of the mill. Henry Watson was a fine fellow to work for by all accounts. For instance on Christmas Eve 1851 he gave all his employees an excellent supper, after which there were toasts to the man and his workers. 'Mr Watson was well known for his many acts of kindnesses concluded the report. The Cotton Famine of the early 1860s brought an end to this partnership which was eventually dissolved in 1869. John Whitaker who lived at Craggs Farm and owned the adjoining Daisyfield Sheds came into procession of Wellington Mill, and carried out a number of improvements. These included the installation of a new compound beam engine with a 20 foot diameter flywheel, by the early 1880s, 36,000 mule spindles and 378 looms were running at the Wellington Mill, and Whittaker was providing employment for 360 hands. Spinning ended in 1907 at Wellington Mill, and a multi storey block that still survives was leased out to various companies as warehouse storage and workshops as it is today. The business previously run by John Whittaker was later turned into a limited company of which John Harry, the only son of John Whittaker was the principal partner, however the firm went bankrupt in 1930, and the business was placed into liquidation ending weaving operations at the same time. John Harry Whittaker was also involved with the Padiham Aerated Water Company and had been from its inception in 1897. Before his death in June 1922 he lived at 'Dene Hill' on the Whalley Road at Padiham, he was also a lifelong member of the Constitutional Club at Padiham and was a member of Padiham Council. Padiham Paints now occupy most of the ground floor premises at Wellington Mill today.

THE EXTRACTION INDUSTRIES
COAL MINING
The extraction of coal is an ancient industry, we have records locally of the fuel being mined as early as 1294 when the monks at Bolton Abbey were working coal at Trawden in East Lancashire. [xlv] 'Mining' in this sense simply meant extracting the coal where the seam came to the surface, this is known as 'outcropping' and the simplest way of getting at the coal. Later shallow shafts would have been sunk as the miners followed to coal deeper into the earth.

The coal would have then been worked around the bottom of the shaft until it was considered too dangerous, and then another shaft would be sunk close by. This method of mining was known as bell pit workings, the cross section of the shaft resembling the shape of a bell. The relicts of both these types of workings can still be seen at Castercliffe, and ancient hill-fort overlooking Nelson and Colne. The outcropping here is depicted as long shallow troughs where the coal was extracted centuries ago, and the bell pits present themselves as round circular hollows. The first mention of coal in or around Padiham probably occurs in 1434, and in 1515 some illegal coal pits in Padiham were ordered to be closed up. Coal was still being mined and sold outside the township without license in 1537. Mines were leased by the lord of the manor, in just the same way as he leased his mills and pasturage of his land, and were leased for a certain number of years—often though they might be sublet. In 1450 mines were leased at Padiham and the Pendle Forest, and in 1640 a mine was leased to Richard Shuttleworth for 21 years at an annual rent of £2/13/4 per year, the estimated value was £40 per year. [xlvi] In 1617 the rights to mine all the coal in Padiham were leased to Lawrence Sankey—it was not until 1826 that John Hargreaves the Burnley coal master leased the coal seams in Padiham.

John Lomax of Clayton-le-Moors was the last to give up his local coal mining rights to Hargreaves in 1840. In the early 17th century a number of coal pit shafts were sunk by the Shuttleworth Family of Gawthorpe Hall. The shafts were circular, and about six feet in diameter, stone lined. One of these was hard by Brookfoot Farm on Grove Lane in Padiham, and worked the coal by the pillar and stall method. It is interesting to note that that part of what is now Grove Lane before the present Town Hill Bank and Grove Woods itself was once named Duckett Lane, probably after the Duckett's who worked Padiham Quarries nearby, and Hill Farm. The Towneley Family also had a coal mine at Hapton on lands belonging to Hapton Hall Farm and Hapton Clough sunk by Charles Towneley in the year 1779. 'A contract was drawn up between Charles Towneley Esq., and Richard Robinson, of Padiham, Harry Winterbottom of Goodshaw Chapel, James Thomas Tattersall of Oswaldtwistle, John Whittam of Pheasantford, and Norman and John Cooper, 'Burnley Gentlemen'. 'They proposed to take the mines and beds of coals situated in the Parish of Hapton belonging to Charles Towneley, except such parts called the John Mines that are under the farms in the occupation of John Collins, as tenant'.

The 'Padiham Thick Seam' lies roughly between Dean Wood, off the Blackburn Road to the west of Padiham to Pendle Hall farm, to the east and to Higham, the seam reaches a thickness of 10 to 11 feet. In the mid 17th. Century a small coal mine existed at the junction of Grove Lane and Garden Street in Padiham, which worked the Padiham Thick Seam. The shaft of this old mine collapsed as recently as January 1967, when the workings could be entered. What was long thought to have been a horse drinking trough in Slade Lane at Padiham was in fact the entrance to an old drift mine that led to the same Padiham Thick Seam. Another old drift mouthing was located twenty yards to the south of the stile and footpaths that goes to Hargrove Farm from Adamson Street. When this area was opencast mined in the 1950s, the coal was exposed and it was found that large areas had been on fire, charred coals and cinders lay among the good coal waiting to be extracted by the diggers. Enquiries revealed that at the turn of the 20th. Century, the area had been affected by Foot and Mouth. This area had long been worked for coal by the locals and farmers to supply their own needs, so much so, that little coal was actually bought, and indeed some was sold. These large cavities that had been mined in the Padiham Thick Seam and they were utilised to dispose of the dead animals, which once placed in the holes were set fire to. When the whole operation was completed, the holes were back-filled leaving no sign of the cremation until the seams were again exposed during the opencast operations. [xlvii]

In fairness, all these mines were small scale and only supplied the local markets, the odd farmhouse or a few cottages. Larger scale mining didn't really begin until the coming of the Industrial Revolution, when the demand for coal as a fuel for the steam engines and the foundries soared. The following are some of the coal mines that worked in and around Padiham, although some are outside the parish they have been included, for by the nature of this extraction industry most coal mining was done in rural areas—you wouldn't after all, want a coal mine working under *your* house!

Bancroft Colliery
This coalmine was besides the River Calder in the woods on the left hand side going up the drive to Gawthorpe Hall, two capped shafts covered with concrete can still be seen near the river. The nearby housing estate on River Drive is called Bancroft Woods estate. The pit is marked on the First Edition of the O.S, Map of 1844-48.

It is not however mentioned in the *"Catalogue of Plans of Abandoned Mines"* which would have given us a few details about the pit, nor is it mentioned in *"Statistics of Collieries in Lancashire, Cheshire and Wales"* published by Mines Inspector Joseph Dickinson in 1854. The mine probably worked the Padiham Thick seam, which hereabouts was between six and ten feet thick. The shafts here were sixty six feet deep and as late as 1965 were only protected by a scant fence and wooden trap doors placed over the pits—as this reports goes to show.

"Danger lurks for children in a bluebell wood less than 150 yards from a row of new houses in River Drive on the Bancroft Woods estate, Padiham. Protected by a few strands of barbed wire fencing is a 66 foot deep mine shaft belonging to the N.C.B (National Coal Board) The wooden door over the shaft is without padlock. The grave danger which the shaft presents to the children has been brought to the notice of Padiham U.D.C by Mr A.S. McMillan...His concern is shared by several, residents of the estate including Mr Harry Fielding who moved to Padiham from Carlisle eight weeks ago "My wife and I have been most concerned at the dangerous state of the shaft ever since I saw four or five children dropping stones down it" said Mr Fielding. "Two sturdy children could easily lift the wooden trap door over the shaft" The Padiham U.D.C. Surveyor, Mr W. Wood has written to the N.C.B. asking them to ensure that the shaft is made inaccessible to children". [xlviii]

Cornfield Colliery

This colliery was also located besides the River Calder upstream of Gawthorpe Hall below Cornfield Farm. There were previous shafts to the north of this site named Palace House situated between Top o' th' Close Farm and Cornfield Farm. These were sunk by the Shuttleworths of Gawthorpe Hall around the 1840s. The 'hey days' at Cornfield Colliery was said to have been in the twenty years, 1850-1870, when the miners were paid in gold sovereigns, the coal was so easy to get, that the men simply filled off what had dropped down as loose coal from the face and pillars sides. While sinking the shafts at Cornfield Colliery, the following coal seams were intercepted, the Four Foot Mine at a depth of 33 yards, the Yard Seam or Three Foot Seam at 68 yards, and the Six Foot Seam at 72 yards. The shaft beside the River Calder was sunk in 1872 by the Exors of John Hargreaves, the Burnley coal owners to the Bing Mine, three foot and eleven inches thick, mainly used for boiler stoking coal.

The agent for the Exors at Padiham in the 1850s was James Diggle. Production at Cornfield pit ended on 9 February 1897, although the shafts were retained for secondary access for Habergham Colliery and for pumping purposes at East Pit, Padiham for dewatering Habergham Pit. The manager at the Cornfield pit for many years was 'Jimmy' Pollard, he succeeded Richard Marshall to the position. 'Jimmy' was connected with the Padiham collieries for 55 years, and lived at the cottages we now known as 'Collier Cottages' on Grove Lane formerly Duckett Lane. The cottages on Grove Lane belonged to the Exors of John Hargreaves, 'Jimmy' Pollard occupied a larger portion whilst next door in a smaller section was the colliery blacksmith, and at other times a collier labourer by the name of Fergus Pate. It was the blacksmiths job to repair any damaged tubs that ran on the ginny track which ran past the doorway coming through Grove Woods. In later years 'Jimmy' Pollard became too ill to do his work as pit manager, and a certificated manager had to be brought in. 'Jimmy' was not dismissed though, he was held in too high esteem for that, and he kept his place at the cottage. From the bedroom widow he could still keep an eye on the tubs as they passed daily in front of the house, he watched the movements as keenly as if he was still in charge of the pit until his dying day. 'Jimmy' Pollard passed away in May 1887.

In March 1933 the shaft at Cornfield Colliery collapsed taking the pumping engines with it. The steam winding engine at Cornfield was controlled simply by letting more or less steam in or out of the cylinder using a simple open/close stop valve. The coal was raised in 3 cwt tubs on an endless chain in the shaft using an engine with two vertical cylinders 14 inches by 24 inches. This same engine also worked the surface ginny at the colliery. The endless chain shaft winding arrangement continued below ground after passing down the shaft operating three quarters of a mile of underground haulage. Steam to the engines here and at the pumping shaft was supplied by three Lancashire boilers and a Cornish boiler located on the surface of the mine. A ginny went over the River Calder and through Grove Wood to the Padiham coal staith to the left of the present day Tesco store. There was a terrible accident to a young lad at the Padiham coal staith in November 1853. He, along with a number of other young lads were messing about near the end of the ginny when one of the other boys pushed him towards the revolving ginny head wheel.

He put his hand up to stop himself when the hand was caught by the moving chain taken into the wheel and taken completely off. In 1890 another ginny was laid towards Cornfield Grove to a turning block and thence to Habergham Colliery—the brick built turning block can still be seen over the wall at Cornfield Grove along with various cuttings for the ginny near All Saints Church. There were a number of incidents which made the news. In May 1872, George Henry Wilkinson was charged with having taken the top of his safety lamp, when there were 100 men below ground—he was fined 20 shillings and costs. In February 1890, Joseph Crabtree lost his life at the pit seemingly through being struck by the arm of a capstan being used for hauling water from the pit. *'Accidental death'* was recorded. No coal was ever allowed to be extracted under the River Calder by any of the Padiham Pits, consequently where coal was mined either side of the river the ground subsided leaving the river higher than the surrounding fields—a strange phenomenon which can still be seen today.

Craggs Colliery
This small colliery was sunk by John Sutcliffe Witham in the early 1870s, and was located in the of Craggs Lane, known locally as 'Th owd' lane' and in field in front of Craggs Farm, just off the Whalley Road before the Barrowford Bypass. John Sutcliffe Witham was formerly a partner in the Hapton Coal Company, in fact he described himself as being a *'Coal Proprietor'* in both the 1851 and 1861 census returns. John Sutcliffe Witham lived at Oakmount on Westgate in Burnley. He also once worked in partnership with Joseph Massey in the worsted spinning trade at Burnley, but the partnership was declared bankrupt in 1840, even though he was able to continue buying shares in various concerns for many years afterwards. He was also a great supporter of the Burnley Mechanics Institution, and a keen game shooting fan. John Sutcliffe Witham 'Gentleman' died 24 March 1881 and was buried at Burnley cemetery in grave number 22272. The manager at Craggs Pit was a John Hargreaves, and the pit worked a small section of the Arley Four Feet Mine at a depth of around 140 feet, and was abandoned before 1876, although there was a fatal accident at the pit in 1875. In January that year 44 year old Robert Wilkinson was taking two tubs down the underground wagon road as was usual until he reached the top of an incline. Here he left one of the tubs and proceeded forward with the other one, when the one he had left behind ran down the incline behind and caught him between the two tubs.

He was badly injured and lost the use of his lower limbs, and the following Saturday died from his injuries. Little remains of Craggs Colliery today save for an area of rough ground surrounded by a dilapidated fence in front of Craggs Farm—the site of the old shaft.

Crooked Leaches Colliery
Also known as Crooked Leeches, or even Crook Leeches was situated somewhere near the Yeoman farm of Hargrove and was working around the mid 1750 under the Shuttleworth's of Gawthorpe Hall. However we know little else about this mine other than it was advertised to be sold by auction in the Blackburn Mail in October 1798 as follows;

"COALS, To be Sold By Auction
(Subject to Conditions) On Thursday 8th day of November at Six o'clock in the evening at the house of Mr John Tickle, the sign of the Talbot in Padiham. ALL THOSE VALUABLE BEDS OF COAL Contained in the freehold estate at Hargreave in the township of Padiham aforesaid Known by the names of Crook Leeches and Marled Earth. The bed is found to be about eleven feet in thickness. The fields are conveniently situated for the Accommodation of the town and other places. Usually served with coals from the neighbourhood. For further particulars apply—in the meanwhile
To Mr Whitaker in Padiham"

The Tickle family mentioned above at 'the sign of the Talbot' were at one time quite prominent people in Padiham's past—Paul Tickle a landed proprietor and an agent for the Gawthorpe estate lived at Hunters Holme Farm, and there was once even a Tickle Street which ran off Barbon Street. Many seams of coal outcrop to the surface, or at least are very shallow around Hargrove and along the line of the present day Barrowford Bypass. These seams were exploited as recently as the early 1950s and 1960s at the Fence drift mines and by commercial outcropping around Pendle Hall. It is also known that a small mine used to operate and supply Hargrove and its adjacent cottages with coal in quite recent years.

Decline Colliery
This pit was a small drift mine located in Badger Plantation off Trapp Lane at Read, the pit is marked on the First Edition of the O.S. Map of 1844-48, although there appears to be no evidence of the colliery today. There was a report of a serious accident at the mine in the local newspaper in April 1857. A man named Pilkington, a collier was going down a drift at the Decline pit in the township of Read. He had gone about 40 yards into the pit when the rope holding his wagon broke and the tubs passed over his body seriously injuring him.

Dugdale Colliery
A pit in Long Plantation between on Burnley Road Padiham between Shuttleworth College and the main drive to Gawthorpe Hall. The pit worked the King Mine two and a half foot thick at a depth of 132 feet at shaft depth. The name is a bit of a problem, it might have been worked by the Dugdales of Lowerhouse Mills to fuel their factory boilers? Dugdale Colliery was abandoned in 1873, and there are no remains of this old pit.

East Pit
The East Pit was situated on Grove Lane, and as you come to Grove Woods itself, the pit was on the left hand side a few yards on behind a broken down gate. An area of rough ground marks its position, and East Pit is one of the few Padiham pits that we actually know something about. The old East Pit Colliery, on Grove Lane, formerly Duckett Lane dated from 1706, and to this day carr water (water stained with iron oxide) leaches out from the ruins of the old shaft. There was an old travelling road 500 yards beyond the shaft further along on the left hand side going towards Brookfoot Farm on Grove Lane running into the Padiham Thick Seam. The entrance to the workings was all stone arched, around 5 foot 6 inches high and about 4 foot wide. This old tunnel was opened up during the 1921 Coal Strike by the local miners' seeking out coal supplies, until news came that easier pickings could be found further up the River Calder where the seams outcropped in Whitaker Clough. A furnace drift was also driven to provide ventilation at the pit, the hot air from the fire drawing the cooler air into the workings, and the date '1706' was cut into the keystone of the arch, which was all built of dressed stonework.

This old furnace drift was visible up till around 1912, when it was filled in, but not before it was explored to some degree by local inquisitives. Fifteen yards from daylight, a large pile of ashes and burnt coals were discovered, beyond which progress was halted by iron bars firmly driven into roof and floor. I wonder if this is the 'coal pit' in which the villains who stole some meat at Burnley found temporary refuge back in 1849. It appeared that one Sunday morning, George Grey and Jonathan Shepherd broke into the butchers shop at Burnley belonging to George Pilkington and stole a quantity of meat. They absconded with their hoard, but later on the runaway robbers were found hiding in a coal pit at Padiham according to a newspaper report. They were both committed to Preston Assizes for trial. At the bottom of the East Pit shaft were three roadways, all stone arched. One went in the direction of Brookfoot Farm, another in the direction of High Whittaker Farm, and the third in the direction of Hargrove Farm. At certain distances along these roads, it was reported, that there were built into the sides, recesses about two foot high containing tallow and wax candles. Each of which would give out a small 'beam' of light, protected from the draught of the ventilation by the recesses. The old East Pit was laid in a derelict situation for many years, from around the year 1840, and it was officially abandoned in 1862, however in 1890, the pit shaft was brought back into use as a pumping pit. At this time a Cornish Beam Engine was installed complete with a single boiler flue. An old water delivery course taking the water from the workings at East Pit into the River Calder was all stone arched and had a datestone 'J.S. 1839' (Janet Shuttleworth) The Cornish Beam Engine house wasn't unique in this area, it was based upon those used at the Cornish Tin Mines. It was a vertical type engine with an iron rocking arm at the top, one side connected to the pistons and cylinder, while the other was connected with the crank arm and flywheel. Other Cornish Beam engines are known to have been put to work at the old Cuckoo Mine near Cliviger.

The shaft at East Pit

The main driving shaft passed through the engine house walls where it engaged into two cogwheels. This then was connected to two wooden arms, which in turn connected with two rocking iron cradles, which controlled the rams on the 15-inch delivery pipes. The engine could be run on as little as 8 lbs., of steam pressure supplied by a little nine-foot diameter single flue Cornish boiler situated close by. When repairs were required to be carried out in the shaft at the East Pit, the shafts men were lowered from the wooden headgear down the pit sat in boson's chairs, or slings. An essential part of the shaft man's equipment was a gong and hammer to tell the person lowering or raising him when to stop or start. Retired colliers with nothing to do would spend hours gossiping in the engine room to while away the time. Levi Heys, the grandfather of George Heys worked on the pit top at East Pit when he was aged just eight years old. The days of the old pumping engine at East Pit came to an end in 1943. East Pit always seems to be linking to the pumping operations of a number of other local collieries, such as Habergham Pit and Cornfield, but it must have been a pit in its own right at one time, because it predates both the above mentioned pits by many decades. The pit was worked by the Exors of John Hargreaves, the Burnley coal-owners.

The abandonment plans indicate that the working were connected underground with the Nook I' Th' Holme Pit nearer over towards the River Calder. The coal seam at both pits was not named, but it was abandoned in 1862, but evidence suggests that the seam worked was the Burnley Four Feet, alias the Arley Mine at a depth of 120 feet. The shaft of Cornfield Pit besides the Calder further upstream was sunk in 1872, and a decade later than when Nook I' Th' Holme and East Pits were abandoned, so it is more than possible that the old shaft at East Pit was brought back into use for pumping or even secondary access. In March 1863, a Mr Shackleton was following his employment in the East Pit, when a large coal fell upon him and broke his thigh—this is the only known accident at East Pit.

Eyses Colliery
This was a pit situated at the end of Park Road between the allotments and the River Calder, it was sunk originally in 1850, when there was a party thrown to celebrate the event, recorded in the Blackburn Standard 29 May as follows:

> *"On Friday last a handsome treat was given by L. N. Starkie of Huntroyde on the opening of a new freeholds mine in Hapton, the property of the above named gentleman. The masters, colliers, banksmen, carters etc, of the Hapton Coal Company, to the number of 160 were treated with an excellent dinner provided for them at Mr James Whitaker's Starkie Arms, and Mr James Kelly's Swan Inn, Padiham. The whole day was spent in great harmony, and gave general satisfaction to the whole party"*

The pit worked the Arley Mine, and it appears that two more shafts were later sunk on or near the site to rework the seam in 1883 by Robert Sagar and Company. One of these partners was Richard Parkinson of Padiham Green, who in 1880 was returning from work and on entering the house simply dropped down seriously ill—and died almost immediately. Sagar and Company were also involved in pits at Padiham Green and the Hapton Collieries. The agents for the Hapton Coal Company in the 1850s were Richard Radcliffe and George Witham. I also mention here John Earnshaw who served the Hapton Coal Company 21 years as a faithful servant until his death aged 53 years in November 1849. The Eyses Colliery was officially abandoned 5 March 1887, the area around the former pit has all been landscaped and there are no remains.

Gawthorpe Colliery
A pit worked by the Shuttleworths of Gawthorpe Hall located in the woods on Burnley Road below Shuttleworth College. It was noted that a shallow trench runs for quite a distance through these wood, which might be the remains of a horse drawn tramway used in connection with the pits hereabouts. The pit is marked on the First Edition of the O.S. Map of 1844-48 and also shows two buildings. The colliers and other workers at the pit were entertained by Sir James Kay-Shuttleworth at Gawthorpe Hall on New Year's Eve, January 1862.

> *"The colliers had meat pies and spiced ales, and their wives had meat pies, currant bread etc. After the repast the colliers sang songs and danced simple step dances on a platform, and were addressed by Sir James. The occasion was rendered both profitable and entertaining. The songs began with Rule Britannia and ended with God Save the Queen, both in full chorus. The Padiham Volunteer Band attended and contributed to the entertainment"* Continued the report.

The pits worked by the Shuttleworth's appear to have been in charge of Janet Shuttleworth, for instance she had pits at Ightenhill in 1842 as well as the Gawthorpe pit. Both these pits employed children underground, two were aged ten years old, one was eleven years old and three were aged twelve years old. Their hours of work varied from eight to ten hours a day, and their wages averaged 3s.11d per week. They had no regular times to eat while they were underground *"They eat when they can"*. Boys under the age of 10 years were banned from working underground in 1842, and females banned altogether, only under the Tories Maggie Thatcher's reign (1975-1990) were women allowed to go back underground in Britain's coalmines. There was a report of a local strike at the Padiham pits in March 1860, when the colliers at the three pits in Padiham struck work on account of six of the men being discharged through their recent strike for an advance (pay rise) The report went on to say that some knobstickers, or strike breakers came in to take the men's places. In May 1979, Lancashire County Council set aside £8,000 to look into the safety of old shafts around which extensions to Gawthorpe School was to be built.

The Mines Inspectors Report for the year 1854 also tells us that a young lad named Fort aged 14 years old was killed at a pit in Padiham—this might have been Gawthorpe Colliery?

Lomax Colliery
This was a pit worked by the Exors of John Hargreaves, the Burnley coal owners and was located almost due south of the former farm named Middle Fields off Grove Lane Padiham. It was probably connected underground with East Pit and perhaps the coalmine named Middle Fields near the farm mentioned below. Little else is known of this pit, there were scores of small mines in and around Grove Wood and the surrounding fields. This is probably the old shaft 'found' in the back garden of 'Collier Cottages' on Grove Lane a number of years ago.

Middlefield Colliery
An old colliery located beside the farm of that name off Grove Lane, worked by the Exors of John Hargreaves at one time. It was working in 1887, for there was a report of an accident there in that year. Fifty five year William Scott was changing the buckets at the Middle Fields pit, when the rope broke and his hand was taken completely off. Scott also worked the Middle Fields farm nearby, which consisted of 17 acres. George Heys in his *'Geology of the Burnley Coalfield'* in Burnley reference library states that the colliery was closed down on 8 May 1877—if this was the case, then clearly William Scott must have reopened the pit to work it on his own account. His son, Walter was also listed as being a coal mine labourer. Middle Field farm has now gone, and only a pile of rubble indicates its existence, a slight hollow close by might indicate a shaft belonging to the Middle Field Pit, or perhaps a water lodge in connection with the mine. There is a tale told of more recent times about a farmer at Middle Fields Farm. He began to notice a large crack appearing in one of the gable ends of the farm—this got bigger and bigger over the coming months. The farmer scratched his head and at last came up with a solution. He managed to get hold of a good length of old haulage chain off the ginny track down by Grove Lane and he got it up to the farm. There, with a good deal of effort he wrapped the chain around the building and fastened the ends together—rather like tying up a large parcel. It seems that the solution to the crack in Middle Field farm failed, for it's now a pile of rubble!

Nook I' Th' Holme Colliery

This mine was on the Burnley Road side of the Bendwood footbridge, in fact the footbridge is on the site or at least very near a bridge over the river belonging to the former ginny track which ran from Nook i' Th' Holme pit to some of the Padiham cotton mills. The pit was sunk around 1815 down to the King Mine and was almost due east of Padiham Bridge. The colliery *may* have belonged to the Shuttleworth Family, it being almost on their doorstep at Gawthorpe Hall, or possibly worked under lease from them by the Bancroft's. However, the abandonment plans were listed as being with the Exors of John Hargreaves, the Burnley pit owners. There were three shafts sunk at Nook I' Th' Holme Colliery, for it was large enough to be marked 'colliery' on the 1844-48 OS Map and they were all stone lined. Two of these pits for ventilation purposes were located in Bancroft Plantation, (Bancroft Pit?) and the third in the present day Bancroft Close. Other seams worked here included the Fulledge Thin, and maybe the Padiham Thick Seam (?) All three shafts were fitted out with wooden headgearing and winding wheels, and worked the coal underground towards the Burnley Road at Padiham. A number of shafts are also known to have existed in the small plantation besides the bottom lodge gates running to Gawthorpe Hall, but these have little significance, as the coal crops out here, or at the least is very shallow. A surface chain road ran directly from the Nook I' Th' Holme Colliery across the River Calder by a wooden bridge. An alarming occurrence took place at the colliery around 1855, when sand and gravel from the bed of the former River Calder (the course of the river has been moved on two occasions) burst into the workings of the mine filling the tunnels to the roof. Happily there appears to have been no loss of life. Incidentally, the first footbridge at Bendwood was installed in 1930, and following some flood damage in January 1984 was replaced by a second-hand footbridge from Penwortham near Preston where it used to span a railway there.

Simonstone Colliery

We venture a little over the Padiham border to include these mines at Simonstone, because of the close proximity to Padiham. The main Simonstone pits were located Coal Pit Lane, now an indiscernible grassy track at the end of Craggs Lane, but all traces of the pits had been obliterated during opencast mining during the 1950s.

A ginny ran up towards the Whalley Road for distribution of the coal going towards Whalley and Clitheroe, coals for Simonstone and other local use used the short section of Coal Pit Lane back towards the Blackburn Road. Other shafts in connection with the Simonstone Pit were named Ambrose, Edge, Fault, Nook and Star which worked during the early part of the nineteenth century. The colliery owners in 1841 were Messrs Hargreaves and Whittaker, and their agent was George Waddington. The firm employed two children, aged 11 and 12 years old. One was a wagoner, the other a gin driver which suggests the use of a horse gin for winding coal, miners and equipment to the surface. One lad 17 years of age was working 10 hours a day getting coal but could earn 18 shillings a week on piecework. The total workforce consisted of 30 men and boys, but only 14 of those employed could read it was recorded. Underground the coal was drawn either by horse or adults, and the seams varied in thickness from three feet to twelve feet. The Simonstone Pits were abandoned some time before March 1883. The Old Hey Opencast Mining site of the 1950s must have uncovered some of the old workings here, but so far I have found no record of this. There only appears to have been one coal miner in the 1880s at Simonstone, Richard Bickerstaffe of Railway Row.

Whitaker Clough Colliery
A small pit which worked along with a few others on the North western side of Grove Lane. As its name suggests the pit was in Whitaker Clough, the wooded area to the right of the track from Grove Lane up to High Whitaker. The pit was interconnected underground with East Pit as well as several other small pits named Dick, Fault, Folly, Harry, Heys, Lomax, Smallpage and Tunnel, and it was one of the Exors of John Hargreaves collieries. There were of course a few other small mines which operated in and around Padiham over the many years, but the ones mentioned above are the main ones, and are enough to give the reader an insight into this old industry.

OPENCAST MINING

By the end of WW2 Britain was on its economic knees with massive debts and production levels at an all-time low. To get the country up and running again it needed fuel to feed the factories, the workshops and the domestic fires.

The coalmines of the country were run down, they had little investment for decades, rumours of Nationalisation saw to that. The coal owners were not going to invest *their* money in a business that might soon belong to the country—but this went on for decades, even before the war. At last a decision was taken to Nationalise the country's coalmines, and on 1 January 1947, which became known as Vesting Day the Government took over the British coal mining industry. From the very start work began with great speed, locally pits thought to have a long life and good reserves were installed with the latest mining equipment, these included Bank Hall at Burnley and Hapton Valley Colliery Old pit with few reserves were closed down, the Towneley Pit at Burnley being one of the first in the country to fall under the axe. New drift mines were opened up, by driving inclined tunnels into new reserves of coal. These included new mines at Red Less, to be named Salterford Numbers One and Two, and drift mines at Fence and Higham. These were Fence Number One, Fence Number Two, and Fir Trees Drift. But opencast mines provided a cheap alternative to deep mining. A National Opencast Executive was set up and 34 sites around Burnley stretching from Deerplay to Higham were earmarked for the extraction of an estimated 4m tons of coal. One site at Higham was in production by October 1949. On site was a huge drag-line excavator, weighing 380 tons, a Monigham 4W. Its job was to strip off the overbearing rock and earth covering the coal seams. The machine comprised a 40 feet by 25 feet high cabin, a gigantic jib 135 feet long and 19 feet wide at the base—the five and a half yard bucket could snatch seven and a half tons of earth at each grab. This mammoth machine was originally designed for use dredging the depths of the Mississippi River in America. The machine was brought to Higham in thirty wagon loads from the Midlands—it took four months to dismantle, transport and re-assemble on the Higham site. The drag line crane carried four men, an engineman, a driver and two greasers. One of the main hazards during the early days of opencast mining at Higham was the tremendous weather conditions the workers had to endure, it was one of the worst winters on record. There were also many complaints from the locals at Higham—the mining went on 24 hours a day, with blasting operations even smashing windows in the village—complaints also came thick and fast over the massive opencast wagons using Grove Lane daily to and from the site . For Bob Phillipson, the farmer at Pendle Hall Farm it was nightmare existence that was to last 11 years.

The opencast works took 63 acres of his 230 acres including some of his best meadows. Where his sheep and cows once grazed was replaced by a massive gorge. The only 'perk' he confessed later, that he would miss after all the work was done and the site was being restored was the opportunity to nip out of the door and help himself to a bucket of coal for the fire! All the opencast sites were reinstated when the mining was done, when the opencast operations moved on site a small brook at Huntersholme Clough disappeared. But during the restoration the stream bed was remade using hundreds of tons of boulders to form a new stream way as part of the new drainage course. The water course was fenced in and new saplings planted outside the fence to make it as natural as possible—one thing they did not replace was the miles of natural dry stone walls that had to be removed for the mining operations. Whilst the mining operations were ongoing at the Pendle Hall site a 220 million year old fossil tree was discovered, by the Padiham miner and geologist the late George Heys. Enthusiastic as always, George had the fossil removed to the back garden of a house at 25 Grove Lane. The fossil tree attracted quite a lot of attention, and even aroused a plea from Manchester Corporation who wanted the tree to grace their new centre—but George insisted that it *'Stay's where it wur put'*.

By 1957, the Wimpy Group working under contract to the National Coal Board were mining 300 acres around Gawthorpe Hall. A major task here was to divert the course of the River Calder to, what turned out to actually be the original course of the river nearer to Gawthorpe Hall. It was Lord Shuttleworth who diverted it to the course nearer to Grove Woods around 1820 as it was affecting his gout! The river today however is back on its original course. Another task that Wimpy had to do was to provide two new football practice pitches for Burnley Football Club, and an all-weather pitch with floodlighting. All this was so that the mining operations could continue without interruption beneath the bed of the river. However, there is also some evidence that mining under the river bed itself *might* not have taken places after all! It was intended that the Gawthorpe opencast would mine almost right up to the door of Gawthorpe Hall. Because of objections about fears of damage to this historic hall this never came to fruition and mining stopped short of the hall. The Minister of Power, Sir Ian Horobin toured the Gawthorpe opencast site in 1958, and paid particular attention to *'Marion'* the massive 'walking' 800 ton excavator working on the site.

"It is one of the largest things I have ever seen" he remarked. The *'Marion 740'* excavator was one of two purchased by George Wimpy from the Australian Government Joint Coal Plant for the large Benbullen Opencast Coal project in Australia, which was carried out by Wimpy. Both machines were purchased in December 1951, and on completion of the Australian Opencast contract, having no further use for the machines in Australia, Wimpy shipped them to the U.K. in 1955. One was erected in Maesgwyn in South Wales and the other at Gawthorpe Hall opencast site. The Gawthorpe Hall *'Marion'* stayed at the site until June 1966 when she too was moved to South Wales. Some Padiham folk may still remember *'Marion'* working the opencast site. We also have some remarkable statistics about this marvellous machine;

Total working weight of the machine—1,275 lbs.
Ballast required, included in the above—250,000 lbs.
Total horse power of electric motors—700 h.p.
Length of drag-line boom—175 feet
Capacity of the D/L bucket—12 to 13 cubic yards
Weight of empty bucket—approx 2,500 lbs.
Weight of full bucket, depending on materials—60 to 70 tons
Diameter of circular base—31 feet
Walking shoes—36 feet 6 inches long by 6 feet wide
Total width from both shoes—44 feet 6 inches
Diameter of walking shaft—18 inches
Length of step—6 feet 2 inches
Travelling speed—0.15 miles per hour.

The opencast sites around Burnley and Padiham had to all intents and purposes finished by July 1961 and restoration work was begun in earnest and was expected to take 12 months. Besides the Gawthorpe and Pendle Hall sites, others around Padiham included land around Old Hey farm to the west of Craggs, the sweetly named Cuckoo Hall site, near Wall Green, Whitaker Clough, and West Close near Higham.

Marion, the giant excavator
(Duncan Armstrong)

QUARRYING

Padiham Quarries were situated in two parts, one smaller quarry off Grove Lane and a larger one to the rear Garden Street. Town Hill Bank now takes place of the smaller quarry, the vent pipes on the 'green' there is a legacy of former landfill on the old quarry site. The larger quarry has also been filled and now a small football pitch and a children's play area take most of the space of the old quarry. Quarry Street however recalls its existence. It fair to say that Padiham Quarries provided the rubble, the stone, the flags and the ashlar (dressed building stone) to build the Padiham we know today. The rows and rows of stone built terrace houses, the massive mills and factories all obtained their building stone from Padiham Quarries—although there were other stone delphs locally. The site of Padiham Quarries is on Shuttleworth land, and it was probably worked by them for stone for various ventures in connection with the hall in the distant past, for instance during the redesign of the hall in 1850, or for building the cottages in the grounds. We know that the quarries were on Shuttleworth land because after they were closed down, a Mr Lee of Garden Street Padiham purchased part of the old quarry from the Shuttleworth Estate.

He then spent a great deal of time transforming it into a wonderful garden—it became quite an attraction, and was often used for fetes and fundraising activities. The Padiham Quarries are marked on the First Edition of the O.S. Map for 1844-48, but soon after this date leases were granted to various people to work the quarry on a commercial basis. These included the Duckett's of Hill Farm, and Cornelius Anderton, *'a master stone mason employing nine men and two boys and a farmer of eight acres'*. He lived at 28 Albert Street, Padiham, and I think that he may have worked the smaller quarry at Padiham Quarries, as well as a delph on the Banks, or *'The Bonks'* as it is known locally. He married Margaret Edmondson at Burnley in 1844, his son Servetus was also a stone mason. At the time of Cornelius's death in May 1891 he had been a contractor for between forty and fifty years, among his works was the building of the present day St Leonard's Church, St Matthew's Church, Burnley, St Anne and Elizabeth Church at Padiham and the schools there, as well as Higham Church and the Unitarian Chapel, at Padiham.

The larger of the Padiham Quarries appears to have been worked by Davies and Crawshaw around the 1880s. James Davies of Garden Street appears to have been the more junior partner in the concern and worked as a stone mason for the firm. Aaron Crawshaw who was born in Higham around 1834 describes himself as a *'Master Quarryman'* and lived at Grove Terrace, his elder brother John was also a quarryman. Grove Terrace occupied a site on the steep banking running off Grove Lane, it was cleared in the late 1960s. Aaron was a dedicated worker for the Cross-bank Wesleyan Chapel and a regular attendee at that place of worship—he married Sarah Hartley at St Leonards in 1857, and from the union a number of children were born. Four sons and four daughters that we know of, but it was the death of his daughter Mary around 1902 that really affected Aaron. This overwhelmed the Aaron, and in 1904 he too passed away. Padiham Quarry was last worked by George and John Duxbury, brothers of Simonstone—John was a mason and George was a contractor and quarry-master. By 1894, the mills had been built, the rows and rows of terraced houses had been completed, every back street was laid out with stone setts, and Padiham Quarry fell into disuse.

Bricks were then being produced at a much more competitive rate than quarried stone, especially from Accrington which led to the downfall of many local quarries. We have a few more details of the quarries that add a bit of interest. In June 1846 a quarryman named Richard Waddington of Read was killed at the Padiham Quarry through a fall of rock, a verdict of 'Accidental death' was recorded at his inquest held later. There was a strike by the Padiham Quarrymen in July 1853 for an advance (pay rise) of four pence a day, but neither the master nor the men were for giving in, and in August 1881, John Hirst was injured through a fall of rock at the Padiham Quarry, the earth fell and broke both his legs as well as otherwise injuring him. The abandoned Padiham Quarries must have been left quite deep, and an obvious danger to both children and the general public. There was a report of a man named Brown, aged 38 years who in December 1896 was found at the bottom of the quarry having fallen 100 feet. It was stated that he had been out drinking and strayed from the footpath and fell through the fence, which was said to be quite rotten surrounding the quarry—he was of course killed. Another local quarry was the Whitegate Quarry just over the border on the Burnley Road which was worked by Tomlinson and Bridge, by way of Thomas Hyde Tomlinson and Ralph Bridge.

Mr Tomlinson of 810 Padiham Road, Burnley had been in the quarry business for over forty years, and also worked quarries at Read. He was a native of Colne and came to Burnley in his youth about 1862. He started out in the Railway Side Quarry off Accrington Road at Burnley before opening up the Whitegate concern. He was well known in the 'Chepside' district as it is known to the locals, and was an ardent supporter of the Fulledge Conservative Club. He died in 1928 at the grand age of 76 years and was buried at Burnley Cemetery. His partner Ralph Bridge was a Liverpool lad who moved to Burnley in his teens and was living on Coal Clough Lane in the 1880s working as a stone dresser at the nearby Pickup Delph Quarry off Every Street. By the early 1900s at the age of just 36 he was able to retire from quarry work. The entrance to the Whitegate Quarry and that used by a small mineral tramway is now marked by a wooden fence between two massive gateposts just below the bus turning circle on Burnley Road at GR 805-333 Alt, 383 feet. The tramway went across the main Burnley/Padiham Road to a stone yard where the bungalows now stand on Keats Fold, and in later years under the road to a brickyard in the same area. The tunnel under the main road was probably brought about with the coming of the tramlines.

The Whitegate Quarry besides producing stone and bricks also made the *'Gate Brand'* of scouring stones. Some older folk might remember these, they were also known as 'Donkey Stones' and were made from reconstituted stone mixed with a little cement to form blocks about 2 ½ by 3 inches. They were the forerunners of the more modern 'Brillo' pads and other scourers—but many folk used them to whiten the edge of their doorsteps and even window bottoms. The author can remember these as a child under his grandma's sink. They were grey in colour, but there were also rusty brown ones, but it was the grey ones that his grandma always used. In later years these stones were given away by the rag and bone man in exchange for a few old rags—or you might get a goldfish in a bag. In November 1894, Charles Nash who had only worked at the Whitegate Quarry for three weeks was killed in a rock fall whilst he was getting some stone down. Lumb Quarry was another local quarry and could be reached by a gateway between the more modern 136 and 138 Victoria Road and used to be between the backs of those houses and Green Brook. A footpath further up Victoria Road towards Burnley also gives access to the site which is now an open space.

The main access road to Lumb Quarry though was via the path immediately before the railway on Dryden Street going downhill. In times past this wended its way directly into the quarry and its workings. Lumb Quarry had been worked for over a century for ashlar and sandstone, and in later years up to 1968 was used as a landfill site. There is hardly any evidence of the old quarry today. There were also a couple of stone quarries at Read, one in Shady Walks near the top of Trapp Lane on the left, and one just beyond the four lane junction a little further on the right hand side. We know that Thomas Tomlinson of Whitegate Quarries worked a stone delph at Read—but which one is another matter. The following advert for the sale of a quarry at Read by auction appeared in the Burnley Gazette 2 July 1904 and gives us some indication of the type of machinery in use at a quarry at that time.

"TOWNHEAD QUARRY READ, near Whalley. To Quarry Masters and Others. Expiration of Lease.
Mr John Duckworth is favoured with instructions to sell by auction on Tuesday 5 July 1904, all the QUARRY PLANT, comprising of one ten ton steam crane, 60 foot guised vertical Steam Engine 8 inch cylinder. Steam Boiler ten feet by five feet diameter, two hand cranes, Pulsometer to lift 5,000 gallons per hour, Steam and water taps, steam piping, chain blocks, sheath blocks, wall boxes and hangers, fire bars, wagons and metal, chains, wire rope, three pairs of blacksmiths bellows, anvil and stand, tongs, sets, wedges, picks and spades, crow bars, platform weighing machine, spring cart, box cart, useful pony and trap, several sets of gears etc.
Sale Commences at two o'clock. Townhead Quarry is 10 minutes walk from Simonstone Station."

ENGINEERING IRON AND STEEL TRADES

Foundries.
James Blezard and Sons Limited
Was the largest of the Padiham foundries and was established by James Blezard, a former joiner and wheelwright who came to Padiham around 1840 and Thomas Blezard. James took his sons, Norman Thomas, John and James into the firm which started out in a small way in 1859, in an adapted foundry near the Enterprise and Industry Mills.

This appears to have been in the enclosed yard to the rear of Enterprise Mills, although the red brick building of today seems to be later additions. The firm became known as James Blezard and Sons in the mid 1860s, Thomas Blezard in 1876 chose to withdraw from the family partnership and start his own foundry business in Livesey Street. The father James born 29 May 1779 and later of Grove House, Padiham died 20 June 1871 leaving his sons Norman (1842-1901) and James (8 December 1832-13 October 1879) and John (1839—6 December 1906) in charge. Norman lived in some style at Bendwood Grove with his wife Mary, their three daughters and son Wilfred. He was a staunch temperance supporter and had never touched a drop in his life—he was also a member of the old Padiham Board, and when the new Liberal Club opened in Burnley Road he became a trustee there. Norman was a great one for new inventions, in 1880 for instance he patented some improvements to folding chairs, long backed seats and forms—there were other improvements to hot water heating apparatus which the firm made. Norman died in July 1901 and was buried in the family vault at cemetery on St John's Road. From the premises near Enterprise Mills the foundry was moved to what was to become known as 'Guy Foundry' or 'Helms' Old Factory' also known as 'Warm Spout' on Factory Lane and Ightenhill Street in 1869, ten years after the firm was founded. A decade later the business was making things such as cast iron hot water boilers, cast textile machinery parts and loom accessories and even school furniture.

In 1890, James Blezard and Sons were able to move to even larger premises at Grove Mills, bought by Norman, John and James Blezard—a decade later the firm was employing over 100 people. [xlix] This was the peak time of James Blezard and Sons, and the range of products also increased, they were then making greenhouse boilers, and water heaters, cast iron public house tables and chairs and stools and many other products. Three years later however, after a depression in the trade the firm was offered for sale as a going concern, part of which, the temple making side of the business was bought by Lupton Brothers of Accrington who continued working at Padiham until the 1920s. The family struggled on trying to make a go of the existing part of the business that was still left. On 6 September 1906, the last of the founders' sons, John Blezard died. Wilfred Blezard, the son of Norman, he had taken over the business carried on by his father and uncles in 1901 following his father's death.

To try and make ends meet he took into partnership Mr Walter L. Eddleston as a junior partner, which brought in a welcoming £250. Eddleston however pulled out in 1909, and the following year Wilfred was before the Burnley Bankrupt Court. Walter Eddleston meanwhile had become a traveller for Lupton Brothers, and at the end of WW1 was able with Harvey and Harold Eddleston to establish a storage firm and mill furnishing business at Bridge End Mill. Wilfred Blezard had recommenced business in a small way at Rosegrove and then at Railway Arch Padiham. In the late 1920s, the Eddlestons were able to purchase the firm of James Blezard and Sons from Wilfred and the whole operations were transferred to Bridge End Mill, but still under the name of James Blezard and Sons. In the 1930s this company moved lock stock and barrel to the Victoria Mill. By the end of WW2 Eddleston and Company Limited ceased trading, whilst James Blezard and Sons Limited concentrated on the sale of boiler from source made by other manufacturers. In 1989 The Eddleston family sold all the business concerns to their manager when operations were moved to Enterprise Mill—the business finally closed down in the early 1990s, ending almost on the very doorstep of where it originated 130 years previously.

Thomas Blezard's Green Bank Works
As noted above left the partnership he was involved with at James Blezard and Sons Limited to start his own business in 1876 on Livesey Street, later moving what was known as Green Bank Works, on Station Road which was a foundry as early as 1868. In 1883 when living at 32 Railway Street (now Russell Terrace) Thomas was employing nine men making power loom temples. But even at this time Thomas was approaching his late fifties, and he took retirement around the early 1900s. At that time he described himself as being an iron and brass founder, school furniture maker and temple maker. In 1901-02 Thomas sold the business to James Herbert Robinson, formerly a foreman in an iron foundry, who then traded under the name of Unity Wood and Iron Company. Among the customers who had taken the heating boilers manufactured by the Unity Wood and Iron Company were these Burnley institutions; The Co-operative Society, Hammerton Street Burnley and various branches. The Mechanics Institute, Manchester Road, The Weavers' Institute, Charlotte Street, Bethesda Chapel, Hollingreave Chapel, St Mary's School, St Mary's Church, St Mary Magdalene's new Church and Schools.

They also heated Park Hill Chapel, Empress Hotel, Bull Hotel, New Market Hotel, St Stephen's Schools, Mr Robinson Esq., J.P. of Reedley Hall, Alderman Dickinson, J.P of Healey Mount and J. Butterworth of Oak Mount Westgate. In January 1910 Thomas Blezard passed away at his home on Partridge Hill Street at the grand age of 85 years. A decade later and the works on Station Road ended as a foundry, it later became the Padiham Chemical Company Limited which manufactured fire lighters, and later still it was occupied by the Edenfield Spinning Company.

Victoria Foundry
Formerly Spa Foundry, near the Spa Mill off Burnley Road was worked by Francis Helm who established the works in 1868. Francis served his apprenticeship with relations of his, Henry Helm and Sons at Smithy Gate Mill as a mechanic. Afterwards he moved to Barrowford where he worked for a number of years for Messrs Berry, cotton manufacturers. Later he went into partnership with Mr Haighton of the Walverden Ironworks at Barrowford, a partnership which was dissolved in 1868. In the same year Mr Helm removed back to Padiham where he commenced in business on his own account and erected the workshop and foundry near Spa Mill. [l] The foundry went on to produce works such as washing machines, wringing machines and kitchen ranges by the 1880s. Extensions were made to the foundry in 1890, and in 1894 Spa Mill itself was purchased and used in connection with the foundry business, although the weaving shed was leased out to tenant cotton manufacturers. Further extensions were made over the years by Helm. After WW2 the company was taken over by Morley Products, and five years later over 220 persons were employed making washing machines and water boilers for the domestic market. Major extensions to the east of the site were made in the mid 1950s. In 1955 Morley Products was taken over by Glover and Main of London, and production at the Victoria Foundry ended, and the place was used for storage. Later the same year the buildings were taken over by Newmark Limited who manufactured plastic products for the home and garden. A fire subsequently destroyed the old spinning sheds and adjacent buildings. [li] New housing now occupies the site of the old Victoria Foundry.

Wyre Street Foundry
Was a small foundry, the site of which is now taken by Cooke's Oils at the very end of Wyre Street on the right hand side. The foundry was started by John Morris in 1885. Morris was a native of Brierley Hill in Staffordshire, he came to Padiham in August 1877 and started a fish business which he carried on for a number of years before opening the foundry. The firm employed nearly thirty workers, but was eventually sold to James Blezard and Sons for the production of cast iron fireplaces. The original owner John Morris died in November 1910 at his home on Garden Street, when he was still the owner of the foundry—he was 77 years of age and was buried at the Church Cemetery on Blackburn Road.

Gothic Works (Baxi, Main Morley)
A large mainly single storey factory started in 1955 by Glover and Main Limited who had recently taken over Morley Products. Following a number of difficulties the site at the very end of Wyre Street, Padiham was not finished until 1960. The factory was built on a former football ground where Padiham Football Club originated, and the building was constructed to a design by Houston and Forbes, a local firm of architects. Equipment was moved from the Victoria Foundry at Padiham and from Croydon, South London. Five years later a workforce of 500 people were employed at the works making washing machines, water heaters, spin driers and boilers. Main Morley was taken over by Thorn in 1965, and renamed Main Gas Appliances. The manufacture of gas fires was also introduced at the works in 1966, and a tumble drier plant was erected in 1974. Further changes in ownership took place in 1986 when the business was taken over by the Myson Group, and again in 1990 when it became part of the Blue Circle P.L.C. organisation. A research establishment was erected in 1986, and the following year Economic gas fire makers was acquired, and the manufacture of oil and gas boilers was begun in 1992. Ownership of the factory passed to Potterson Myson in 1991, and then to Baxi of Preston, and finally to the Baxi-Newmond Group to become the largest single employer in Padiham. [lii] In 2007 when the Baxi Heating firm employed 387 persons on the shop floor and another 113 in management and office staff the business announced closure of the plant in order that they might concentrate production at their Club Street works at Preston.

In March 2007 a rescue plan put forward by Union officials including staff taking a one pound an hour reduction in wages and a reduction in overtime rates were rejected by management. Some of the workers at Padiham were offered employment at the Preston works, but the closure would have a devastating effect on the local economy said local traders.

Blacksmiths

In the early days of horse drawn traffic the smithy was an essential part of any village, town and city. The obvious shoeing of horses took a greater part of the smithy's time, other time was spent making and repairing agricultural machinery and general mill and factory equipment. Padiham was no exception as regards having a number of smithies, and the one on Guy Street was still in use in living memory, Dennis Haworth was running that place in the 1950s—we also have details of other blacksmiths around town. One of the busiest times for the blacksmiths must have been in the 1850s, and the height of the Industrial Revolution. We know that there were at least five smithies in Padiham at this time. John Ainsworth had a smithy on Mill Street, which might have given its name to Smithy Gate (the way, or street to the smithy) John Ashworth kept his smithy on North Street, and Robert Pickles had a smithy on Church Street. James Sagar's smithy was on Burnley Road and William Waddington had his on Bank Street. Notice all the smithies are on or near the main thoroughfares in town. Thirty years later in the 1880s there were six smithies in town—Ellen Ainsworth was running the blacksmiths at 28 Mill Street, formerly run by her husband John, who I presume had then passed on. In reality she was only the figurehead, her son John was the blacksmith, all others in the family were connected with the cotton trade, except the mother Ellen who was classed as being a housewife. We also have now the first reference to the smithy at 12-16 Guy Street, although doubtless it was here before the 1880s. At this time this smithy was being worked by Higham born Dennis Haworth who actually lived just around the corner at 25 Moor Lane with his wife Anne, also Higham born. Dennis, who was also a wheelwright had been at Guy Street since at least the 1870s, and by 1891 was describing himself as being a 'master blacksmith'. Padiham born Hindle Ingham had taken over the smithy shop at 73 Burnley Road by 1883, although he had actually been a blacksmith since the 1850s. His smithy was replaced by the old Co-operative Stores on the corner of Burnley Road and Sowerby Street.

Hindle was very well known in Padiham and was a member of the fire brigade for over thirty years and had reached the rank of Lieutenant. He often did work for the Gawthorpe Estate and when he died in January 1890 Sir Ughtred Kay-Shuttleworth wrote to his family expressing his sympathy. He was buried at the Church Cemetery on Blackburn Road when members of the fire service attended at his graveside. John Shacklock, a Hapton lad had a smithy at 7-9 Green lane, which was just behind the Bridge Inn, and was able to employ a man and a lad to help him out at his work. The lad was probably Richard, his son who was listed as being an apprentice blacksmith. F & G Sutcliffe were both blacksmiths and wheelwrights who had a shop on Morley Street off Burnley Road, and Tom Wardleworth had a blacksmiths shop in Sowerby Street. Blacksmiths in 1911 included John Bradshaw at Garden Street, T. Barritt, blacksmith and wheelwright at Sowerby Street and Green Lane, Dennis Howarth was still at Guy Street. Bill Middlesbrough had a blacksmiths shop on St Ann Street and Howarth Wilkinson had the smithy on Mill Street. By the mid 1950s though there was only the smithy on Guy Street being worked by Dennis Howarth. There was just one saddler and harnesser in town in 1911, and that was Robert W. Hargreaves whose shop was at 21-23 Church Street, although he lived at 2 Shuttleworth Street. Robert was known locally to everyone as *'Bob Saddler'* and was born at Clitheroe, although he was still a child when his parents moved to Whalley. In about 1871, when he was aged twenty, Robert moved to Padiham and took on an apprenticeship in the saddling trade. Later he started on his own account, and at one time had no less than three shops in town. Robert was also a founder member of the Padiham Agricultural Society, of which he was a member for 47 years and secretary for 23 years in close association with R.T. Whitehead, Thomas Sagar of Simonstone and others. As regards the Parish Church, Mr Hargreaves was a bell ringer there for fifty years, as well as being associated with the Padiham Liberal Club, of which at the time of his death was honorary chairman. He passed away in 1924, and was buried at Padiham Church Cemetery following a service at St Leonard's Church.

Hill 'Special' Cycles.
We can't leave this section on metal trades without including a piece on Hill 'Special' Cycles—the Rolls Royce of the cycle world which were made in Padiham. The business was founded by Adam Hill.

Born in Rochdale in 1914, Adam was the son of Thomas a coal miner and his wife Marie, the father died young, and it was left to the hard working mother to bring up the family of four. Soon afterwards they moved to Padiham, and at the age of fifteen Adam got a job as an apprentice engineer. Even at this tender age Adam was a passionate cyclist, and his first major success was winning the arduous National Hill Climb against more senior riders from the village of Sabden to the Nick of Pendle in 1926—he was 12 years of age at that time. In the years that followed he had many more cycle racing records and achievements—some still stand. With Walter Holcroft, his brother-in-law to be, he completed the Padiham to Blackpool—Blackpool back to Padiham tandem race in three hours, seventeen minutes 36 seconds, slashing 12 minutes 15 seconds of the previous fastest time. Just one week later he was back! This time he did the 75 mile round trip solo. Setting off at four o'clock in the morning, he was back in Padiham in time for breakfast. His time? Three hours thirty six minutes and forty seven seconds cutting thirteen minutes and twelve seconds off the previous record. The solo run was made on his very own Hill 'Special' cycle.

As part of his interest in cycles, Adam Hill was of course repairing bikes, and this quickly moved on to him actually making bikes—by 1933 he was making the all chrome racer 'to the envy of all other manufacturers'. It was said that Adam started his own business because of a 'bad tempered boss' when he was only seventeen years of age. The manager of the firm where Adam was working had left his cycle in the workshop for some repairs by the older craftsmen. Adam started to tackle the job with his usual enthusiasm, and when the boss found his cycle was being repaired by a mere apprentice he kicked Adam in the nether regions. *"This sort of thing happened in those days, but I wasn't putting up with it"* Adam stated later. Adam went home, and encouraged by his mother decided to start up on his own account, but not before going back to the factory and telling the boss where to stick his bike. During 1936-37 Adam had studied metallurgy at Manchester, a skill which was put to good use in his business, and he worked in the aircraft industry during the War. Plans had originally been made for Adam and his brother Tom to go into business together, and in fact a company was formed just before the war and was named the 'Hill Brothers Cycle Engineering'.

However, the partnership never really flourished, and Tom went his separate way, but Adam decided to retain the name of the business which was used during the 40s and 50s. Soon after the war premises were obtained at 22 Burns Street, Padiham just two doors away from the family home. A friend Ron Dicken joined the firm as a frame builder and finisher. It was also Ron's job top take the finished bikes to the dealers each Saturday. Billy Hill, no relation was another employee and an innovator in the technical expertise for which the company was fast gaining a reputation. From 1948 Adam Hill was exhibiting his cycles at shows at Earls Court and the standard of his products flourished and his reputation spread wide. Adam was a founder of the Lightweight Cycle Manufacturers Association, set up to give the smaller cycle manufacturer and frame builders a footing against the stronger and more competitive mass producers of cycles. It was in the early 1950s that Adam Hall was able to get premises in an old former warehouse on Eccleshill Street in Padiham, and from then on the firm became known as The Clarion Cycle Works. The change of name was brought about because Adam was a member of the very popular Clarion Cycle Club, which was in almost every Lancashire town at that time, and indeed nationally. We need to remember that cycling at this time was a great way for the ordinary worker, the weavers, the miners, the foundry workers to 'let their hair down' at the weekends and get out and about and enjoy the fine country air and away from the place of work.

There was no looking back—production grew and grew but they struggled to meet demand. Another feature was the large number of chrome cycle frames that were being produced, quality and workmanship where 'money was no object' was being supplied to cope with the demand. In the 1950s during a recession in the cycle trade Adam Hall heard that a friend of his Claud Butler was in some difficulties, he drove to London and bought the tools and the goodwill of the firm from Butler. Unfortunately, Adam Hill and his company were also having difficulties, and a few years later meeting of the creditors was held in 1958 to review the situation. The high esteem by which the company was held can be judged from the fact that Adam was told to carry on business, and to pay any debts out of future profits. However, Adam Hill at this time was not in the best of health and decided to call it a day, the Clarion Cycle Works was closed down and the production of cycles ended at Padiham.

In an effort to improve his health Adam moved to Jersey to join his brother Tom, he then moved to the Lake District where he and his wife ran a guesthouse for a while. He soon returned back to Lancashire and opened a retail shop on Padiham Road, but cycling was then in decline. He briefly turned the shop into a gent's outfitters, but that too was short lived—after this he became an inspector at Main Gas at Padiham.

Adam's son, Dennis who had been helping his father in the past, had joined the air force and was also a keen cyclist. For instance he won the 1959 Lancashire Evening Post Tour of the Lakes. In 1978 Adam Hill moved to Blackpool, and after 'testing the water' in the cycle industry he set his son Dennis up, along with two colleagues from Harbri Engineering in a new company, which started trading in 1980. The 'Hill Special' name once again lived on. But the business climate was not quite right for the manufacture in volume for lightweight specialist cycle frames and the company closed. The Hill Special name was finally sold on by Adam Hill to Jack Wright of Middridge Engineering in Stockton-on-Seas. Despite advice to the contrary Adam could not get the cycle business out of his system and revived cycle frame building in his own name by opening new premises in Spring Street, Rishton. It was a short term adventure though and in 1983 the remaining stock was sold off together with frame making equipment and spray booths which was purchased by an enthusiast in Liverpool. The latter was able to continue to make cycle frames for a further ten years. Adam now took well earned retirement, and after re-occurring heart problems died in 1990. His son Dennis toured the Continent, and in between had short spells of cycle frame-building for various firms, but was sadly killed in a road traffic accident whilst driving his camper van in 1998. The name of 'Hill Special' lightweight cycles still brings a beam to the face and a glint to the eyes of many an enthusiastic cyclist even today. The firm was not a conglomerate of multinational companies, it was just a small independent firm which produced quality cycles, and one which Padiham folk are still very proud of. [liii]

LESSER TRADES AND INDUSTRIES.

Mineral waters and brewing.

Padiham is not well known for having a brewery, but it did have one albeit a short-lived affair. The Bridge End Brewery was started around 1850 by brothers Bowers and Henry Bertwistle, builders in Padiham.

Bowers also stated that he was a master carpenter, later he became connected with the stockbrokers firm of Mr Gahegan at Burnley, which later was carried on in the style of B. Bertwistle and Company. I assume that the brewery business was connected in some way to the Bridge End Mill, or at least was close by. The brewery was capable of producing around 130 barrels of ale and porter a week, but in November 1853 the partnership between Bowers and Henry Bertwistle was dissolved. Henry Bertwistle later went on to become the landlord at the Kings' Arms at Top o' Town, and the brewery was later offered for sale by auction, but appears to have had no takers, and thus was confined to the pages of the history of Padiham.

Padiham Aerated Waters.
This company was founded by Josiah Monk (1844-1907) who was the son of Mr and Mrs Edmondson Monk of Brookfoot Farm along Grove Lane. The Aerated Water company had been well established by 1880—when Josiah was also farming the 22 acres of land at Brookfoot Farm. Josiah had married Mary Pickup (1847-1895) his first wife, at Burnley in 1873. She was the daughter of James Pickup of Fenny Fold Farm, Stonemoor Bottom. Josiah was a leading figure in Padiham Liberalism. His second wife was Lizzie (Elizabeth) Denbigh, the daughter of Richard and Bridget Denbigh, a well known Padiham grocer at 65-67 Church Street, and a respected businessman. Josiah and Lizzie who married in 1896 at Burnley Registrar Office had several children together. The mineral waters company appears to have moved to Smithy Gate Mill around 1897, we know that he was still manufacturing the mineral waters at Brookfoot in 1890, but he must have moved to Smithy Gate soon after this. A partner in the business was John Harry Whittaker who was also involved with the Wellington Mill. Josiah made a good living out of the mineral water trade, and retired to 'Hazenthorpe' Norbreck near Blackpool about 1902. He was leader of the Liberal party in town, at a time when they were almost unrivalled, he was chairman of the District Council, he was a County Councillor, and a Justice of the Peace as well as being a trustee of the Wesley Chapel and the Wesley Chapel at Hall Hill, and chairman of Padiham Agricultural Society for over twelve years. Following his death at Blackpool in 1907, his body was brought back to Padiham and after a service at the Wesley Chapel interment followed at St James Church Altham in the family vault.

The Padiham Aerated Water Company which Josiah had founded continued after his death and in 1928 was taken over by Grimshaw's Brewery of Burnley, a firm amalgamated into the more famed Massey Brewery at Burnley the previous year in 1927. In June 1965, Massey announced that it intended to purchase all the shares of the Aerated Water Company not already owned by them. *"The Company were confident that the fact that Padiham Aerated Waters would in future be supported by the full organisation of Massey Brewery and its subsidiary companies would enable the service given to its customers of Padiham Aerated Water Company to be maintained and extended"* a press release stated. It was not to be, the following year production at Padiham Aerated Waters at Smithy Gate Mill ended when the mill was sold off to Padiham Urban District Council for £4,250—£250 less than the Aerated Water Company paid for it in 1951. Demolition followed soon afterwards and by 1968 the site of the old mill cleared and landscaped.

Hill's Mineral Waters
Not quite as large as Padiham Aerated Waters, this firm was located in buildings in a yard behind the chip shop on Stockbridge Road—now used by a firm of taxis. The firm was founded by Thomas William Hill a native of Kildwick, near Cross Hills, Keighley in Yorkshire. He came to Padiham when aged twenty around 1881 and subsequently set up the mineral waters firm. He married Lily Davy, a cotton weaver, at the Wesley Chapel in 1886 she was born at Sutton near to where Thomas was born—she was the daughter of George, a tailor and Ruth of Railway Terrace, now Russell Terrace. As the business prospered, Thomas was able to move from 40 Stockbridge Road where his wife Lily ran a drapers shop to 3 Shakespeare Street and then to the large house named 'Rycroft' on Burnley Road. Thomas was able to take retirement from the firm around 1926, although he still remained the head of the firm now named *'T. W. Hill and Son'*. Thomas was a regular attendee at Padiham Liberal Club where he went every day after retirement to enjoy a game of dominoes. It was at 'Rycroft' that Thomas William Hill passed away in February 1936, had he lived another few months until August he would have celebrated his Golden Wedding Anniversary—but it was not to be. He left a wife a son and a daughter, and was buried at Padiham Cemetery.

The firm continued for many years after Thomas's death and was carried on by his son Tom who continued to live at 3 Shakespeare Street. Certainly the firm was still in existence in 1959, and probably for a good few years after that date.

Saw Mills and Joinery Works

Railway Saw Mill
Was established by James Bertwistle about 1874 and is probably the longest running firm in Padiham today. Bertwistle is an ancient name hereabouts, and as farmers they came from yeoman stock, a direct line from James Bertwistle can be traced back as farm tenants of the Huntroyde Estate four hundred years. The name Bertwistle was the oldest on the Huntroyde books, and James Bertwistle had been a tenant farmer at Old Hey Farm just beyond the turn off to the bypass on the Whalley Road since 1870 up to the time of his death in 1910. James carried out many major joinery contracts in his lifetime. He did work on the Parish Church and assisted by his sons did work in connection with the Pendle Street Room and Power Companies Mill at Nelson, then the largest weaving shed in the world. He worked on Peel Mill at Rosegrove, the Station Hotel, the Craven Bank, Burnley Wood Council Schools, St Leonard's Schools at Padiham and restoration work at Whalley Abbey. Besides all of this he was a dairy farmer of 60 acres at Old Hey milking 30 head of cattle a day. James lived at 20 Whalley Range on the Whalley Road in later years, and was a regular worshipper at the Parish Church. In public life he served several terms of office on the old Padiham Local Board, and on the Urban District Council. For instance, he was chairman of the Gas and Water Committee in 1892 and had the pleasure of accepting a gold key at the opening ceremony of the new waterworks at Church Clough at Sabden. By the 1880s James Bertwistle and Sons were employing nine men and five boys and an additional two men to help out on the farm. The firm founded by James Bertwistle still survives as funeral directors in the town and has only recently (2010) moved into a new funeral parlour on Burnley Road next to the old White Horse public house. James Bertwistle died 9 November 1910 at a good age of 79 years and was buried at Padiham Church Cemetery on Blackburn Road—he left a widow, Ann nee Bibby whom he married in 1855 at St Leonards (died 31 March 1914) and two sons and two daughters to mourn his loss. However the 1881 census returns shows three sons, William Rennie, Joseph and George Pickup.

The latter died 24 June 1893, and three daughters, Alice E., Annie who died 20 June 1914, and Margaret, when the family were living at 1, St Leonard Street. One of the sons, William Rennie went on to follow his father by working at Old Hey Farm, whilst the son Joseph followed his father in the joinery and sawmill trade as James Bertwistle and Son. Isaiah Davies who lived at 30 Garden Street in the 1920s and traded as Davies and Company were probably James's only rival in Padiham at the Victoria Sawmills on Ightenhill Street and Guy Street. The plant at the Guy Street works was powered by a 20 horse power gas engine which was offered for sale by auction in 1910. Davies was the son of a stonemason named James Davies and his wife Mary. [liv]

Ropewalks
There were two ropewalks in Padiham, so named because the lengths of twine were laid out (walked) along the ground before being twisted into ropes. Ropes were an essential part of the Industrial Revolution, ropes were used to lash down the bales of finished cotton on the lorries and used as driving ropes for the huge steam engines. The larger ropewalk in Padiham was on the right hand side at the top of Moor Lane and was known as 'Mount Pleasant Ropewalk'. Some bungalows now take the place of this ropewalk. This was worked by Henry Myers, 'rope and twine manufacturer' who also had a confectionery shop on Church Street. He was actually a Skipton lad, but in 1876 at St Leonards had married Mary Speak, a Padiham lass, daughter of Alice Speak, a farmer's wife who used to live at the Arbory Lodge at the top of what is today Arbory Drive off the Whalley Road. In September 1883 there was a meeting of the creditors of Henry Myers at the offices of Artindale solicitors of Burnley. Mr Mossop auctioneer acted as receiver in the matter and produced a statement of affairs which showed that Myers had £483 in liabilities and just £70 in assets. Liquidation was arranged, but not in bankruptcy. Edward Stevenson Innkeeper of Padiham was appointed trustee, with a committee of inspection. I think Henry Myers had died by the 1890s and the confectionery shop was being run by his former wife Mary and the rope works had been taken over by James Cooper a Burnley rope manufacturer. The rope works survived until around the start of WW1 when economic conditions brought about its decline. Cooper was fined 10 shillings in 1889 for employing a under the age of 13 years at his rope-works without a certificate of school attendance.

The only other ropewalk in Padiham was directly behind today's Bridge Inn, and is marked on the First Edition of the O.S. Map of 1844-48, but little else is known about it.

Tripe Dressing Works
The trade of tripe dressing was something of an institution in Padiham especially when it came to the Bradshaw family. Tripe was extremely popular amongst the working classes as a delicacy during the two wars. It could be served as tripe and onions or with lashings of salt and vinegar or even with warm milk. Just after the Second World War there were no less than eight tripe dealers and dressers in Padiham. There was Austin and Company of Ightenhill Street, Bradshaw Brothers of 65 Burnley Road, Unice Hill, 43 Shakespeare Street, Mary Hudson of 2 Green Lane, Wallace Knowles of Park Road, Thomas Parkinson of 8 Victoria Road and Joe Wild, 133-35 Burnley Road. [lv] The best know of all Padiham tripe dressers though was Bradshaw's, a firm founded by the grandfather of Stanley Bradshaw. It was said that the grandfather started off boiling offal on the kitchen stove in the house. Later all five sons and even the daughters got roped in to making tripe. What is not so well known is that all the Bradshaw's were great sportsmen. Stanley Bradshaw was a professional footballer for Blackburn, Nelson, Burnley and Accrington. Another brother, William (Billy) was a former Blackburn Rovers international left half back. The youngest brother who left for Australia in 1924 also played for Accrington Stanley, and later for Blackpool. The best known brother was perhaps Ernest, and he too was formidable sportsman in his younger days. At the age of 15 he joined the Belvedere Club and signed for Accrington Stanley the following year. At the age of 17 he was signed for Blackburn Rovers before moving onto Nelson three years later—there he captained the reserve side for several seasons. He was a former president of Padiham Sports Club, and a national sprint competitor until he was nearly 30 years of age. He also took on board his fair share in public life, he was a councillor, and chairman of Padiham Urban District Council 1941-42, and a past president of Padiham Building Society. He was a Liberal in politics and a Freemason. Ernest of Clough Croft Simonstone died at a Nelson nursing home in February 1973, just a month short of his 86th birthday. [lvi] Ernest Bradshaw had taken retirement for the old established family tripe business back in 1968, and the firm was later taken over by Les Hayhurst who ran it until his death in 1997.

The tripe works was off Clitheroe Street behind Enterprise Mill, the red brick buildings, although these may be later additions in a small yard with the stub of a stone chimney. The following year John Marks, along with a former employee at the works, Andrew Ingham who worked at the tripe works for ten year bought the business with hopes of reopening it. The partnership spent £30,000 bringing the old firm up to scratch in order to meet the EEC regulations, which included installing new equipment to filter out smells. This was always a major problem with tripe works as fats were rendered down they cause objectionable smells—especially Bradshaw's which was almost in the very heart of Padiham town centre. The officially opening of the new firm was performed by the Mayor of Padiham and which retained the Bradshaw name as *'Bradshaw's Quality Food'* took place in October 1998. [lvii]

CHAPTER FIVE

Strikes and Disputes

A meeting of the Burnley weavers met at the Burnley Market as part of a county wide movement to see how best to get the best wages out of the manufacturers in August 1852. Further meetings followed including one in Fulledge Meadow which raised a demand for a 10% increase in wages. The spinners joined in the agitation and 6 August 1852 held a great demonstration at Padiham. The masters at Burnley appeared in the first instance to accept the demands, and the leaders of the mill operatives agreed that some of the workers who were on higher wages should suffer some reduction—such a happy settlement was not destined to last however. In common with other Lancashire manufacturers the Burnley mill-owner decided to form a 'Masters Association' on 15 August 1852, and in doing so bound themselves on a large penalty to be loyal to each other and resist all the demands of the workers. Inevitably trouble arose and on 28 October the masters declared a lockout. Fifty six mills closed down in Burnley and Padiham, and 12,000 operatives were thrown out of work. Tempers flared throughout the county, riots ensued in Wigan and there was much unrest in Bacup, Preston, and of course Burnley and Padiham. At a mass meeting held on 29 October at Burnley the riots at Wigan were condemned but they refused to accept the advice of Radical Charles Owen who was anxious to establish the right of each individual to make his own contract with the cotton masters.

This was going to be a long bitter dispute, and a relief committee was set up and raised £112 to be distributed in food among 2,000 families. The public in general were for the operatives. On 19 December the masters held a meeting at the Bull Inn at Burnley and agreed to open the mills and pay the rates to be posted at the factories when work was started. The master would not however allow collections to be made at their mills for strikers in other towns. The Burnley and Padiham operatives were glad of any concession—their leaders resigned and a new committee was formed. When the rates were published at the mills they showed that the spinners had made a 10% increase, but the weavers none at all. For a considerable period after the dispute the mills ran on a four day week. [lviii]

There were the inevitable disputes in the main industry at Padiham, the cotton trade as the operatives tried to better their lot. A strike in the town beginning in March 1859 over equal pay with the operatives working in the same trade at Blackburn and other places was to last a full six months. It became known as the 'Ten Per-cent Movement'. Its claims were (1) The adoption of the Blackburn List, which the Padiham operatives claimed were as much as 12% higher than the average Padiham rates of pay. (2) The right of Mr Pinder to enter any mill. (3) And the right of Mr Pinder to negotiate terms and conditions on behalf of the workers. The Padiham manufacturers backed by the Masters Association declared that such a scheme was not practicable on account of local conditions such as the price of coal and distance from Manchester and Liverpool. On the subject of Mr Pinder the masters would not enter into any agreement on his right to enter mills or negotiate on the weavers behalf. On 2 March 1859 a meeting was held by the power-loom weavers at the Oddfellow's Hall to decide on the question of calling a strike. It was decided that should the masters not give them the same terms as the Blackburn weavers then they should give notice of strike action. Mr Pinder, the secretary was then asked to serve each master with a fortnights notice on behalf of the hands. The whole town was in an excitable state while these proceedings were going on, and the hands at Thompson and Sons came out on the following day, but on being told the situation they returned to work the following day. However, the masters refused to move and the strike was called, all the mills in town were brought to a halt save for Temple and Company and Mr Hindle's mill who agreed to give what was asked for. Further meetings were held by the weavers and it was resolved that there would be no return to work until they got the pay of the Blackburn standard list.

Other weaving towns agreed to give support to the Padiham weavers whilst they were out at a rate of 6s per week each whilst on strike. By the end of March many of the Padiham operatives had found employment elsewhere, but those still on strike were determined to maintain their position against the masters and hold out. By the middle of April Messrs Knowles and Company who employed more weavers than any other mill on strike and which was the only mill that stood fully idle commenced running although by but a few hands. The total amount collected for those on strike amounted to £311, being a full £40 more than the previous week. Out of this the strikers were paid six shillings each besides sixpence to a shilling per head in the case of distress—support for the strike was also coming from the Preston weavers at a rate of 2d per loom and the Blackburn weavers at 1d per loom. The following week a total of £322 was collected in support of the strikers. On 19 May 1859 a large meeting was held at the Albion Inn on Church Street Preston regarding the condition of the operatives on strike at Padiham, and what assistance, beyond what had already been given could be afforded by the Preston operatives. Mr Pinder, secretary of the Power loom Weavers' Association reported that at last the Padiham masters were giving way. One of the masters had conceded to the wishes of the operatives who however could not work on account of the beams being empty. Another master had made an offer to the strikers—and the men on strike were grateful for the support they had received and the sympathy they got from outside areas. After paying all out that week they had £62 in hand—weavers were paid 7 shillings each, tenters 3 shillings and six pence, and over £26 was distributed amongst the children. The Rev., Mr Verity of near Burnley made a speech on behalf of the hands on strike and contended that they were justified in the action they had taken.

The strike was soon in its tenth week. A crowded congregation of striking operatives packed Habergham All Saints Church to hear a sermon preached by the Rev., Verity who went on to say that he had heard that there was going to be a collection. He was not anxious that a collection should be made for fear that the employers might say that he was actuated by pecuniary motives. He would however test the sense of the congregation on the subject—those in favour of a collection were asked to hold up their hands. The whole congregation held up their hands and a collection of £5.10 shillings was raised.

The Rev., Verity supported the operatives throughout the strike to the condemnation of cotton masters and the church alike. By the fourteenth week it was generally believed that the masters were giving way, but a few workers had agreed to go back to work only to find that the masters would not pay the rate of the Blackburn weavers, and the operatives found themselves back out on strike. At Burnley Edward Wilkinson was bound over to keep the peace by the courts for having threatened and intimidated a Padiham man named John Whittaker who was at work at Messrs Hull and Ingham's mill. The complainant stated that when returning from his work about five minutes past six in the evening he saw a crowd of about 200 assembled a hundred yards away from the mill. Wilkinson, who was one of the crowd went up to him and said *"Damn thee devil as thou art, when it comes dark we will pay thee for working, and we would do now if it were dark"* Wilkinson then followed him to his own door 400 yards way using similar threats to him all the way. The crowd followed and hooted. By early August the strike was in its twentieth week and neither party, the master nor the weavers looked like giving way. However, on 10 August the master spinners and manufacturers agreed to appoint a committee to look into the claims and demands of the Padiham operatives. Finally after 25 weeks in September 1859 an agreement of sorts was finally reached to end the strike when the Padiham operatives gained the standard list.

The Cotton Famine had a disastrous effect on the cotton industry in Lancashire, however by 1873 things were looking up and the masters agreed to recognise the Burnley list, or standard rates of pay. But this did not last long and a depression in the trade from 1875 made many of the masters consider a reduction in pay to their employees. In March 1878 the Masters Association decided on a general reduction of 10%. This was naturally rejected by the operatives in Burnley and many other towns, and on 17 April a strike was declared. At first it was a case of a bit of hooting and name calling, but as the strike lengthened then tempers frayed. On 13 May some violence was shown as a large crowd attempted to rescue prisoners going to Preston for trial on Standish Street in Burnley. On 15 May large crowds at Burnley went to hear the president of the Union Mr Holmes make a speech on the matter, and appeal for a continuation of a peaceful strike. The large crowd got out of hand and marched to John Kay's mill in Parliament Street and smashed all the windows there.

The town clerk was forced to read the Riot Act in Springfield Road, but still the crowds refused to disperse. The police baton charged the crowds who then went up Todmorden Road to Mr Kay's residence where more windows were broken. On 17 May a mill was burnt down in Haslingden, and rioters at Burnley and Accrington were arrested. At Padiham a riot was anticipated, and a troop of infantry from the barracks at Burnley was sent to the town. The Volunteers and others were sworn in as special constables, and other arrangements under the direction of Major Starkie were being made for the purpose of retaining order. The infantry 44, in number and under the command of Captain Frampton arrived at Padiham around six o'clock in the evening of 17 May 1878. Their arrival was greeted with much hooting as the troops made their way to the National Schoolrooms where they were to be stationed in case of any outbreak. Padiham had previously been quiet as far as the situation was up to that time, and a large crowd complained bitterly about the presence of the troops in town. They insisted that the presence of the soldiers would only aggravate the situation and cause angry feelings where none existed before.

At seven o'clock Major Starkie came out of the drill room where people were being sworn in as special constables and addressed the crowds. He said that he respected the people of Padiham, and that they did not expect any disturbances, but if there were any disturbances then it would not be by the Padiham people—of this he was perfectly satisfied. The assembled crowds however were not so easily pleased and shouted and hooted for the soldiers to be taken out of the town. A quarter of an hour later a boy aged around 12 years old came through the streets with a rather dilapidated effigy said to be a representation of one of the local manufacturers. A large crowd followed and hooted the effigy, the police watched on without interference. Later that evening at about ten fifteen Major Starkie was forced to read the Riot Act after a large number of windows were smashed at the Starkie Arms where the Major was staying. Even after the Act was read the violence still continued and all the windows fronting the inn were broken. A large group of special constables were drafted to the place, and the Sergeant addressed the crowd telling them to move on. A spokesperson in the crowd said that they would move on if the police did the same. Soon after this the stone throwing ceased and the streets were cleared.

On 25 May a ballot was taken amongst the Lancashire weavers which showed a heavy majority still in favour of continuing the dispute. But the coffers of the Union Funds were then empty and no more strike pay could be made. Over the next few weeks the weavers were forced to drift back to work. The strike had been a victory for the masters and the weavers went back to work on a reduced pay, there were further disputes but by the end of 1879 all the weavers were earning up to 25% less in wages. There was an interesting case during this strike which ended up in the courts. Riley Kenyon, John Mann and Amos Yates were charged with having on the 11 June demanded with menaces the sum of one shilling with intent from Mr John Whittaker cotton spinner and manufacturer. It was stated that there was a considerable amount of turmoil in Padiham at that time because of the strike. Mr Whittaker it was said had rendered himself obnoxious during the strike. On the day in question, the three prisoners along with two other men had gone to Mr Whittaker's house and asked him to give them a shilling. Whittaker refused, whereby Mann made the threat that if he did not give them any money he would have a mob at his house that night and pull him to pieces and the house would be pulled down. At that moment Mr Whittaker's man servant came out of the house and the mob ran away. This was the case for the prisoners—however Mr Whittaker version of events differed slightly. He stated that he saw the prisoners at his house with two other men. He found them in the kitchen, the other two men being outside. They were drunk and said that they wanted to sing a song. Whittaker said that he wanted no songs and told them to get out of his house. They refused, and then he pushed Kenyon and Mann out of the house. Kenyon asked him for a shilling. Whittaker said that he would give them nothing and told them to go on their way. Mann then uttered the threats *'If you don't give us anything we shall have a mob here at half past eleven tonight, we will pull you out of your house and pull the building down'*

Yates repeated the threats, but Kenyon said nothing. Whittaker said that he would bring the police and the prisoners surrounded him as he tried to leave—Mann saying that they would tear him from limb to limb. After hearing other evidence, the judge summed up the case and the jury consulted for a few moments before returning a verdict of *'Not Guilty'* and the prisoners were then discharged.

There was a localised strike at Padiham at the Orchard Mill in April 1883. Mr Whittaker the proprietor of the mills brought in a number of hands from Burnley to take the place of the weavers on strike. This caused a great deal of anger among the strikers, and crowds gathered outside the mill and as the Burnley weavers were leaving work they were greeted with hoots and the throwing of stones. The threats continued the next day and in anticipation of a disturbance a large force of police was sent from Burnley to Padiham and a bus was brought into use to convey the Burnley weavers' home. The strike was called by the Padiham weavers on account of Mr Whittaker reducing the rate of pay to that of the Burnley workers. Previously the rate paid was slightly higher at Padiham. The strike breakers from Burnley had been going to the mill at Padiham every day by train, and returning at night either by tram or train. The Manchester Times on 28 April announced *"The strike at Orchard Mills at Padiham is virtually over"* but his appears not to have been the case. Reports in May that year tell of P.C. Hickling who was in the habit of meeting and escorting a family from Higham who worked at Orchard Mill each working day. This same family complained of being assaulted by a tape sizer named John Smithson of Forrester's Court Padiham, who worked for Mr Stuttard of Clover Croft Mill at Higham.

Also at Padiham a 'Public Reception' was given to Christopher Hudson who had been serving a month in prison for an alleged assault on a policeman during the disturbances. A large number in the town turned out to greet the young man who was then driven around the streets in a wagonette proceeded by a brass band. Eventually several thousand people assembled in a field near the railway station and presented the man with the sum of £5 to recoup him of the losses incurred whilst he was in jail. There were further reports in June of the 'continued disturbances at Orchard Mill' whereby crowds composed mainly of children and women were still assembling and shouting to the 'knobstickers' who continued to come from Burnley to the Orchard Mill. Each evening they were marched under the protection of the police to the railway station, and were met with them each morning. The police it was stated had been there over two months.

Following a reduction in wages there was another strike called in March 1885 which took place at several mills in Burnley, the Rossendale Valley and at Padiham. On 23 April a meeting was held at the Spinners' Institute at Blackburn in aid of the workpeople of Burnley and Padiham in resisting attempts to reduce their wages.

It was resolved to contribute one penny per loom for a few week to assist any weaver bold enough to resist encroachment. There was a strike called at the Riverside and Albert Mills of Messrs Ingham and Sons in June 1890—the dispute appears to have been about the attitude of some of the management towards the operatives and a wage structure. Several mass meetings were held by the workers at the Assembly Hall, Mr Joshua Borrows occupying the chair and Mr Dean the secretary was also in attendance. The strike lasted several days and was settled on Tuesday 24 June and was a victory for the operatives. There was a curious strike at Thomas Catlow's Orchard Mill in March 1896 seemingly over the quality of the work. The employer, Thomas Catlow was inspecting some of the cloth wove by one of the weavers when he noticed a 'float' or 'flaw' which he tore out. The weaver followed Catlow into the warehouse, where the two had heated words and almost came to blows. The whole of the weavers then held a meeting and decided not to return to work until they had seen their representatives. Later that day Theodore Robinson the weavers' secretary was seen and he arranged to hold a meeting that very same evening.

At the meeting Mr Robinson recommended that the weavers return to work the following day and tender a weeks' notice of strike action. The weavers agreed to this decision, but when they turned up for work the following morning they found the mill doors locked. Mr Catlow came and said that he intended to speak to the weavers before letting them into the mill, but after waiting some time he did not appear and the workers went home. Various meetings were held, some between the masters association and some between the weavers' representatives and some between both parties. Mr Catlow was asked to pay the weavers wages for the day that he 'locked' them out of the mill, this he refused to do and the meetings ended up in deadlock. Further meetings were held and eventually a compromise was reached and the workers returned to their employment.
There was an even stranger affair at Slater and Son's Greenbridge Mill in September 1896. The dispute arose from the weavers, who when short of warps were not allowed to run each other's looms and work alternatively but were required to work even if they only had one loom running which did not pay them enough in wages. Consequently one of their numbers was discharged because he failed to turn up for work and all the hands at the mill came out.

Further trouble ensued as the masters refused to employ any worker who was a member of the union, they then secured the employment of other weavers from Burnley, Colne, Nelson and the surrounding districts. These strike breakers arrived each morning around six thirty at the railway station and were met by crowds of Padiham people who 'hooted' them all the way to Greenbridge Mill. On one day up to 4,000 congregated around the mill as the new hands departed from the works. One family from Colne who had taken up residence in Hill Street were followed home by a large crowd. The police were called to the scene. The occupants of the house then opened a window and threw several halfpennies into the crowds. This taunting angered the crowds even more and stones were thrown through the windows of the house—several panes of glass were smashed. The police had some difficulty in moving the angry crowds on. The following day there was an uncanny silence in the town—thirty extra police had been drafted in. The mill stopped at a quarter past five in the evening and the strike breakers were got to the railway station before the other operatives at other mills finished work.

    A smaller crowd had assembled at the station and there was some hooting before the train pulled out of the station. A meeting of the Weavers' Committee was held when it was decided to keep the workers out until the masters decided to take them back, or they found other places. This whole affair just seems to have fizzled out, a week later it was reported that things appeared to be going normal at the mill, there were a few pickets, but nothing like the former week. A few placards had been put up in Burnley stating that a few looms were vacant, and that the average earnings of the waver were 5s.8d per loom per week. Days later only a few looms were standing, since a large number of applications had been made for work. Several of the other original workers had got work elsewhere in Padiham and one family had left town. A week later all the looms at Greenbridge Mill were at work.

A dispute took place at the Perseverance Mill in February 1911 over the dismissal of an employee, by which 4,000 operatives came out on strike. The employers at the mill refused to give any details of the dismissal stating that they had no reason to do so. The local Weavers Association then caused all the other weavers at the mill to come out. This in turn resulted in all the Padiham mills federated to the North and North East Lancashire Manufacturers Association having notices posted stating that there would be a lock out at the mills.

Hasty meetings were called between the operatives and management which were to last a full three hours. Eventually the following communication was issued;

"Whilst the employers are not prepared to waive the right of withholding, if they think fit, the reason why notice is given for the termination of employment of any of their workpeople, and in the hope that in future the Padiham Weavers Association will strictly observe the joint rule between the two central Associations, the employers state that as they had no feelings against the weavers whose employment had been terminated at Perseverance Mill, they were prepared to give an assurance that she should not be at disability but reason of what had happened, but should not receive the same consideration upon applying for employment at any of the Federation mills in Padiham, as would be given to any other weaver. One of the employers subsequently, on his own initiative offered to give the weaver in question the first chance of employment in his mill when a vacancy arises. It was therefore mutually agreed to recommend that all notices would be withdrawn, and that work should be resumed at all the mills at six o'clock and that conditions of employment at each mill should be as heretofore". One cannot help feeling that the weaver dismissed and the operatives in general came out worst in this, and nearly all the other disputes.

Miscellaneous disputes

Mining Disputes

We do not have much information about mining disputes in Padiham mainly because all the pits there had been closed down by the mid 1870s. To get some idea of the miners' way of life, we might state that the men worked 12 hours shifts in 1850, four o'clock in the morning till four o'clock in the afternoon, although this was reduced in 1872 to a ten-hour day. An Act of 1872 also made it illegal to employ boys under the age ten and that lads of ten to fifteen should work no more than 54 hours a week. During a national dispute in 1840 there was a demonstration held at Padiham. "The procession proceeded down the main street in Padiham, and as it was lunchtime the factory hands were keen to get a glimpse of their friends. The streets were literally crammed, the procession having arrived shortly before one o'clock when the whole population turned out to welcome them and Mr Roberts the miners' attorney.

They moved through the town maintaining the strictest order and returned to the Dun Horse Inn where Mr Roberts addressed the miners in a large room of the inn. A carriage was then ordered to take Mr Roberts back to Burnley. There was a local strike of all the colliers at Padiham employed by the Exors of the Late Colonel Hargreaves in March 1860 called in consequence of the dismissal of six of their number who had been appointed delegates to the trade union. Sir James Kay-Shuttleworth agreed to mediate in the dispute, and the men were called to Gawthorpe. On arrival they were requested to select nine men, three from each pit to negotiate with Sir James. A meeting followed lasting four or five hours in which the matters of the dispute were discussed. Finally a memorandum was drawn up and read to the colliers at the hall which they concluded was a statement of their views and wishes. The document also contained details of how their wages were made up and the rates of advance which they might expect if the price of coal should rise. Sir James then offered to become their mediator and to assure their masters that the men had unabated confidence in their judgment and kindness if *'Bygones might be bygones'* and a reasonable consideration was shown to their wishes. This offer was accepted and a letter was forwarded to Ormerod House at Burnley. The following day Mr Thursby entered with his agents into the whole of the representation of the colliers and returned to Sir James Kay-Shuttleworth an answer. In consideration of this reply a meeting of the colliers was called at the Oddfellow's Hall at Padiham, whereby it was resolved to return to work the following day.

In November 1873 a deputation was sent from the Padiham pits to the Exors of Colonel Hargreaves to make a request for an advancement in wages in consequence of a recent rise in the price of coal. They were then informed that those in the Union must leave, and that those having lamps must returned them. A strike was then called and the Padiham men joined forces with the Burnley miners' who were already out on strike. What followed was one of the most bitter disputes in local mining history. Soon the local mills were shutting down due to lack of fuel, the colliery master then began to bring in 'knobstick' labour from as far away as Cornwall and Devon offering those men a two year contract at 7s per day. The Union leaders were charged with 'conspiracy' for trying to dissuade the 'knobstickers' to go home and in court they were found guilty, although no fines were imposed.

By May the following year, 1874, it was clear that the strike was failing as far as the men were concerned, many colliers left town, some joined the army, some entered other industries. In August after holding out for almost 12 months the men had to admit defeat. The strike had cost the Union over £20,000 and the 'Burnley and Church Branch' of the Union was dissolved.

The Engineering Industry.
Various strikes in the engineering industry were called over the decades, but most were short lived being settled within days, sometimes to the advantage of the men, other times to the masters. None of these strikes had a particular influence on the history of Padiham—but we might mention a few of the more recent disputes. A strike at Main Gas Limited in 1979 appeared to be a strike that no-one wanted, and it had been called by the national executive. What made matters worse was the fact that many of the men and women employed at Main Gas were actually on more money than the national minimum level, and the only thing they were likely to gain through the strike was a reduction of one hour per working week. A ballot held at Main Gas showed that 56% wanted to return to work but could not because the strike had been called by the Amalgamated Union of Engineering Workers. Soon the strike had spread to Kirkstall Gear on Rossendale Road, Lucas factories and even Prestige. The strike lasted about a week. In August 1983, the same firm at Padiham, then known as Thorn E.M.I., went on strike again, this time in support of their annual pay claim. Mr R.T. Heywood the general manager said that plans to take on extra staff had been put on hold because of the strike. A 24-hour picket line manned the Wyre Street premises waiting for the management to make the next move. However, the management refused to budge on the offer of a 4% deal, and for days the situation was deadlocked—although a final settlement was agreed eventually.

CHAPTER SIX
Essential Services, Electricity, Gas Water and Sewerage.
Electricity Supply, Postal Service.
Padiham was not supplied with electricity until December 1926, even though its little sister Hapton had become the first village in England to be lit by electricity as far back as 1888.

The Local Board at a meeting held in 1889 put forward a motion that they should apply to the Board of Trade for a provisional order authorising the Board to supply for public and private purposes. The U.D.C had also looked at the matter and the probable costs of installation in 1899, but no action appears to have been taken at that time. An Inquiry was held at Burnley town hall on 24 February 1924 by the Electricity Commissioners to decide what scheme they would decide upon for a new power station. Initially, Burnley appeared to have the upper hand as to where this should be, and was supported by other authorities, apart from Padiham who had negotiated a supply from the Lancashire Electricity Power Company. As the inquiry progressed it soon became apparent that the L.E.P. scheme had been put together more carefully, and they had already bought a suitable site. Burnley's plan was for a site to the south of Simonstone railway station, a smaller site than the L.E.P.'s and the water and waste ash would have to cross a main road.

In May 1924 the Commissioners granted permission for L.E.P. to construct their power station. Formal consent was given on 25 July and work was soon in progress. The supply to Padiham U.D.C. was switched on when the power station was opened on 9 December 1926 on 20 acres land below that occupied by 'The Old Parsonage' to the north of the town. The Chairman of the U.D.C. Councillor Coe performed the opening ceremony. The new power station was to be called Padiham 'A' Power Station. The Lancashire Electric Power Company was also responsible for the laying of cables and all the building work and ran the works on behalf of the council. To this end an Electricity Committee body of the U.D.C. was formed to look after customer accounts, connections and the general running of the electric side of the business. It appeared that they would have their work cut out—in 1926 there were only ninety local people prepared to have electricity installed in their property. Electricity demand in the 1930s was almost entirely taken up by domestic lighting and industrial power. Padiham U.D.C. had a mere 25 cookers to supply and nine water heaters and boilers. At the power station there were six boilers, four on one side and two on the other side of the firing isle. They had a working pressure of 250 lbs per square inch. The engine room was at the end of the boiler house and at right angles to it, it contained two 7,500kW turbo-generators, with a third 15,625kW generator being installed in 1928.

The station used tried and tested equipment, once coal wagons had arrived at the station they were marshalled and moved to the unloading hopper by an electric loco worked off overhead cables. The wagons were then tipped using electric rams and the coal was fed into skips on an overhead ropeway. This lifted the coal to the top of the 50 ton bunkers where it was tipped automatically. The station was simple in design, and not expensive to construct costing around £390,000. When the L.E.P., acquired the land for Padiham 'A' Station it was much larger than necessary, and by the end of the 1930s a planned extension of the station was then obsolete. Power Station design and size had improved much over the previous ten years. So, a proposal to build a new power station next to the old one was put forward—to be named Padiham 'B' Power Station. However, the outbreak of war curtailed any development, but plans were brought out again when hostilities ceased. Following Nationalisation of the electricity industry in 1947, it was thought that Huncoat power Station was be sufficient to supply local needs, although planning for Padiham 'B' continued apace. In 1952 a new site was considered between the River Calder and north of Altham church and the railway. However, the old Calder Colliery workings were under this area. Efforts were then concentrated on the 'A' site and more land was purchased to the west of the site. In 1956 much of the design work had been completed and outline consent was given for a station with two 120mw turbo-generators, two boilers and cooling towers.

Formal consent was given for Padiham 'B' was granted on 30 May 1957. Towards the end of 1959 the contractors had constructed banking alongside the river stopping flooding which had been a problem in the past. The actual buildings were completed by the end of 1960 at a cost of £2.5 million. Despite a number of industrial disputes the No.1 Unit was finally synchronised on 30 December 1961—the No.2 Unit almost a year later on 5 November 1962. The coal fired station was an efficient generator of electricity from the start. In later years it was converted to using oil, and the station appeared to have taken on a new lease of life. However, the price of oil rose dramatically for 1979 which resulted in a steep decline in use at Padiham 'B'. In 1980, it was declared 'cold' and required seven days notice before it could be put back on load. Consideration was given to converting the station back to coal firing, but this was dismissed. Trials were carried out mixing fine coal with oil which could be used with conventional oil fired boilers—but these were unsuccessful.

From 1983 the unit was only used occasionally for the next eight years and only ran the odd time—it was on load for the last time on 9 March 1991. Privatisation of the industry took place and National Power plc took over operations at Padiham 'B' in March 1991. A proposal was put forward that the station might be able to burn, a bitumen based fuel, but pollution emission control equipment that would have had to be fitted to the station rules this out on account of costs. With no other way forward a decision to close Padiham 'B' was taken in September 1993. Seventy jobs went with the closure, most taking voluntary redundancy. In 1998 a plan was put forward to create up to 500 new jobs on the site of the old power station with an injection of £2.5 million coming from Europe. Work started in 1999 on the new industrial estate which was named 'Shuttleworth Mead'.

Gas Supply
Without doubt gas was being used at Padiham by the turn of the 1800s and by the 1840s, a 'gasometer' shows up at the Old factory, or the Guy Yates Mill run by the Helm's on the map of 1844-48. In August 1845 a meeting was held at the Swan Inn at Padiham to decide whether to form a gas and water company. A company of this type had previously been proposed but without success. However it was then thought that 'This thriving little town should have street lights like many other towns'. A company was thus formed and 12 months after the following notice appeared in the Blackburn Standard of August 1846;

> "To Iron-founders, Gas Fitters, Braziers, Glaziers &c., &c. Parties desirous of contracting for lamp posts gas lamps and fittings are informed that the inspectors for lighting the town of Padiham are prepared to receive tenders for the above named articles on or before Thursday the third day of September next when the lettings will take place at the towns' office Burnley Road, Padiham at two o'clock in the afternoon. A pattern for the gas lamps will be ready for inspection on or after Friday the 28th instance on application to Mr Bramley at the National School adjoining the above office. The lamp posts must be similar to those adopted by the Accrington Gas Company"

The Padiham Gas, Light and Coke Company was bought out by the Local Board in 1875. The gas works in 1895 were on Station Road between the bridge and Burnley Road—in fact that part of Station Road was once known as Gas Street. The gasometer was on the site of the present day Health Centre, with the actual production side being on the site of today's fire station. Plans had been put forward to build a new gas works as far back as 1884—in 1887 a plot of land was acquired at the bottom of what is now Park Road for the new works, and due to the urgent need a new gasometer was erected there in the same year. Plans for a completely new gas works was submitted before the authorities in 1895, but at a cost of £26,000 it was shelved on account of the expense. [lix]

In 1895 gas consumption had risen dramatically to 41 million cubic feet per annum. There was a serious incident in August 1898 when a couple of men were moving a boiler from Great Harwood to the gasworks at Padiham. The men, John William Clegg of Burnley and William Wilson of Gray Street Burnley were coming down Burnley Road with the boiler on a lurry drawn by two horses when they reached the steep section near the 'Top Bank'. Wilson slackened the brake on the lurry and it gathered speed, the horses were pushed forward with the extra weight and a lamp post was knocked down, there was also some slight damage down to the bank building. Clegg grabbed hold of one of the horses' heads in order to try and calm it when the animal lost its balance and fell taking Clegg with it. The animal fell on top of him, his head was badly crushed and he suffered serious internal injuries—he later died from the effects. In January 1905 a little before midnight a fire broke out at the gasworks, the fire brigade were quickly on the scene when an explosion occurred. People who had gathered to watch the blaze panicked thinking that the whole works was going to go up, and raced away to safety. Happily there were no serious injuries incurred to anyone—but almost a year later there was another smaller explosion at the works in which Mr Harrison the gas engineer was burnt on the hands and face.

These events brought forward the need for a completely new gasworks. An Act of 1908 applied for by the Padiham Urban District Council authorised the building of a new gas works at the bottom end of Park Road—it would also supply Read, Simonstone, Higham and Sabden with gas. The authority was obliged to purchase the mains and services of Read Parish Council.

The gas supplied to Higham and Sabden was done so in a pressure of two pounds to the square inch—one of the first installations of high pressure distributions in Northern England. The extent of the land purchased on Park Road for the purpose was 16,560 yards and adjoined the railway on two levels, the lower level being 15 feet below the higher level. To achieve this some 20,000 cubic yards of earth had to be removed, the material excavated was used to level up land adjoining which also belonged to the council. When completed the higher level was used for the production of tar and enabled to tar to run down by gravity into the railway wagons. Also here were the purifiers, the weigh office for the coal, the essential ingredient for the production of gas and a sulphate plant. The lower level contained the offices, boiler and compressor house and scrubbing plants. All the buildings were built from Accrington brick with sandstone inserts. The new works was opened on 19 October 1910 by the Chairman of the Gas Committee Mr Thomas Riding which was followed by a banquet at the Co-op Hall. The Gas Act in 1948 brought in by Clement Atlee resulted in the Nationalisation of the British gas industry which resulted in 1062 private gas companies being merged into 12 gas board areas. In this area it became the North West Gas Board. Until the last day of September 2010 the site of Padiham's old gas works was used by Lancashire County Council as its recycle centre—its future use still looks uncertain at the time of writing. [lx]

Water Supply
Prior to having water on tap, the folks at Padiham depended on wells or springs for their water supply. There are a number of wells marked on the first edition of the O.S. map of 1844-48. Well Street off West Street is aptly named, for there was a well nearby, and another well further down the road near the Alma where you can still hear running water to this day. This may have been 'Grimshaw Well' for a short street near here was named that! There was a well besides the road near Slade in addition to a couple on the 'Banks' and Spa Street off Padiham Road recalls yet another well. In comparatively recent times a well was discovered, or rather rediscovered in the cellar of Trevelyan House on Church Street. I have to say here, that apart from the latter, the wells we are talking about are not the 'Jack and Jill' type of wells with a deep shaft and a roof over them, but more springs of water from the hillsides.

The water here was collected in stone troughs, and there are still a few examples to be seen around the Lancashire countryside. However they were still deep enough to cause the deaths of infants—take the case in August 1838 by which a 3 year old child named Ellen Hudson was found drowned in a well near the Hare and Hounds, where the inquest was later held. The usual verdict of 'accidental death' was recorded. Padiham was expanding at this time in the 1840s, and expanding fast, there was a real need for a proper water supply to meet the growing population. In August 1845 a meeting was held at the Swan Inn at Padiham to decide whether it would be practicable to form a company to establish a public gas and water company in the town. Mr William Waddington occupied the chair, and a committee was formed to look into the matter. It was stated that an attempt was made some years before to accomplish the same objection but to no avail. However, it was some years later before the Padiham Water Works Company was formed in 1854—although initial surveys had been carried out the previous years. The company was founded on 600 shares of £10 each, the money raised was to be used for the building of a new reservoir at Wall Green at the bottom of the Sabden Road up Slade Lane. The remains of this old reservoir can still be seen to this day in its walled enclosure.

An office and house was secured for the secretary of the new company on Mill Street—the directory of 1868 states that the secretary at that time was one John Blackburn, who incidentally also worked as a clogger. The Padiham Waterworks Company obtained an Act of Parliament for the construction of this reservoir at Wall Green in 1854—its capacity when completed was to be 11,000,000 gallons and it had a gathering ground of 240 acres. In 1873 the Padiham and Hapton Local Board was constituted, and in the following year promoted a Bill through Parliament for the purchase of the water company—at the same time it was also promoting another Bill to extend its gathering grounds. However this was rejected and the Local Board was thrown back to its position and resources of 1854. The Board was obliged to call in engineers who made a report of supplying water to Padiham with a reservoir at Cavaliers, on the Sabden Road near Black Hill. Also at this time the Board was considering a scheme for the construction of a reservoir at Hapton a scheme which they finally adopted and promoted a Bill in Parliament for that purpose. But this was strenuously opposed to by the landowners, and rejected by the Committee of the House.

The Board was once again obliged to look at other means of supplying water to the town and engineers were once again called in. They recommended the construction of a reservoir at Churn Clough on the side of Pendle and above the village of Sabden, and this was accepted by the Board. Accordingly a Bill was presented to Parliament once again which received Royal Assent in April 1882. The new reservoir was to be charmingly situated at Churn Clough a short distance above Sabden from which a fine view of the valley could be obtained. Its capacity when completed would be 112,000,000 gallons and it would have a gathering ground of 440 acres—all of which was open moorland. The quality of the water had been tested and said to be the finest in the land. The new reservoir was said to be capable of supplying a town with a population of 20,000 and more than suited Padiham's needs, and should it be required was capable of being extended should the need arise in the future. The original amount estimated to be spent on the new waterworks was put at £41,000, but owing to unseen difficulties this was exceeded.

The new reservoir was not before time, it was reported as late as 1880 that the water supply at Padiham contained 'water wolfs' and various kinds of animalcule, it was disagreeable to look at and the smell was almost unbearable—the Board must take steps to improve it or the people will have to give up its use!. In the same year, it was stated that the people of Padiham are badly supplied with water as regards quality and it was feared that unless the Board take steps to improve it will become very noxious. A sample recently drawn from a water tap was placed before the Board and found to contain a leech two inches long. A resident on Clay Bank Street was drawing water when he too found a leech two inches long. Even later in 1899 it was suggested that the water at Padiham should be analysed, but one witty councillor declared that he doubted that there was enough water to analyse. Work on the new reservoir began in earnest and was to take until 1892 before it was fully completed. In 1886 there was a supposed outbreak of smallpox among the navvies constructing the Churn Clough reservoir, alleged to have been taken there by a tramp. However an investigation by the relieving officer revealed that this was not the case and that the 'infection' in one of the huts proved to be nothing more than a water rash. The following year in November 1887 there was a fatal accident at the reservoir.

A number of navvies were engaged in the excavations when one of their numbers, a man named John Heydon was overcome by a fall of earth. Every effort was made to extricate but he was pronounced dead when he was got out. Others near to him also had a narrow escape, and one name William Pool had both his legs broken. He was taken to Blackburn Infirmary, and the body of the deceased Heydon was taken to the Black Bull to await an inquest. He lived at Barrow near Whalley and was an army pensioner with several war medals to his credit having been decorated with the Victoria Cross and The Legion of Honour for his efforts during the Crimea. In 1888 a Government Inquiry was ordered concerning an application by the Padiham and Hapton Local Board to borrow an additional £30,000 to complete the Churn Clough reservoir. The following year in late July 1888 a man was seriously injured at the new works. He was engaged in loading a wagon and had one of his legs hanging over the side when the wagon ran back on the rails and caught him between the buffers, his hip was badly smashed. He was carried to one of the huts where medical aid was procured, and was then taken to Blackburn Infirmary where amputation of the limb was possible.

In 1889 one of the contractors for the new reservoir, Alexander and James Tullis was taken to court at Burnley for storing gunpowder without having a licence—they were fined £5 and costs. In July 1885 there was a report stating that "The pipes having been connected with Churn Clough, the people of Padiham are now in procession of a good supply of pure water. This connection was only just effected in time to prevent a general outcry, as the former supply was insufficient and very impure and within a few days of the supply being entirely exhausted" This must have been a temporary 'quick fix' for the reservoir was not officially opened until March 1892. The opening of the reservoir in March 1892 was a lavish affair which included the presentation of two gold keys and a banquet afterwards at the Starkie Arms. A description of the new waterworks was given at the time. The embankment was about 490 yards long, and the greatest width at the base (or Old Brook Level) was about 500 feet. The cubical content of the embankment was about 249,000 yards. The average depth of the reservoir was 26 feet 6 inches—the length was 820 feet and water surface when full was 15 ½ acres. It was a fine day for the formal opening of the new waterworks, and two large wagons provided by the Burnley Carriage Company set off from the Starkie Arms at eleven o'clock.

The drive four in hand went by way of Simonstone, Read and up over to Sabden climbing up the hill towards the reservoir. A tour was made first of the embankments, and Captain Bear insisted that all take a first draught of water from the reservoir—he provided a portable flask and two silver cups. The party then proceeded to the light girder bridge on the reservoir for the opening ceremony proper. Various speeches were made and the Clerk of the Local Board Mr Smith called upon Josiah Monk to present a gold key to Mr Ingham, the chairman of the Local Board to mark this important ceremony. Mr Ingham and several members of the Board then proceeded along the girder bridge to the valves which were duly unlocked and turned on the water—here the party was photographed before their return, and they then made their way to the sieving chamber. Here another gold key was presented to Mr James Bertwistle in order that he might open the measuring chamber. More speeches followed before the ceremony was completed and the officials moved off to the Commercial Inn at Sabden where a light luncheon was served. Then it was back to Padiham for a banquet at the Starkie Arms. At the end of the day the result was a fine one—Padiham had at last a supply of clean fresh water.

One of the most difficult jobs involved in the construction of Churn Clough reservoir was getting the water over Black Hill and into the town itself. To this end a tunnel had to be driven right through the hill. The difficulty of this undertaking can be seen in the fact that two of the contractors ended up bankrupt—in the end it had to be completed by the Local Board Engineer Mr John Gregson. After the tunnel was driven 12 inch pipes were throughout its length to take the water over into Padiham. In 1960 these pipes were replaced by concrete pipes and the tunnel was backfilled. In the same year a new reservoir was built capable of holding 1 ½ million gallon at Cavaliers on the Sabden Road as well as the new water treatment works attached. Possibly the last major undertaking of the Urban District Council was to lay a nine inch supply pipe from here down through the Huntroyde Estate to supply the new industrial site at Simonstone and the power station there. Padiham Waterworks along with all the other water boards in the surrounding areas was amalgamated to form the Calder Water Board in 1963—this in turn was merged to form North West Water in 1974. Things changed yet again in 1989 when North West Water was privatised, and the following year Norweb, the electricity supply company was also privatised. Finally United Utilities was formed by the acquisition of Norweb in 1995.

Sewerage Treatment
After the Local Board had been established in 1873 there were enormous problems to be sorted out in the town—not least of these were the problems associated with the antiquated sewerage system where it existed, and in most cases it did not exist at all. Waste water including human waste was often simply flushed away along open stone sewers in the streets feeding directly into the River Calder or Green Brook. Here it was expected the effluence would be washed away—but this was not always the case. In times of drought or slight rainfall it lay festering on the riverbed or collected behind the various weirs and dams built by the mill owners. The stench on hot summer's days must have been unbearable. This was the situation for almost twenty years after the Local Board had taken over. The Local Board were actually taken to court over the matter of polluting the River Calder in 1892. Not until the new sewerage works at Altham were built in 1894 at a cost of £16,000 did the Board come some way to alleviating the problem. John Gregson was the Local Board Surveyor, and responsible for aspects of sanitation, he came from Darwen and had served for a few years with Darwen Council. For many years he lived at Cragg Villa, Whalley Range on the present day Whalley Road. Besides being the Surveyor at Padiham he was also the Water Engineer and Captain of the Fire Brigade. Even when he 'retired' in 1919 at the grand age of 72 he was retained as Consulting Engineer for the next five years because of his great knowledge in such matters. In fact it was John Gregson who introduced the 'Pail System' to Padiham. This system, as the name might suggest, involved the residents putting their household and human waste into pails provided by the Board which were emptied by the night soil-men on a regular basis. This system was even looked at by other Lancashire towns such as Accrington to see if the system would work in their town—however not all were satisfied with the 'pail system' and a correspondent in the Burnley Advertiser of 26 October 1878 had this to say;

"Sir, we hear such a glowing account of the benefits of the pail system on its introduction in to Padiham and were so satisfied of the cleanness that would ensue, that we welcome its advent with much satisfaction. No more were we to be pestered with the stench arising from an overflowing ash pit. No more was the health of the family to be jeopardised by an unwholesome effluvia.

Every week the ashes and night soil were to be taken away in the pails which were to be substituted by clean ones. Now, however instead of the realisation of the bright dream we had pictured before us, we find that the pails are returned unwashed and in most cases with a disagreeable and unhealthy odour rising from them. This might easily be remedied by taking cleanly washed pails in exchange for the dirty ones. And, in order to promote the health of the town, I should suggest to the Board that they direct the night soil men to put chloride of lime at the bottom of the pails. This has been done in most places adopting the pail system with the happiest results, and I trust that our Board will adopt the same plan. Yours &c.
HEALTH."

There was a horrible accident in a Padiham sewer just a few days before Christmas in 1892. Early in the morning, a labourer named William Chadwick was working cleaning out a sewer between the two mills of Messrs R. Thompson and Mr J. Whittaker when the walls of the sewer collapsed and buried him. It was over an hour before rescuers could get him out by which time he had expired. He was taken home to his residence at back St Giles Street—he left a widow but no children.

The Postal Service.
We only have scant details of Padiham's early postal services, but the Starkie Arms appears to have supplied a mail service from the early times. We also know that the position of postmaster vacated by the resignation of Mr J. Whittaker was conferred upon Mr John Simpson, grocer in December 1853. A mail omnibus service was started in 1863 between Burnley and Padiham running twice a week. In 1879 premises at 82 Burnley Road were listed as being the post office and a sub post office in 1896. The main post office however was located at 8-10 Church Street and also served as the registrar office for births death and marriages. For many years the registrar, printer and postmaster was Michael Servetus Holland, a position he held for 42 years. Michael came from a large family of Padiham folks, being born in 1829 at the old Wesley chapel on West Street, the youngest son of Thomas Holland, who at the time was one of only two grocers in the town.

When Michael was only 24 years of age he started his own business as a newsagent on Church Street, and in 1850 was appointed to the position of registrar. Michael married Miss Rushworth who died in 1886, they had one daughter Endora Sarah Anabel. It was recorded that Michael in all his 42 years as registrar never slept away from home, and never had a holiday. He died in December 1900, and was buried at the public cemetery St John's Road, Padiham. After Michael's death the post office was moved to 32 Station Road, the postmaster being Edward Barnett Carnie, who remained at this position till around 1908. The Post Office, on Station Road and besides the River Calder bridge was constructed in 1914, was built by the local building firm Duxbury and replaced premises on Burnley Road, where the Postmaster was Francis Whinnerah till his death in 1917. The post office on Station road continued to be used certainly into the 1950s. There was also a sub-post office on Church Street in the mid 1950s, here the sub-postmaster was James Arthur Bulcock, who in May 1954 was elected to the chair of Padiham Council. Councillor Bulcock was also the president of the Burnley and District Retail Newsagents for over 20 years, as well as being the president of the Burnley and District Sub-postmasters Association. In November 1967 a planning application was submitted to the council to knock two buildings into one at 24 Burnley Road and 46 Mill Street. Permission granted, the premises became the present day Padiham post office on Burnley Road in 1968, a position which survives to this day. The post office block on Victoria Road carries the datestone of 1898.

CHAPTER SEVEN

The Railway, Bridges etc.
The idea of a railway line running between Burnley and Blackburn connecting with Padiham and Great Harwood was first conceived in the early 1860s. The proposed route was surveyed by Sturges Meeks a well respected engineer responsible for the surveying and construction of many of the Lancashire and Yorkshire Railway routes. In December 1865 Meeks estimated the cost of the Padiham to Blackburn section of the proposed line to be £200,000. The section from Rosegrove to Padiham was later estimated to cost just short of £69,000. Following approval by two Acts of Parliament in May 1866 and July 1967 the way forward was eagerly planned. The new line was nine miles long from Great Harwood Junction near Blackburn to connect with the sidings at Rosegrove Station, Burnley—the work was put out to tender.

The Blackburn to Padiham section was priced at £94,980 by Thomas Stone and Sons, a price accepted with work commencing in April 1870. From the outset there were numerous unseen problems. Nearly all the cuttings were at the Blackburn end of the line and all the embankments at the Padiham end. This entailed transporting ton after ton of earth from one end of the line to the other, much of this was clay which turned into running sludgy muck when wet. At Martholme a viaduct was required to be built over the River Calder, in addition there was coal underneath which might be mined in the future from Martholme Colliery close by. The railway company therefore ordered that the viaduct be constructed of wood to save on costs—but later decided that might be a false economy and opted to built the structure in brick and stone. To avoid any subsidence the railway company also purchased the coal under the proposed viaduct. There were other difficulties, at Duxbury Wood an embankment over 50 feet high broke into some old mine workings and a brick culvert had to be built over them. The Padiham to Rosegrove section of the line was completed without any major incident by James Gregson and Company with a tender of £33,000, the iron bridges at Dryden Street, Shakespeare Street and Green Lane being built by William Thompson at a price of £3,300.

This latter section was opened for goods traffic on 1 July 1875. The contract for the station was let to Thomas Stone on 18 August 1876, the engineer stating at the time that it would take another two years to complete the project. On 16 September 1875 the Padiham Local Board passed a resolution requesting the Lancashire and Yorkshire Railway Company to open the loop line from Rosegrove to Padiham for passenger traffic, up to that time the line had only been opened for goods traffic. And on 1 September 1876 the loop line from Rosegrove to Padiham was eventually opened—*"it had been a long time in completing but it will be a great accommodation and the station is a model for convenience safety and neatness. The Local Board went to Rosegrove by the first train"* the press reported. In June 1877 goods traffic was able to run on the Padiham to Blackburn section, this length being inspected by Major General Hutchinson in September 1877. The gentlemen inspecting the track left Blackburn to inspect the line from there to Padiham. Particular attention was made on the track where it crossed over or under bridges. Another party followed them in two powerful engines each weighing 40 tons each and they were used to test the strength of the bridges.

When they arrived at Padiham Station there was a large crowd to greet them and lunch was provided by Mr Bertwistle at the Bridge Inn. On 15 October 1877 the first through train as a passenger line to use what had become known as the North Lancashire Loop ran between Rosegrove and Blackburn. The journey time took 22 minutes. The Padiham to Blackburn line might have been a more scenic route than that running through Accrington, running through some fine countryside and over the viaducts across the River Calder, but it was ill favoured by heavy traffic due to the steep incline. The 1 in 40 climb from Padiham to Rosegrove tested many a steam engine pulling coal and other heavy goods up the incline, and they often had to be backed up with an additional train banking at the rear. To see the trains straining and puffing with a large and heavy load behind them was always something of an atmospheric scene to all those who loved railways—that was the great magic of steam. There was a remarkable incident in May 1964 involving a runaway train on the incline going to the power station—happily no one was seriously injured. A steam train hauling 35 wagons of coal weighing in at over 500 tons from Bank Hall Colliery at Burnley, was on the last leg of its journey, and had been diverted off the main track onto the power station sidings, which ran parallel to the main line.

	For some reason the train got out of control and gathered speed and momentum racing towards the buffers near the entrance to the power station. The 'checker in' at the power station was George Latham—his job was to count the number of wagons as they came into the power station sidings yard. George watched awe struck as the steam engine came towards him at great speed—he knew that something was wrong as the train at this point should have almost been at a standstill and just easing the wagons into the yard. As he gazed back up the track he saw the fireman Rengi Tanganika, of Nelson, and the driver Edward Shackleton of Lowerhouse Lane, Burnley jump to safety, quickly followed by the guard Fred Hall of White Bull Street Burnley. The train and its heavy load carried on rushing forward and smashed through the steel buffers and ploughed into a six foot deep embankment running part way up before finally stopping just yards from the main Padiham to Clayton-le-Moors road. The train actually ended up at a remarkable angle near the main road, with the now tangled coal wagons reared up behind it—just a few yards away was a power cable carrying 33,000 volts serving the Clitheroe area.

This was switched off as a safety precaution, and power diverted to Clitheroe from a different source. Seventeen year old John Bailey who was of work with a broken wrist was in his garden at Dean Range when the accident happened. "My first reaction was that the train was going too fast" he said. "Then there was a terrific crashing sound, I though the train was going to end up on the road" The three man crew were taken to hospital for a check up, but all were later discharged. Only fate had prevented a much more serious accident taking place here. Had the train gone a few yards more up the embankment and onto the main road with its busy traffic, who knows what the consequences might have been? Happily, this was not the case, and there were no serious injuries that day.

A fatal accident, possibly the first to occur on the line occurred in December 1886 to a man named Robert Robson a labourer from Bolton. He was employed with two other men named Dart and Neil making an excavation for the erection of a signal post. Robson was stood close to the rail, or inside the rail talking to the other men who were in the hole when an engine dashed down the incline in the direction of Blackburn. Robson was struck by the engine buffers and carried about 20 yards. He was terribly mutilated—he was a married man and left a widow and a child aged four months. An inquest was held at the Railway Inn where a verdict was recorded of "Accidental death by being run over by a train". There were other fatal accidents on the line. In August 1892 a twenty year old lad named John Thomas Southwell was struck by the buffers of the Yorkshire train and hurled down the embankment suffering fatal injuries. On the last day of September 1895, two lads aged about 12 years old were in charge of a horse drawn greengrocers cart in the goods yard at Padiham Station when the horse took fright on the screeching of some moving wagons. Both horse and cart were dashed against the moving parts of the train which smashed the cart to pieces. One of the lads, Robert Law was killed instantly, and the other lad named Harrison the son of one of the firm Harrison Brothers, fruiters to whom the cart belonged was badly injured by having both his legs broken. The closure of the passenger services on the railway took place on 2 December 1957 following a gradual rundown the railway. In its hey-day it often had up to 15 trains a day running each way, some even travelling on to Nelson and Colne, Skipton and Todmorden. The Loop line was used occasionally after this for summer trips to the coast avoiding the delays on the Accrington line until 1963.

The line closed down for all traffic in November 1964, although the section from Rosegrove to Padiham power station survived for some time after this. After closure the line became a dumping ground and an eyesore. In October 2006 plans were put forward to make the disused line into a linear park for walkers and cyclists running from Rosegrove through to Padiham Memorial Park—a project completed in 2010. The old railway is now a valuable asset to the town and is used on a regular basis by hundreds of people each day.

Crowds of people waiting for the train at Padiham railway station

Bridges.
Padiham as we know it grew as a settlement because of its important position at a crossing point of the River Calder for the road joining three central medieval places, Blackburn, Burnley and Whalley. The Calder also provided water for the animals and for the crops—and many years later power for the water wheels of the manorial corn mill and steam engines of the Industrial Revolution. No one can say for certain just when Padiham Bridge was built, but the first known reference was in 1530. Like all stone structures the bridge needed care and maintenance, and in 1647 when in 'a state of collapse' it was repaired at a cost of £10 at a burden to the parish. In 1754-55 the Padiham Bridge became part of the turnpike road leading from Blackburn to Burnley thence on to Yorkshire, thus ending that burden on the parish.

The present day Padiham Bridge, excluding the widening of 1904 possibly dates from soon after this date, around 1760, when an advertisement in the Daily Register of Commerce on 8 March recorded the following;

> *"Miscellaneous Article. Notice is given to persons inclinable to undertake the rebuilding of Padiham Bridge over the River Calder"*

The direct route to Whalley only came about with the construction of an entirely new road in 1810. Even many decades later Padiham Bridge was still causing problems, this time to the tram company in the mid 1880s. In April 1887, at the Preston Sessions, *"Colonel Starkie urged upon the court the necessity of altering Padiham Bridge over which the tramway passes. The bridge was on a curve which was most dangerous for the carriages, and there had been at least two narrow escapes"*. The angle of the bridge in relationship to the road was so sharp, almost at right angles that the trams had to come to a halt at the Bridge Inn on a number of occasions, especially in icy or snowy weather—although the lines, single at first were laid as far as the present town hall. The Bridge Inn also became the 'Tram waiting rooms' for many years. At last, after many years of debating in 1903 plans were finally approved to widen Padiham Bridge, and the inscription on the parapet walls tells us that this was achieved in the following year. It was not simply a case of widening the existing bridge though; it was also a matter of altering the acute bend in the road from 130 degrees to 240 degrees. This is best seen from underneath the bridge via the new riverside walk at Padiham, the alterations can be clearly seen in 'blue' engineering brickwork. It must have taken the County Bridge Master, quite a few sums, and a lot of headaches to calculate these angles and degrees for the bridge widening. The alterations were estimated to cost around £3,000, and took the width of Burnley Road to 65 feet, double what it was previously. There were fears for the safety of Padiham Bridge during the storms of September 1877. The rising water had undermined the bridge to a depth of seven feet and it was feared that the flood would carry the bridge away. As the water subsided however the damage was found not to be too great although a number of cellars were flooded—that of Ainsworth Whittaker to a depth of five feet.

At the cellar of Mr. Bertwistle at the Bridge Inn water had also rushed in, as it did at Charles Waddington's mill, although there was no serious damage. However the Bridge Master made an inspection of the bridge the following month and reported that the masonry on the south abutment beneath the springers had been washed out and rendered that portion of the bridge insecure and required immediate repair. He also reported that the bridge had been built twice, the east portion being the more ancient structure. The span of each arch was 35 feet, the position of the bridge in respect of the River Calder is such that the wash of the river was along the south abutment the bed of the stream under the north arch being raised by large deposits brought down from the hills of the Pendle Forest, thus nearly the whole of the flow goes through the south arch. Later in October 1888 the Local Board made an offer of £200 towards the repairs of the bridge. In March 1881 there was a remarkable occurrence at Padiham Bridge. A furniture van with two horses one in the shaft, the other behind was passing over the bridge when the horse in the shafts was startled by a gas lamp suddenly lighting. The horse mounted the bridge and went over the parapet wall and fell a distance of about seven yards onto the sand below. Fortunately the gearing on the van became dislodged, and although it mounted the bridge it detached itself from the horse. The man in charge was riding on the front and had a marvelous escape.

Running round the river they were amazed to see the horse walking up from the river bed none the worse for its remarkable leap. The carter placed the horse back in the shafts and proceeded on his way as if nothing had happened. Another, more serious accident happened in January 1860. Fourteen year old Ann Blezard and her grandmother were walking along the banks of the River Calder when a sudden gust of wind blew her bonnet into the flowing waters. Ann cautiously went to the edge of the water to try and recover her bonnet when another gust of wind blew her into the icy waters. The water was high after several weeks of rain and the poor child was instantly swept away. Her screams were heard by several men working at Mr. Waddington's Mill who rushed to her aid—one of them succeeded in getting the lass out, but she was so exhausted that she died within a few minutes. An inquest was held later at the Starkie Arms where a verdict of *'Accidental death'* was recorded. On the Bridge Inn side of the bridge in the little walled area by peering over the parapet you may be able to see two lines of substantial timbers below the water line.

These timbers are as thick as the old telegraph poles and about three or four feet wide, are well preserved even though they are under water—however their purpose has yet to be determined. Upstream from Padiham Bridge is the Bendwood footbridge, which was first constructed in 1930—although it has been replaced since that time. The idea for a footbridge at this place was first suggested as far back as 1900 in order to assist the weavers and mill workers to get to the mills and factories on Lune Street and Wyre Street. The cost of the 1930 bridge was put at £850. This bridge had to be demolished in January 1984 following structural flood damage, it was replaced by the present structure which came from Penwortham near Preston where it used to span a railway. It has a remarkably lengthy single span. Further upstream still is the latest bridge to be built over the Calder in 2002, near the former stepping-stones near Pendle Hall. Stepping stones had been at this spot since time immemorial and were traditionally the responsibility of Higham village, but over the decades prior to the mid 1890s they had been reduced to just a few stones making passage impossible save for the driest of weather.

There was an angry dispute here in 1895 because local folk wanted a right of passage restored over the River Calder here by way of some newer stepping stones. But the owner of the land Colonel Starkie of Huntroyde refused to submit to the request as it would bring *'Poachers in large numbers'*. Following this a local Footpath Preservation Society under the chairmanship of Thomas Blezard one of the directors of Blezard and Sons, the iron founders at Padiham held meetings on the matter. The society decided to reinstall the crossing over the Calder themselves and backed its purpose up with a petition containing over 2,000 signatures. Meetings between the society and the agent for the Starkie estate Daniel Howsin were also arranged to ask Colonel Starkie to build a bridge over the river, but he refused. Six iron boxes were then made at the Blezard foundry and in June 1895 the boxes were taken by horse and cart down Ightenhill Park Lane. The notices put up by the Huntroyde Estate threatening action for trespass against anyone who interfered with the river or its bed were ignored, but a severe thunderstorm put an end to the first attempt to put the boxes in, but the following week eight boxes had been put in place on the river bed. The next Monday however news came that men from the Huntroyde Estate were breaking up the boxes on the riverbed.

A large crowd reported to be around 300 in number descended from Padiham, Higham and Burnley and threatened to throw the Huntroyde workers in the river unless they stopped. Only the intervention of the police and members of the Footpath Preservation Society prevented a nasty scene. Another meeting was held by the Footpath Preservation Society on Whittlefield Recreation Ground where upwards of 15,000 spectators attended. Demands that Colonel Starkie be removed from the magistrates' bench, and that questions should be asked in the Houses of Parliament were put forward. Colonel Starkie in the end relented and although still refusing to recognize the right of way the following year 1896 installed at his own expense stepping stones cross the river. Gates and notices appeared either side of the stepping stones indicating that this was still private land, and that the Colonel had the right to closed one day a year. The stones were put in place at the end of May 1896, that Sunday over 7,000 crossed the stones. The stepping stones were replaced by a bridge in 1928. The next bridge downstream from Padiham Bridge is the fine two-arched bridge on Station Road—this was constructed in 1875, the rather strange inscription on the bridge tells us so. I say 'rather strange inscription' because this is on the river side of the parapet wall and to view the inscription you would need to either stand in the middle of the river in fear of drowning, or risk life and limb by hanging upside down over the parapet. I am fairly sure that the builder who did the bridgework would have received a severe reprimand for this mistake.

The inscription actually reads;

"This Bridge was erected at the expense of Major Starkie of Huntroyde, and the free use of the same given to the town of Padiham for the benefit of its trade and commerce. A.D. 1875"

The bridge was built in anticipation of the increased traffic from the new railway which was planned to be fully operational two years later in 1877. The only other way to gain access to that part of town was by the narrow Green Bridge on Green Lane. Green Brook was formerly known as Lodge Brook, and runs from the Lowerhouse Lodges through Padiham, it was never the same obstacle as the River Calder—but nevertheless it was an obstacle which had to be overcome if the town was to expand.

Green Brook was passed in ancient times by a footpath crossing at a stoney ford, and in 1602 a bridge replaced the ford—look for the inscription "Green Bridge" on the wall of the present day bridge. Further up Green Brook is what is known as the Levant footbridge near the Levant Mill at the bottom of Pendle Street—this was constructed in 1898 and replaced an old wooden handbridge, which had become so dangerous and mossy that people were slipping off into the water. The new bridge "was strongly built of steel girders and timber, with a cement path and brick built pillars" we were told. But even this bridge has been replaced over the years—again, it saved the weavers and other workers a long detour to get to work. A footbridge over the railway on Pendle Street was opened in 1896, with much the same objective in getting people to work. They didn't like folk turning up late for work tired in those days—tired people didn't produce as much in output! This railway bridge was built following a petition signed by four or five hundred of the ratepayers in town. Yet another footbridge over Green Brook at the bottom of Palmerston Street connecting with Thompson Street was authorized in 1905—even though the residents of 87 Thompson Street objected. In order to open up the Dryden District of town by building a bridge over Green Brook, or Lodge Brook as it was then known, the Urban District Council had to apply to Local Government to borrow £600 for its construction back in 1910. There is still a poster that survives telling us all about it, which can still be seen in Burnley reference library—it reads;

"The Padiham Urban District Council
PADIHAM
Whereas the Urban District Council of Padiham have applied to the Local Government Board for sanction to borrow £600 for the construction of a bridge over the River Lodge at Dryden Street, Padiham, and the Local Government Board have directed Inquiry into the subject matter of such Application.
NOTICE IS HEREBY GIVEN that A. G. Drury, Esquire, M.Inst.C.E, the Inspector appointed to hold the said Inquiry, will attend for that purpose at the Council Offices, Padiham, on Tuesday, the first day of March, at a quarter past ten o'clock in the forenoon, and will then and there be prepared to receive the evidence of any persons interested in the matter of the said Inquiry.
H.C. Monro,"
Secretary
Local Government Board
15th February 1910.

The Inquiry into the loan was successful for the Urban District Council for the bridge was in fact built—again this is inscribed on the wall *"U.D.C.P.B. Erected 1910, James Horne Esq., J.P."* James Horne was a prominent local councilor and Justice of the Peace at that time. Prior to the building of the Dryden Street Bridge the development of the area beyond was very much hampered, and a decade before this there were only a few houses at Levant, Oat and Wheat Streets, the latter is where Thompson Street actually finished at that time. The Council might have been criticised for their borrowing of money for the bridge—but in the end their wisdom and judgment proved correct and a whole new area of Padiham was opened up for fresh development, which included amongst other things, the houses around Cambridge Drive and beyond. Access to the Jubilee, Holme, Levant Mills and other places of employment was also improved.

CHAPTER EIGHT
Leisure and Entertainment

Padiham Memorial Park.
The idea of a public park at Padiham was first aired at one of the Local Boards meetings held in 1877—a site was suggested at the Banks. However members considered that this place was too steep, it would cost a fortune to lay out, it was also too near the River Calder and the town's sewerage outlet. Various ideas were toyed with over the next few decades. In 1908 the Health Committee of the Urban District Council once again looked into the question of acquiring land at the Banks for a public park. The owner of the land Lord Shuttleworth said that he was prepared to give the land at the Banks for such a use. However another six years were to pass before more rigorous efforts were ploughed into the reality of a public park for the town. Landscape architect Mr T. H. Mawson was asked to draw up plans for a new park at Padiham—he had previously drawn and designed parks at Southport, Blackpool and St Anne's'. The park we see today is essentially a product of a bequest made 1915 at the height of the atrocities of WW1 in the will of Thomas Clayton of Burnley. It was also decided soon on that the new park should be a memorial to the fallen in the Great War. So who was Thomas Clayton—and why did he, indeed why should he, have left money for a park in Padiham?

To solve this puzzle, we need to go way back, almost two hundred years to 21 June 1825 and to the tiny hamlet of Sabden Fold nestling under the shade of old Pendle. It was on that day, the longest day of the year that Thomas Clayton was born. His parents were farmers in the little hamlet and also ran a small grocers' shop. Most of the customers at the shop, being handloom weavers, and times were hard, very hard indeed. The basic everyday food for the weavers was oatmeal, three times a day if they were lucky, once or twice a day if they were not. In 1851, at the age of 26, Thomas Clayton married Ann Speak, at the beautiful St Nicholas Church in Sabden, the church being only around ten years old at that time. Ann was the daughter of Hill and Peggy Speak who worked the Dean Farm close by. Dean Farm in fact still exists, and is probably one of the oldest houses in this area bearing a date of 1574. By a strange coincidence the very first marriage at St Nicholas's Church was also by a couple from Dean Farm and Sabden Fold by way of the union between William Bailey of Dean and Betty Smith of Sabden Fold on 19 May 1849. After their marriage Thomas and Ann went on to work at the Copthurst Farm near Higham and afterwards at Northwood which was close by, off Fir Trees Lane as a tenant farmer of Col. Starkie of Huntroyde for 30 years.

Although Thomas Clayton bred cattle in his farming career, his greater love was breeding horses and he became exceptionally well known at both the cattle and horse fairs between at Clitheroe, Skipton and beyond. Thomas was a great supporter of the established church, and while at Northwood he was a churchwarden at St John's Church Higham, and at Padiham St Leonard's. It was at Northwood however that tragedy struck on 19 December 1879, just a few days before Christmas in the form of the passing of his wife Ann at the age of 59 years after 28 years of marriage. Thomas was grief stricken, there were no children of the union, and although he himself was just 54 years of age, he decided to retire from farming and move to Southport. The seaside was not for Thomas though— his love was for the open air and the countryside, and in less than a year he returned back to East Lancashire and settled in Burnley. At first he got a house on St Matthew Street, but soon moved again to 'Sunny Hurst' at 275 Manchester Road. Here, one of his greatest joys in his autumn years was take a leisurely evening stroll in Scott's Park at the rear of his house.

The park, as many will know was the gift to the town of Alderman Scott, and I think this had a great influence on Thomas when deciding what to do with his money after his death. Indeed, he once said to George Clayton, a Wesleyan Town Missionary, a great friend of Thomas and later one of his trustees whilst walking in Scotts Park, that he didn't know what to do with his money. George, the Missionary advised him as best he could. First, he recommended seeing that all members of his family were not left in want. Secondly, to look after the church, which had looked after his spiritual needs in life. Thirdly to think of the hospital that looked after the sufferings of people. But Thomas Clayton wanted to do something for Padiham, and when the outline of his will was drawn up with the bequest for a park there, a number of potential problems had to be sorted out. The main one was that the District Council of Padiham might not want to accept it on the grounds of cost of maintenance. If this was the case, then Thomas Clayton stipulated that the money should then go towards a church in the parish of Padiham. Thomas Clayton passed away at the grand age of 90 years on 11 July 1915 at his home on Manchester Road. A funeral service took place at St Paul's Church which used to stand in Saunderbank across from the town hall—and then Thomas was taken to be reunited with his wife Ann, at St John's Church at Higham. In September 1915, the will of Thomas Clayton was published with the following provisions, of which St John's Church Higham was favoured very well—but which also provided funds for a Memorial Park at Padiham.

£2,000 to be paid to the Ecclesiastical Commissioners of England to be applied towards the stipend of the resident clergyman for St John's Higham. £1,000 for, or towards the building and furnishing of a vicarage to be used and occupied by the resident clergyman for St John's Higham. £100 to be invested with Burnley Corporation, the income from which to be applied for providing an annual tea for the members of the church choir in connection with St John's Higham. A similar bequest was made for St Paul's Church at Burnley and St Mary's Church Newchurch-in-Pendle. £1,000 to the Burnley Victoria Hospital for the endowment and maintenance of a bed to be called 'The Thomas Clayton Bed'. £2,000 for the purpose of buying or erecting and furnishing a building, or buildings to be used by the Burnley and District Blind Society, and the Burnley and District Deaf and Dumb Society.

The proceeds raised from certain specifically named properties are to be used to pay the income arising of his niece, which after her death is to be expended towards purchasing land within or near the area of the urban district of Padiham, and for laying out the same for a public park. If this bequest should fail, the proceeds are to be paid to the Ecclesiastical Commissioners of England towards the cost of erecting, finishing and furnishing a new church of the Established Church of England on a site approved by the trustees in the parish of St Leonard's Padiham". It was clear indeed that Thomas Clayton had heeded well the words of advice given to him by his friend George Clayton. The trustees under the will were Thomas Clayton's niece Miss Sarah Jane Smith, and his two friends, Joseph Pickles, secretary of Burnley Borough Land and Building Society, and George Clayton, town missionary. On the death of Mr Clayton's niece, a company of Padiham folk who had taken over the ground rent bequest began to take steps to secure suitable land for the new park. What Thomas Clayton had not foreseen nor for that matter the committee, is that the war had a dramatic depreciation effect on the ground rents. At the time of the bequest the ground rents were expected to have raised £10,000 or £12,000, but by 1921 they were worth only £4,000 or £5,000.

Thus, a scheme was devised whereby a group of Padiham gentlemen advanced the capital required for the new park on behalf of the Council, the ground rents then being used to pay them the interest on their money. In this way the Council would be able to put the ground rents on the market at a more favourable time. In 1921 land was eventually acquired at Knight Hill along with the house of that name, the former home of Edward Drew, a member of the Drew family, the calico printers of Lowerhouse. Edward moved on to live at Simonstone Hall, a mile or so down the Whalley Road. A little over an acre of land was also purchased from the Huntroyde Estate. There was more than a little grumbling from the townsfolk when it emerged that money had to be spent on acquiring a bit of land off the Starkie's Huntroyde Estate—one of the largest landowners in Lancashire. Surely they could have made a gift of the small piece of land—especially as it was going to be used as a memorial to all the local lads who had given their lives in the war! The deeds to the land and property at Knight Hill were eventually handed over by the Thomas Clayton trustees at a special Council meeting held on Wednesday 6 April 1921. The park was officially opened on 18 June 1921 to a design by Thomas Mawson, an influential and prolific landscape designer.

The idea that the park should be a memorial to the victims of the war was supported soon after the Thomas Clayton bequest became known. A body was set up on 29 August 1916 at the Technical School, Padiham and named *'The Padiham War Memorial Committee'*. It wasn't until 7 September 1920 however that the following resolution was passed. *"That the towns' war memorial should take the shape of a scheme for supplementing the Parks Scheme as provided by the Clayton Bequest"*. The fine house at Memorial Park, Knight Hill went on to become Padiham's Museum with many exhibitions including famous water clock until it closed down as such in 1952. Entrances to the park were made on Blackburn Road, Bridge Street and a footbridge was negotiated across the River Calder and the railway viaduct giving access from the recreation ground. A piece of land was put to one side for the towns war memorial, and after the demolition of some old farm buildings the cenotaph was officially opened in October 1921 by Hon., Rachel Kay-Shuttleworth. A fitting tribute for she herself had lost brothers in the Great War. The memorial was built out of red granite, and the money for the project was raised by public subscription in memory of the 300 plus servicemen of Padiham who perished in the conflict.

One of the two public shelters in the park is also a memorial to those who died, the other shelter being in memory of Thomas Clayton and were opened in 1925. Yet another memorial to the fallen was opened in September 1927 in the form of a bandstand and was paid for by the War Memorial Committee. Band concerts in the park were extremely popular even before the bandstand was built. The bandstand was built in a 'natural amphitheatre' overlooking the Unitarian Chapel, the sloping ground was laid out in terraces and provided with seating at the Council's expense. The bandstand itself was of the 'shell type' rather than the more unusual circular structure, and had a steel frame encased in oak. It was 29 feet wide, just over 18 feet from back to front. The terraces which could hold 500 people cost £400 which was borne by the Council whose workers carried out the task of laying it all out. The terraces were built up of Clitheroe limestone and bounded at the rear by a privet fence 'to keep the draughts out'. The contractors for the bandstand itself included Messrs Helm, masonry, and J. Bertwistle and Company the joinery, and it was constructed at a cost of £600.

Unfortunately, 29 years later in September 1956 the bandstand was destroyed when it was burnt down in a fire thought to have been started by children playing with matches. The last scheduled concert at the bandstand was in August 1950. Today the old bandstand and the terraces where so many Padiham folk flocked to on warm summer days in the past is now covered in the undergrowth as nature takes back what was once its own. The Memorial Park is also hopefully also the last resting place of what surely must be one of the most travelled water fountains in the country. The fountain which now stands in between the two public shelters in the park was a gift to the town in 1888. It originally stood at the junction of Victoria Road and Burnley Road being a gift of Sir Ughtred Kay-Shuttleworth by way of the Metropolitan Drinking Fountain and Cattle Trough Association as a supply of drinking water for horses and members of the public.

    By the beginning of the Great War however, the fountain was in a sorry state, the drinking cups had disappeared, the taps were inoperable and the local kids were using the horse trough as a mini paddling pool in the summer months—motorists were even filling their car radiators up at the fountain. It was moved to the entrance of Whitegate Park in 1937, in order that Victoria Road could be widened, this being the last time that water flowed in the fountain just before its removal. It was moved yet again in 1969 to Park Road with the opening of the Padiham Pool. Finally, what was left of a fine water feature was removed to the Memorial Park in 2008. The fountain when in its original position on the corner of Victoria Road was also topped with a fine piece of 'street furniture' by way of a 'Gawmless' type street lamp. The Memorial Park in recent years has won the Green Flag Award a number of times, it is popular with the residents and is a living and growing memorial to all those men and boys of Padiham who perished in past conflicts.

Whitegate Park.
Was built on land that was purchased by the Council in 1921 which was originally intended for use as council housing. This area was being developed fast, the first of Padiham's Council houses were being erected on Dryden Street at this time. However, the Council saw a need for an open space for the residents and decided to open out the land as a public park—and it was on a much grander scale than we see today.

It had a large roofed pavilion overlooking a bowling green and a couple of tennis courts, a putting green and a miniature golf course as well as a small children's play area. The park was scheduled to be opened in October 1930, but the local Sunday schools made a request that the children's play areas be closed on the Sabbath as they were afraid that Sunday school attendance would be affected. It was also felt in some quarters that noisy children might affect the enjoyment of older folks using the park and might drown out the playing of the bands in the park. These objections caused considerable delays in opening the park, and it was only finally opened on 28 March 1931. [lxi] There was a considerable outcry in September 2006 when items of play equipment were removed from the park for health and safety reasons.

Theatre and the Cinema.
In September 1875 the Padiham Local Board passed a resolution that they take steps to prevent a license being issued to perform theatricals. Little wonder then that we do not normally associate Padiham with things to do with the theatre. However, there were at least three attempts to get theatres going in the town. The first was in February 1883 when a license was granted to John Bennett Preston for a period of three months for the performance of stage play in a building that was proposed to be erected in 'Mow Lane' (Moor Lane) to be named the *'Alexandra'*. In April that year Mr Preston advertised in *'The Era'* for the leader of an orchestra, and *'He would be glad to hear from stars with their own pieces and picture posters and other novelties'*. Mr Preston's attempt at establishing a theatre in the town appeared not to come to fruition, and we hear no more about him. But, the following year in March 1884 we were told that the new theatre erected behind Webster's Buildings in Moor Lane was opened and since has been extensively patronised. The owner was Mr Charles Reeves. This *may* have been the premises established by Mr Preston previously? In August 1888 another advertisement appeared in *'The Era'* as follows;
"Wanted, for Fred Lichfields 'Alhambra' Theatre, Padiham Lancashire. Entire company, scenic artist, also band. Open all year round"
Unfortunately these appear to have been the last attempts to establish a theatre in Padiham, although there was a Unitarian Drama Society connected with that church in later years—various groups have also put on plays at the town hall and other places and there was also the 'village plays'. Concerts were given in the town from the earliest of days.

For instance in February 1861 when Henry Russell, late of M. Jullien's bands, gave one of his grand vocal and instrumental concerts at the Assembly Rooms assisted by Miss Fanny Edwards, contralto, Mr Hazeldine, baritone, and Mr Wilson. In 1893 in order to raise funds the Conservatives held a concert and ball at the Constitutional Club in which appeared the following. The solo violinists, Miss May Paget Moffatt, Mr Fred Pollard, Mr J. Winter, Mr George Slater, and Mr William Townley. These were seconded by the male voice choir of St Peter's Blackburn. Several high class selections were also given by Mons. Vladimir Hefft, the violinist, when Mr Tattersall of Blackburn conducted and accompanied. The concert was preceded by a tea party.

Cinema
Padiham was at one time blessed with two cinemas, the Globe on Mill Street and the Grand on Station Road. The Globe opened in 1920 and was built on the site of the old Dun Horse Inn on Mill Street—originally both the Globe and the Grand which opened a few years previously in March 1914 only showed silent films although the Grand was able to convert to 'talkies' later on. Also because there was no electricity in Padiham until late 1926 both cinemas had to generate their own electricity using a gas engine. The Grand was generally considered to have been one of the best cinemas in this part of Lancashire at that time. During its lifetime it not only served as a cinema but also a nightclub and a bingo hall. The Grand lived up to its name, it was far superior to the Globe with its handsome facade and lush interior, and it could hold in the region of 900 patrons. The glory years at the Grand were the 1930s and before the Second World War. It was extremely popular during the week as a means of spending a few pleasurable hours for the working class, and of course the courting couples on the back rows. The usual showing was a cartoon, a newsreel, a B rated movie and then a main film. These main films would be changed mid week to attract ever more filmgoers. The Globe Cinema was a large building and it too could hold 900 people—it was also used for other purposes such as concerts and the occasional public meeting. The Globe closed as a cinema in 1934 and never showed a 'talkie' but the building still stands and in 1946 it was acquired for use as an industrial unit and renamed 'Globe Works'. Firms such as Cox Chase Globe Limited occupied the premises from 1949 to 1973, and the furniture retailers Clayton Sales Rooms for ten years from 1976. [lxii]

There was a sort of little mini boom in the 1980s for cinema goers and it became the in thing to go and watch the latest films. A firm at Burnley had just opened the new Studio 1-2-3 and soon turned their eyes towards the old Globe at Padiham. However 50 years of neglect had taken its toil and it would need a great deal of work to revert the old cinema back to its old usage. However, planning permission was given and it seems that it was then up to the business end to get things moving. But by July 1988 it appeared that things had reached a stalemate position, with both the owner and the leaseholder at deadlock—each blaming each other for the stoppage. The building at this time belonged to Handley Building Corporation, one of the partners of this concern was Burnley businessman John Turkington. The company which wanted to refurbish the cinema was Facealpha. It appeared that Hanley Building Company had stopped work on the building because Facealpha had not signed the lease for the property. Therefore they were not giving the Burnley man a return on his £10,000 money spent, and because work carried out before Mr Turkington took over was condemned by a building inspector from the Council. Both parties did state that they would both be willing to carry on with the project if they were able to sort out the problems involved. Sadly this was not to be, and the former cinema remained closed as such. In June 1990 the Government awarded a £63,000 grant towards the conversion of the old cinema into workshop units and offices. It was to be given a new lease of life by the firm of Colway Contracts, office fitters. This firm ceased trading in 2008. The former Grand Cinema which had become the Stork Bingo hall in the 1960s was finally demolished in 2003 and on the site was built new houses between the former telephone exchange and the police station—it is a building still mourned by many a Padihamer in its passing, but fond memories remain no doubt.

Roller Skating and Ice Skating.
Both these activities were immensely popular in their day amongst the working classes. At a time when the weather was much colder than it is today in spite of all the gloomy predictions, the River Calder would occasionally freeze over providing a fine opportunity for free entertainment. Clogs, the footwear of the working classes made excellent skates whether clad with irons or rubbers—but irons were best.

A skilful kid would soon learn how to raise his heels while on the ice and skate along at a great pace. There were of course the obvious dangers of skating on ice, especially thin ice, which resulted in many fatalities. A good number of deaths occurred whilst youngsters or adults took to the ice on mill lodges or reservoirs with the inevitable results. For instance there was a narrow escape for one fellow at Foulridge Reservoir in January 1895. A large number of people were engaged in skating on the frozen lake when the ice suddenly gave way. A number were plunged into the icy depths, and one fellow was seen to be in trouble. If not for the quick intervention of a local accountant, Mr Ellis the man would without doubt have drowned. Others were not so lucky, in one incident in December 1887 five people drowned while skating on ice at an old quarry at Ightenhill. On a more commercial scale two enterprising Burnley men rented out a room in the Smithy Gate Mill and used it as a roller skating ring and for a time it was very popular. James Hargreaves, or as he was more popularly known 'Jimmy Nobber' who also tenanted part of Smithy Gate Mill used to loan out skates in the winter months and buy them back again at the end of the day.

For a period at the turn of the 20th century the Urban District Council also experimented with flooding part of the recreation ground to a depth of a few inches and allowing it to freeze over as an alternative to the dangers of having both children and adults skating around on the frozen River Calder or mill lodges. Skating reached fever pitch by the late 1900s with skating rinks opening all over the country. In October 1909 Padiham at last got its very own roller skating rink, by way of the Empress rink on Station Road. The opening ceremony was performed by Mr B.W. Granger J.P., and afterwards luncheon was served at the Starkie Arms. The new building was composed of wood and galvanised steel on brick walls and was erected on ground near the railway station. It had a skating area of over 5,000 square feet. On one side and one end there was a balcony with seating accommodation for the spectators and room for an orchestra in the middle of the side balcony. On the opening night the rink was packed to capacity and many would-be skaters had to be turned away. Inside the building had been 'prettily decorated' and there was provided a cafe cloak rooms and skating office making it one of the best rinks in the country.

The Recreation Ground
The idea of an open space where residents could go and travelling shows and fairgrounds could be set up was considered as early as 1883. A field known as the 'Eases' was a natural choice, part of which once had been used for Padiham Races which last took place in 1856. This field was situated between Whittaker Street renamed Park View in 1928 the River Calder and the Railway. [lxiii] Basically, where the swimming baths are now and the skate-board park. The first indications of the recreation ground actually coming into fruition at Padiham can be gleaned from the Local Board Meeting held in June 1890. The meeting was held to consider the recreation ground that Colonel Starkie had promised to give to the town in exchange for a diversion of a footpath that ran through the grounds of Huntroyde. Colonel Starkie had first approached the town some two years previous promising that if the Board would take steps to divert a footpath through the grounds of Huntroyde, he in return would give a piece of land for use as a recreation ground. A lease which had been drawn up by Colonel Starkie's solicitors was shown to the meeting. It was to give the land known as Eases over to the Board for 999 years at a nominal rent of two shillings and six pence per year. There were several clauses in the draft in which Local Board member Mr Blezard took objection to.

He thought that they should have a right to erect a bridge over the Calder for vehicular traffic. Colonel Starkie reserved all the rights to the minerals on the land, and to sink a pit—but Mr Blezard objected to these rulings. He (Mr Blezard) also objected to another clause which stated that the land should only be used as a recreation ground and that no buildings were to be erected without permission of the donor—and also that the grounds should be laid out in 12 months. The matter was not resolved until November 1890, when at last an amicable agreement between the two parties was finally reached and the Board took on the lease of the land known as the Eases. By this time the bridge over the Calder had also been built. The land at Eases had in fact been used unofficially for decades for events such as flower shows, races, fairs and circuses. We have a couple of references to Padiham Race track which are of interest. A report of November 1840 records that a foot-race took place between two men named Douglas and Short for a ten pound a side wager, an enormous sum for the time. Douglas it appeared was the winner of a race held at Enfield near Clayton-le-Moors a few weeks previous, while Short was a Mellor man.

The race was around a course of two miles at Padiham race course and the winner was Short by nearly 50 yards. Horse races were also held at Padiham too by all accounts, and although Padiham races was last held in 1856, there was an incident which was recorded on the track that year in the Cheshire Observer. In August that year it recorded that *'Mr Parker's bay mare 'Young Catherina' met with an accident by placing her foot in a hole while exercising on Padiham race course last Thursday, which will prevent her from running for some time'.*

On 1 April 1895 there was a remarkable incident while the travelling circus was in town which resulted in the death of one of the trainers. 21 year Albert Hartnell one of the elephant keepers with Sanger's Circus was walking along with his elephant watched by a large crowd. The elephant stopped and tried insistently to pick something up off the floor. Hartnell kicked the elephant on the trunk—but not hard, just as a way of encouraging it to move on. Suddenly the elephant wound up its trunk and then extended it with a vicious blow on the chest of Hartnell, knocking him to the ground. The injured man kicked out in defence with his hands and feet, and then the elephant came down on him with its head and tusks, which pierced the trainer's body. The alarm was raised and other trainer's came to his aid, shouting 'Hoiler—Hoiler' the elephants name, the elephant then stopped its attack and carried on its way. The trainer, Hartnell was badly injured and was bleeding profusely, he was rushed to Burnley hospital where he later died.

Padiham Pool, and the area around.
Of course, the area around the Eases looks nothing like an open field today—most of it is occupied by Padiham pool and the tennis courts. The idea for a swimming baths at Padiham was first voiced as far back as 1912 when it might have been included in the proposed new municipal buildings—however, this never materialised. Nor did a plan to convert an old gasometer into an open air pool put forward in the 1920s, and later plans had to be scrapped because of the outbreak of war. It must have been with some relief that residents finally saw plans approved and viewed the drilling operations which were started on the site of the new pool in June 1965. Four test holes had to be drilled to a depth of 30 feet to test the viability of the site for the new swimming baths. The pool was four years in the making and opened on 29 November 1969 at a cost of £187,000.

The style and quality of the new building was second to none—greeting the visitors in the foyer area was an indoor rockery complete with a goldfish pond created by Mr W. A. Speight, the parks superintendent. Mr Duce, the new manager of the baths was able to point out some of the other features at the pool and the new building. Laminated plastic seating was designed as a deterrent to vandalism—and the showers that operated automatically. There was an advanced air conditioning system and water heating which completely replaced the water every three hours. There was speculation that the new pool might 'steal' swimmers from other areas such as Burnley and Nelson who had previously been attracted to the relatively new pool at Skipton. The pool is full size, 25 metres by 10 metres with a depth from one metre to three metres. A putting course was also put in, but this has long since disappeared. In 1999 a ten year old local lad had a near death fall as he plunged through the roof of a building at Padiham pool where he and his friend had climbed up to play—his friend almost followed him as the first lad grabbed hold of him during his fall. He was injured, but happily not seriously. In 2004 the pool received a major overhaul costing £1.3 million dismissing fears that the pool might have to close altogether. More than 8,000 people signed a petition to keep the pool in Padiham, as Burnley Council closed some of its pools in order to save money including Gannow baths and the Thompson Centre. Today, Padiham Leisure Centre is something the town can be really proud of—and now includes sauna, body training, steam room and sun beds.

The Tennis Courts and Bowling Greens.
As people were beginning to have more leisure time to themselves a scheme was put forward in the 1920s to adapt part of the recreation ground to other leisure and sporting activities, such as tennis and bowls. Both these sports pastimes were extremely popular at the time, and it was also a fine opportunity to extend the facilities at the recently opened Memorial Park. The tennis courts were the first to be built, after the Council had applied to the Ministry of Health for a grant from the Unemployment Grants Committee set up to give work for the unemployed. The courts were formerly opened on 24 May 1924 'in the presence of a good assembly of spectators'. Councillor W. Briggs chairman of the Parks Committee said that it gave him the greatest pleasure to preside at the opening of the courts. The 'En Tout Cas' who had erected the courts were looked upon as the A1 firm in the country for this class of court.

At that time they were exhibitors at the Wembley Exhibition. He finished his speech by saying that more people ought to learn how to play tennis, which was a fine healthy game, and that the public should realise that the tennis courts were a part of their own property and that they should use them and treat them as such. At that point the courts were declared open by Councillor Dr. Mackenzie, who opened the first game which was played by members of the Hargrove Tennis Club. Members of the public might for the production of a shilling play tennis for one hour, balls and rackets included. The first of the bowling greens, there were originally two, was opened in July 1924. This one was on the other side of the tennis courts between those and the railway. Four local Councillors played at the opening of the greens. The present bowling green was opened a short time afterwards. A game of bowls cost three pence per person per game, and included the pick of 26 pairs of bowls and a dozen jacks provided by the Council. Receipts of over £180 were recorded in 1928 with nearly 15,000 tickets being issued. A more recent addition to the area is the skateboard park which was brought into use in July 1991.

It was 16 year old Matthew Morris who organised and presented a 500 name petition for a new skateboard park to Burnley Council—and it was he who was one of the first to try out the £15,000 skateboarding ramp. Matthew, of Russell Terrace organised the petition asking for the ramp to allow youngsters to practise their skills away from traffic and other hazards after he broke his collarbone while trying to avoid a car. PC Ken Inckle of Padiham polices said *"The skateboarding park is absolutely brilliant, and the kids have been using it for some time".* It proved so popular that Padiham Police organised a skateboarding competition in the forthcoming weeks. It was not only skateboarding that made the news that week in 1991—Padiham was at last coming into the modern age when a 'hole in the wall' cash dispenser was installed at Bradford and Bingley on Burnley Road. This was Padiham's first such machine, and prior to this it was a six mile journey there and back to Burnley to get some cash out of hours. How did they manage? In August 2003 a *'Haven for the younger folk of Padiham'* was opened by way of the Padiham Youth Shelter in Park Road and marked the end of two years of campaigning. The shelter was alleged to be vandal-proof and fitted with a steel roof and decorated with murals and was to be used as a meeting place for the youngsters of the town.

It was opened by Lisa-Marie Flynn of Padiham, the runner up in the Lancashire High Sherriff Young Citizen of the Year Award in 2001 for her role in the project. A pupil of St Theodore's Sixth form Lisa-Marie also intended to fly to America to help rebuild a nurse's home there.

CHAPTER NINE
Banking, the Post Office Savings Bank and the Craven Bank, Padiham Building Societies.

Padiham like many other towns in the country was suffering badly from a severe depression in trade in particularly after the Napoleonic Wars between 1799 and 1815, and the collapse of Holgate's Bank at Burnley in 1824. Less than twenty years later in 1842, the historian Dr Whittaker recorded that *'Padiham, the poorest village in Lancashire for years has been dependant for its support almost entirely on handloom weaving...the introduction of power* (loom weaving) *has partially improved the condition of the inhabitants but the place still wears a mean appearance'* The first indications we have of a bank proper in Padiham was in January 1859 when steps were being taken to establish a penny bank in the town following a meeting that was held at the Assembly Rooms. A committee was formed to draw up the rules and to submit them to a public meeting. The following February it was again reported that that the bank had indeed commenced operating much to the gratification of the promoters and that between three and four pounds had been deposited.

Craven Bank

By 1868 it was recorded in the Mannex directory of that year that there were two banks in Padiham, the Craven Bank on Burnley Road and the Post Office Savings Bank on Church Street. The latter may have been at the Starkie Arms from where the post coaches ran around Lancashire on a regular basis. The Craven bank was established at Settle and Skipton in 1791 by partners William and John Birkbeck, William Alcock, John Peart, John Smith and William Lawson. The Birkbecks had arrived at Settle a century previous and were wealth wool merchants, leather, and general merchants. The Alcock's were solicitors, it is interesting to note that John Birkbeck was also a pioneer potholer, and was the first to make any real attempt to descend the famous Gaping Ghyll hole on the flanks of Ingleborough Hill in 1842.

"He was lowered on a rope by local farm labourers until he reached a ledge 190 feet down" The ledge is still known as 'Birkbeck's Ledge'. It was another 53 years before Gaping Ghyll was finally conquered by Frenchman Edouard Martel in 1895. The Craven Bank in 1882 was located at 8 Burnley Road, Padiham. This is across from the present day 'Top Bank' and the building still exists being known as 'Hanson Buildings'. The manager here in 1882 was J. Thornton, and in 1890 it was Alfred Popplewell. Alfred who was born in 1855 at Tickhill, Yorkshire worked his way through the banking ranks, from a humble clerk living at Bankhouse Burnley in the 1880s to becoming manager of the Craven bank in Nelson. He succeeded Mr Ingram Johnson to become manager at the Padiham branch of the Craven bank, and on the death of Mr Armistead removed to the Craven Bank at Ilkley, where he remained until his death in June1895, aged just 40 years. Later the Craven bank was moved to the premises across the road which was built in 1893.[lxiv] The manager here in 1896 was Besford Wyatt Granger who lived at 'Fairholme' on Whalley Road—by the start of WW1 he was the manager of the Bank of Liverpool on Hargreaves Street, Burnley. The present 'Top Bank' at Padiham still contains many features from that time, such as the oak panelled walls and stained glass windows.

The manager's office here is virtually unchanged after over a century save for the addition of some central heating radiators, there is even a collection of old banking books on a shelf there. On occasions the bank holds open days where these old features can still be seen. The new bank was built to a design of William Dent, a Nelson firm of architects and constructed of ashlar and polished pink granite with a with a green slate roof. In 1906 the Craven Bank was amalgamated with the Bank of Liverpool, and the manager of the Padiham branch was Frank Ernest Thornton. Another merger followed in 1918 when the Bank of Liverpool merged with Martins Bank Limited, and the title was shortened in 1928 to just Martins Bank. In 1969 Martins Bank merged with Barclays Bank, which it remains as at the time of writing, although always known locally as the 'Top Bank'. We know that branch of the Manchester and County Bank was opened on Burley Road in the early days of January 1876—hours of business Monday, Wednesday and Friday from 10 o'clock to 2 o'clock. The Manchester and County Bank was established in York Street Manchester in 1862.

The address of the new bank at Padiham was 45 Burnley Road, and the manager was Nathan P. Gray of 169 Manchester Road, Burnley. Nathan was a not a local lad, he was born at Eccles in 1845, marrying Mary Fleming in 1868 at St Paul's church Chorlton-on-Medlock Manchester—but he was quite a remarkable man. He was in the service of the Manchester and County Bank for 46 years, being transferred from the Manchester branch to Burnley in January 1873. As manager of the Burnley and Padiham branches he completed 35 years service before taking retirement in September 1909. He was not only a bank manager, but he was also on the Bench of Magistrates, at Burnley and was one of the founder members of the Burnley Victoria Hospital. Nathan Gray died at Torquay in 1922. The 'Bottom Bank' we see today as Natwest is at 47 Burnley Road and was built in 1901, see datestone. By 1935 this bank had become the District Bank Limited (County Bank branch) and Henry Fletcher was the bank manager. In 1970, the District Bank was merged with the National Westminster (Natwest) and remains thus at the time of writing, also part of the Royal Bank of Scotland since 2000.

Padiham Building Societies.
Contrary to popular opinion there was more than one Padiham Building Society. A society named the Padiham Building Company has already been referred to which was formed in December 1845, and in 1876 a winding up notice was published in the Liverpool Mercury of the 'Padiham Cottage Building Company Limited' Building societies arose during the Industrial Revolution, their objectives were to raise money by subscriptions for building or purchasing dwelling houses for its members. In this respect, the predecessors of both the Burnley and the Padiham Building Societies were among the forerunners of the movements. The formation of a "Padiham Union Society" was instigated at a meeting held at the Starkie Arms on 6 March 1823. The original trustees of the society were all well-known businessmen or members of the more 'upper classes'. These included Paul Tickle, a land agent, who was also a partner in the consortium that built Smithygate Mill on Mill Street in 1834. Others were Elijah Helm, a cotton manufacturer and one of the first occupiers of Smithygate Mill, James Bertwistle, a joiner whose business still survives, and another manufacturer James Hoyle, and Thomas Riding, a cordwainer. The "Padiham Union Society" was a "terminating" society, that is, that once the objectives of the society had been achieved, the society was then terminated.

A document relating to the rules of the Padiham Union Society was in the procession of the later Padiham Building Society for many years. One of the rules provided for fines to be imposed on all members who attended club premises during the hours of business 'disorderly in liquor' or those who might use offensive language or indecent language, and the fines for such offences had to be paid with the subscriptions on the due dates. A fine of five shillings might be imposed upon a member who should fight or strike any other member whilst in the club. Later societies were in general "Permanent" which carried on the business of helping others to buy or construct houses.

The "Padiham Permanent Benefit Building Society" as the society was originally called, was registered under the Building Society Act of 1874 on 8 November 1877 after a series of meetings by interested parties. Local businessmen and well-to-do trading families were again represented on the board. Richard Crawshaw was elected to the Chair, other members included James Moorhouse, who was probably the grocer who had a shop at Adamson Street. There was Peter Laycock, a clogger and shoemaker, who lived at Whalley Range, Richard Bertwistle, a joiner who lived on Burnley Road, Josiah Monk, farmer of Brookfoot farm, and later the first Chairman of Padiham Urban District Council. There was the school attendance officer, Henry Bridge, and George Green a cotton manufacturer of Banks Terrace, and Eli Whitehead, a joiner and builder along with others. The first recorded meeting was held in the Temperance house at the Commercial Room of the Padiham Coffee Rooms and Commercial House Company Limited, Burnley Road, Padiham on 19 September 1877. Their bankers were the Craven Banking Company, of Padiham, later Barclay's Bank—and the first offices of the new building society were at the "Local Board Office" Burnley Road, almost exactly on the site of the later new headquarters of 1958 at Padiham on the corner of Burnley Road and Station Road. The first mortgage application to be accepted was that of 10 December 1877 which was in respect of the houses at Stone Moor Bottom. The following year in 1878, rooms in the old Liberal Club across the way were secured at two shillings per week. Six years later in 1894 a cottage on Sowerby Street was obtained and in 1901 the assets of the society passed the £100,000 mark. Soon after this date additional premises were purchased and a brand new office was built on Sowerby Street, which was to remain the Head Office of the society until 1958.

The name of the building society was also changed and shortened to the Padiham Building Society on 21 February 1924, the society also had branches at 124 Colne Road at Duke Bar in Burnley and a branch at Colne. It was in 1958 that it was decided that larger premises were needed to meet demand, and a site on Burnley Road was purchased from Padiham Urban District Council. On 31 May 1958 the official opening of the new Head Quarters was performed by Sir Harold Parkinson. K.B.E., J.P., of Hornby Castle, a businessman who had for many years been associated with the National Saving Movement. He was also, the then President of the North Western Association of Building Societies. The building was built in keeping with Padiham Town Hall. The major part was of rustic brickwork with a stone façade, which bore the name of the society. However, the 105 year history of Padiham Building Society ended as it was merged with Bradford and Bingley, in June 1983. At the time of writing the former offices of the Padiham Building Society are being used by the bank Santander. There have been many memorable men connected with Padiham Building Society—we might mention Henry Coupland Jackson who became associated with the early days of the Padiham and District Permanent Building Society, and who in March 1882 was appointed secretary there, a position he held for over 34 years.

When he retired in November 1916, his son Henry D. Jackson took over the position previously held by his father. Tom Gill was another person connected with the society and as a director was invited to become a director of the Bradford and Bingley after takeover. Tom will be fondly remembered by many Padiham folk. He sadly lost a leg while serving as a private in the First World War—he rose in position to rank of captain, but decided to devote the rest of his life to education. Besides being a director of Padiham Building Society, he taught at St John's R.C. School at Padiham, and also enjoyed a teaching career at Ashton and Accrington. Medical reasons at a difficult time in his life meant that Tom's other leg had to be removed later. He spent the last few years of his life at Preston, but retained a strong link with Padiham, and was also a regular to be seen at Turf Moor. Tom passed away in January 2000 at a grand age of 82 years.

CHAPTER TEN
Padiham Co-operative Movement

The idea of Co-operatives in Padiham goes way back to November 1848 when about a dozen individuals mainly cotton workers decided to band together and raise an amount of around £25 with which money they began stores for the sale of provisions and clothing. Three years later the movement consisted of 140 members, with weekly business being put at £70. This group, and others like them then tried to form a Co-operative for the erection of a mill for the manufacture of cotton, but most of these failed. This early one seems to have been the co-operative that built the Commercial Mill at Padiham, although this only lasted four years when the mill was being worked by the former manager and in 1858 the mill was bought out.

The roots of the Padiham Co-op shops as we know them go all the way back to 1869, when a group of about fifteen local working class men, including Thomas Oxley subscribed one pound each in shares to start their very own co-operative. They were no doubt inspired by the Rochdale Pioneers who started their own co-operative many years before in 1844. The first job for the Padiham men was to find suitable premises in which to launch their new business. To this end the front portion of a cottage on Calder Street next to the King's Arms off Church Street was acquired on a weekly rental basis. The new co-operative business boomed way beyond expectations, and the new pioneers soon had to seek out larger premises.

A larger shop was opened in Back Lane (West Street) and after a few more years they moved again to Sowerby Street into premises later to be occupied in part by the Local Board. Membership increased dramatically over the next few years, and around 1874 took on the large premises, which many will remember on Burnley Road—this later became the head store. Peter Doyle was the secretary around this time, he was a labourer in a coal mine and lived at Hapton. The stores also began to trade in other things such as drapery, shoes and boots—and in 1879 they were able to open their first branch store in Bank Street in the town on a five year lease. In 1884 the Padiham Co-operative were able expand even more to open their first purpose built store on Peel Street. This property still exists although no longer as a shop, but a private dwelling—however a stone inscription on the building tells of its former use.

The co-operative also built several of the houses on Peel Street at the same time—so we can see it had developed into quite a profitable business.[lxv] There was an interesting case reported in July 1889 concerning the Padiham Co-operative who were taken to court. The charge was one of employing girls in the dress making department from 6 a.m. till 9 p.m., the actual charge is not referred to, although the long hours must have had something to do with it, or perhaps they might have been under age. Whatever, the Co-op was fined 20 shillings and cost in one case whilst the second was withdrawn on payment of costs. By the 1920s, the Padiham Industrial Co-operative Society, to give it its full name was trading in groceries, butchery, bakers, confectionary, fruiterers, fish dealings, tailors, boot shoe and clog making, cycle dealings, ironmongery and dairy products. The Padiham Co-op was a major influence on the town's shoppers, giving dividends at its main store and branch stores which existed throughout town. These included, at various times branch stores on Mill Street, Green Lane, Grove Lane, Bank Street, Railway Road, Shakespeare Street, Whalley Road and the above mentioned Peel Street, as well as part of Vale Mill which was used as the slaughterhouse, stables and stores up to the 1970s. Vale Mill was a former weaving shed which had been worked by Henry Helm and Company—this was purchased by the Co-op in 1894.

They also owned and farmed Bend Wood Farm for dairy products. In April 1886 the Co-op opened its own reading rooms for members in Sowerby Street, in the premises that had been used previously by the Local Board. After alterations the premises consisted of the upper storey which had the reading rooms, conversation room and committee rooms, whilst downstairs there was a smoke room. The reading rooms were supplied with daily and weekly newspapers, and were open to all male members and their sons aged 16 years or over. Something which would cause a positive outcry today. For many years in the 1880s through to the early 1900s, the secretary of the Padiham Co-operative was William Ingham. What was to become the Co-operatives main store on Burnley Road was built in 1874, and remained a common sight in Padiham for 100 years. When the old school at the bottom of Mill Street was vacated in 1905 the premises were bought by the Co-op for use as another branch store housing the drapery department. In later years this became known as 'The Co-op Hall' and by all accounts the upstairs room was used at times as a dance hall.

In 1948 following the closure of the Baptist Chapel on Pendle Street, the Co-op took over the building for use as storage and warehousing—a situation which remained until 1970, when the building was restored and once again used by the Baptists. In August 1974, the brand new 'superstore' was opened on Burnley Road on the site of the old premises by the national director of the Co-operative Retail Society, Mr William Whittaker. The famous Wonderloaf Men were there on the day greeting shopper, and all the first customers all got a free loaf. In 2009 a newly furnished store has taken over near Padiham Bridge—although it is perhaps a little sad that the Padiham Co-operative has had to abandoned the site where over 130 years previous they were able to open what was to become their head store on Burnley Road.

CHAPTER ELEVEN
The Fire Service at Padiham

From the earliest of times tackling any fire at Padiham would have just been a simply hands affair on for all involved. Any 'fire appliances' would have been what was at hand—a ladder here, a bucket or two there and the hope of a plentiful supply of water with which to extinguish the flame. One of the earliest references to a fire in Padiham was in May 1848 when flames engulfed the works of William Waddington, builder and joiner. Timber and other fittings to a value of £700 were destroyed in the conflagration. There was no established fire service at this time in Padiham and the blaze had to be tackled by the engine from Messrs Dugdale Brothers of the Lowerhouse printworks, and by four engines rushed from neighbouring Burnley. By the end of the 1850s a fire brigade of sorts was in operation at Padiham, and a fire brigade proper was formed in 1859 occupying premises under Mr Broxup's brushworks in Burnley Road. In June 1864 the brigade moved to the old Toll Bar House, and a fire bell there was erected in 1865. The brigade removed again to premises in Sagar Street (off Burnley Road) in 1873 and the same years moved again to Smithy Gate Mill. On 4 April, 1874 the brigade removed to Ribble Street where Mr J. Gregson took charge.

The first manual fire engine arrived in Padiham in January 1878, up to that time only a hand cart was used for hoses and other fire fighting tackle. [lxvi]

There was an interesting event in September 1866, whereby the fire brigade were testing a patent fire extinguisher on a plot of land adjacent to Mr Bears' shed. The extinguishers had been supplied by R. Thompson and Son of Manchester. A fire was built containing large quantise of shaving, split wood, old hampers and baskets, tar and tallow barrels and oil. The pile was lit by the brigade, and after being allowed to burn for awhile, the flames were attacked with the extinguishers which immediately extinguished them. The fire was again allowed to gain strength, but the material became so inflammable the second time around that the fluid in the extinguishers was exhausted, and the brigade were obliged to throw water upon it. [lxvii]

In the year 1877 the Fire Brigade became a Volunteer service under the Local Board, consisting at the time of 12 men under the command of the Surveyor of the Local Board, Mr Gregson. The following year they got a manual fire engine which cost £130, even though many expressed that a steam engine would have been better especially since Sir U.J. Kay-Shuttleworth of Gawthorpe Hall had promised £100 towards a steam fire engine. The first fire station was in converted buildings on Morley Street which by all accounts had been a meeting place for the Baptist movement at Padiham, and in 1888 the brigade moved into new headquarters on Inskip Street near the present town hall. The new fire station was made up out of some old cottages which were *'near the gasworks'* which were three storeys high forming a room 20 feet high, 30 feet long and 16 feet wide for the accommodation of a second hand fire engine to be named the *'Fire Queen'*. There was also a harness room, a committee room and cleaning room attached. The committee room there also served as a clubroom for members of the fire service and was supplied daily and evening newspapers and various board games. The second hand horse drawn steam fire engine was made by Merryweather and Company of London, and suffered a few setbacks during trials. It was returned to the makers and a number of alteration and modifications were made including having the boiler re-tubed and improvements to the injectors. The Local Board asked for a representative of the firm to be in attendance at the future trials. The engine was then taken down besides the River Calder near the Banks and the testing was begun.

The fire in the engine was lighted as it left the fire station and by the time the pipes had been connected and all was ready the steam pressure measured 120 lbs. First two jets of water were tried, and then four, all of them sending water to a height equal to any building in the town. The tests were declared a full success. [lxviii]

A second more efficient steam fire engine 'The Calder' was purchased in 1903 capable of delivering 350 gallons per minute to the fire. The firemen were provided with uniforms by the Board, and telephones were installed in their homes also at the expense of the Council. The brigade also served the outlying townships of Higham, Simonstone, Hapton, and Sabden by arrangements with their Parish Councils. Six years after moving into their new headquarters on Inskip Street the fire brigade consisted of fifteen men, a number which had increased by 1924 to eighteen plus one officer. In July 1914, Padiham Urban District Council purchased a brand new motor fire engine to be named as its predecessor was *'Fire Queen'*. The vehicle was a Leyland 50-50 hp., engine with a Rees roturbo twin impeller with a tank capacity of 400-500 gallons, and was purchased through Oswald Tillotson motor engineer of Burnley at a cost of £1,035.00. A demonstration of the new appliance was carried out at the Jubilee Mill, and afterwards at the old gasworks on Station Road.

After the demonstration members and officials of the Council, along with a few friends were entertained by Councillor Holgate, Chairman of the Fire Brigade Committee to an early dinner at the Starkie Arms. A capital repast was served to which the guests did full justice. Afterwards toasts were honoured to *"The Council and Success to the Motor Fire Engine"* Other equipment at this time included a horse drawn hose carrier, a manual hose cart, 40 feet of fire escape, two hand extinguishers, over two thousand yards of fire hose, sixteen branch pipe and eight stand pipes. In February 1925 another light motor type of fire engine made by Morris-Guy was purchased at a cost of £700 and was again put to the test at the gasworks by Captain Bannister. This engine was suitable for use over rougher ground as might be found in the more rural areas of Padiham. After the testing and other ceremonial affairs the group withdrew to the Baptist Chapel for a light lunch and an address by Councillor E. Wiggins, Chairman of the Fire Brigade Committee.

In August 1927 the Urban District Council approved that the siren supplied by Merryweather and Sons be installed at the fire station and that the one in the gasworks be removed and the street alarms be electrically connected with the new one at the fire station. In March 1941 another new engine, a Leyland six cylinder capable of pumping up to 500,000 gallons per minute was purchased. The Padiham Fire service at this time had at hand two fire engines, two large trailer pumps and two light pumps. After the war the Padiham Fire brigade was amalgamated with the National Fire Service and came under the management of the County Council. In November 1963 after six months work in construction the brand new fire station at Padiham was opened, and the old station which had served the brigade for more than fifty years was to be demolished.

Ernest Thompson, the Sub-Officer at the station watched with pride as the fire engine was backed into the new station, but in less than twenty minute the alarm went off and the men were dispatched to a chimney fire. On the eve of the new millennium on Friday 31 December the fire brigade at Padiham were called out to one of its more spectacular blazes in recent years at the Guy Fold Cabaret Club on Guy Street—the building was totally destroyed. It was something of a red letter day for Padiham Fire station when in September 2002, fire fighter Jayne Hinckley passed out after completing her fire training and went on to become the town's first ever lady fire fighter.

In 2006 there were fears that one of the two engines at Padiham could be axed, but in November that year an engine came in as a replacement for the older one. Another replacement engine was also due in the following weeks. The first engine had come from the Burnley Fire Brigade, whilst the other was likely to come from either Leyland or Blackpool. Watch manager at the station Duncan Barker-Brown likened the new fire engine to getting a brand new car. Today, Padiham Fire station proudly goes on protecting the town and its people from serious fire, floods and other accidents.

CHAPTER TWELVE
Notable Padiham Buildings
*Crossways, Knight Hill, Osborne Terrace, Cross Hill (*Trevelyan House)

There are a number of fine buildings in and around Padiham that deserve a mention in this history of the town—however we will not delve into the histories of the halls of the two landed gentries in the area, the Starkie's and the Shuttleworth's of Huntroyde and Gawthorpe respectively as these are well documented elsewhere. We will begin our tour of the notable houses in Padiham at the top of the town and start with Crossways. The houses are in the main much superior at this top end of town, and generally larger with perhaps the addition of bay windows. Today, Crossways, a fine large house is used as a popular restaurant, but the house itself dates from 1899. Prior to being a restaurant though Crossways was always traditionally a doctor's residence. In fact Crossways was actually built in 1899 by a Dr. Owen Fenner Joynson, who previously had a practice at 35 Padiham Road in Burnley, and at 71 Windsor Terrace, Church Street Padiham. Dr Joynson was in practice at Crossways for nearly forty years before retiring in 1936.

During his time there Dr Joynson was also the police surgeon, and responsible for public vaccinations—he was also a former chairman of the Urban District Council from 1899-1900. During that time he was instrumental in the planning and building of the Technical College on Burnley Road at Padiham. Born in Kent he trained at Trinity College at Dublin and practiced at Storrington before coming to Padiham. In 1895 at St Leonard's Church he married Miss Maria Jane Law, the daughter of Dr Law with whom he was in practice with at Crossways. Dr Joynson died in 1950 and was buried at Altham in the family vault—there was one daughter of the union. Following Dr Joynson's retirement in 1936, Dr Harry Simpson moved into Crossways, and served there for many years.[lxix] Doctor Simpson was still there in 1953 and possible for some years after that, but it later became the Crossways restaurant and ran as such until around 1990 when it became empty for about three years. Around 1994 it became Mamma Mia restaurant and continues as such at the time of writing. Just across the road from Crossways is the fine house in what is now the Memorial Park named Knight Hill—a name I have often wondered about. The house itself was built in the 1860s and became the home of Dr John Gregory Booth.

The doctor was born at Accrington and was the son of a cotton manufacturer, being educated at Whalley Grammar School prior to completing his medical training. Dr Booth who first lived on Inkerman street was Knight Hill's first resident. He also went on to become Padiham and District Medical Officer between 1858 and 1885 and was also the surgeon to the 84th Padiham Battalion Lancashire Rifle Volunteers from 1861 to 1880. He married Jane Taylor at St James's Church Altham in 1859. The doctor and his family show up in the 1881 census returns at Knight Hill although he is listed as John 'J' Booth, but there is little doubt that this is the family. He was 49 years old then and a general practitioner, his wife Jane was aged 48 and was born at Hapton. There were three sons, Sidney aged 20 and a medical student, John Gregory aged 12 a scholar, and Charles T., aged five years. The rest of the family included the girls, Elizabeth T. Aged 19 years, Isabel aged 14, a student teacher, Jane Gregory aged 12, scholar, Alice B., aged 9 years, a scholar, Mary L., also a scholar aged 7 years. A young female Catherine Hebbran from Scotland and aged 15 years was a domestic servant at Knight Hill for the Booth's. Dr John Gregory Booth died at Padiham in 1885 aged just 54 years old. In 2003 four benches which had been at Knight Hill and donated there by Mrs Charlie H. Green, the daughter of John Gregory Booth were removed to Padiham Town Hall for use there. A further link to the history at Knight Hill was again made in 2006 when Charlie Booth, the great grandson of Dr John Gregory Booth made the trip from Bury to present to Padiham town hall a portrait of his great grandfather.

Dr John Gregory Booth was succeeded at Knight Hill by Dr Thomas Charles Law, who was born at Accrington but came to Padiham on 7 March 1855. Prior to this he had studied medicine with Dr Edwards of Burnley, and at the age of twenty went to Glasgow for a further course in medicine, being there for about four years. When he came to Padiham he sought and was given the appointment of certifying surgeon under the Factory Acts. For many years he was also the Poor Law Medical Officer for the Padiham District. In 1858 he married Miss Alice Hartley the daughter of Alexander Hartley of Fence at the village church there. There were three children of the union, the only son R.H. Law went on to become the vicar of Arnside, a daughter Maria married Dr Joynson as related to previously, and the third child daughter Alice never wed.

The family show up in the 1881 census returns at Cross Hill, now part of the Trevelyan House, used at that time as the doctor's surgery, but soon afterwards they had moved to Knight Hill. The 1881 census returns lists the doctor and his wife Alice, Maria Jane, the eldest daughter then aged 17 years and the daughter Alice aged 14 and a niece, Alice Maud Johnson aged 14 from Rochdale. Twenty seven year old Mary Pugh worked as a domestic and a groom for the doctor was 20 year old Lawrence Walsh. Dr Thomas Charles Law died in 1905 and was buried at Altham church. The land around Knight Hill at this time was still farmed, the farmer in 1896 for instance being Thomas Anderton. But after the death of Dr Law the Padiham Urban District Council was involved in trying to obtain land around here for use as a park. In 1921 this was achieved and the land secured from the Gawthorpe and Huntroyde Estates, the Unitarian Chapel and Edward Drew who was selling off the Knight Hill estate. The Memorial Park was opened in June 1921 as already related to.

Knight Hill house afterwards became a museum of life in Padiham with part of the house also being used as the residence of the gardener at the Memorial Park. The gardener and later park superintendent and resident at Knight Hill from 1924 to 1958 was Fred Harris, a former gardener at Gawthorpe Hall.[lxx] Following Mr Harris's retirement in 1958 Mr W.E. Speight of 88 West Street Padiham was appointed foreman for the Padiham parks, a foreman at the Huntroyde gardens of the Huntroyde Estates. The museum at Knight Hill itself lasted until October 1952 when Padiham Urban District Council decided to close the museum down because of lack of visitors. One of the more notable exhibits there was of course the famous water clock thought to have dated from 1859—the only other one in the country was that in Kew Gardens in London. Other items included a watch made in 1692, and the top of a Padiham church warden's staff dated 1836. [lxxi] In 2008 after being restored by watch expert Matthew Warburton, helped along with Councillor Bob Clark the famous water clock now stands with pride of place at the Padiham Archives room in the town hall.

Padiham town hall
(Author)

The next buildings of any note are those at Osborne Terrace or 48-52 Church Street, which occupy an elevated position on the left hand side going downhill towards the church of St Leonard's'. These three houses are exceptional as far as other 'terraced' property goes in Padiham and a datestone on the gable of 48 tells us that they were built in 1863. They were built to a design of Padiham architect William Waddington, who incidentally was also responsible for the present day St Leonard's' Church. William Waddington actually lived at 48 Osborne Terrace in the 1860s, but traditionally this residence was the home for many years of Padiham Urban Districts Council Medical Officer of Health. The first such doctor was the Irishman Dr John Weir who was appointed to the post in 1885, he held this position until he retired 1897. Dr Weir was followed by Dr W. Smithies who held the post until 1907. Next came an Indian doctor from the Punjab, Dr Dharmavir who held the post from 1907 through to 1927. The longest serving Medical Officer of Health for Padiham came next in the form of Dr J.W.J. Forsythe, who along with his wife Charlotte, who was also a doctor came to the town in 1927 and served as M.O.H. until April 1964 when he took retirement.

At the beginning of the war the surgery was moved across road to No. 47 Church Street.[lxxii] The Forsythe's lived at Seatland's on Whins Lane at Simonstone. Both 50 and 52 Osborne Terrace, Church Street were used by the more well to do, as large family homes ever since they were built. No. 50 Osborne Terrace for instance was the home to Miss Sarah Hacking her niece Rachael, an assistant school mistress and a lodger Cecil Bromley, assistant curate at Padiham, 1896, whilst No. 52 was the home of Richard Fort in 1883, a barber in the town, and his Irish born wife Margaret—his barbers shop was at No. 12 Moor Lane. Further down Church Street we come to what is known today as Trevelyan House but which used to be called Cross Hill. Names like these are intriguing and make us wonder just where the 'cross' was, Cross Bank is another such local name. At No. 1 Bank Street there was even a Cross Hill Tavern/Inn at one time. Could this be a reference to some ancient market cross? After all we are not too far off the Parish Church and we know that the weekly markets were once held around the outer walls there! Today's Trevelyan House was marked on the map of 1892 as 'Cross Hill' and again by tradition it seems to have been the residence of medical men. The house in the 1881 census returns, although Cross Hill is much older than this, and at this time it was the residence of the surgeon Thomas Charles Law who we already alluded to. Soon after this however, Doctor Law moved to Knight Hill, and he was succeeded at Cross Hill by Dr Robert Horne.

SOURCES OF INFORMATION

[i] Burnley Express 5 July 1950 and subsequent issues, 9, 12 and 15 July. See also photographs of the dig in BRL.

[ii] Bennett Walter "History of Burnley" part I page 25.

[iii] Glenn, Gill "A History of Padiham"

[iv] Wyld Henry Cecil, "Place Names of Lancashire" 1911.

[v] See Blackburn Standard 30 October 1875.

[vi] Mitchell, Newman, Newman and Darlington 'Padiham Historic Town Assessment' 2004.

[vii] Bennett, Walter "History of Burnley, Part II" page 57,

[viii] Bennett, Walter "History of Burnley, Part I" page 139,

[ix] St Leonard's Church Records.

[x] Burnley News 12 April 1924 page 5

[xi] Bennett, Walter "History of Burnley, Part II" page 249,

[xii] Northern Life magazine 'Perfect Padiham' 27 July 2009.

[xiii] Glenn, Gill "A History of Padiham"

[xiv] Whitehall Evening News 17 February 1780.

[xv] Notice in Blackburn Standard, 28 September 1842.

[xvi] Higginbothan, Peter "Workhouses of the North"

[xvii] Burnley Express 4 October 2003, page 4, 'Plaque plan to honour Wesley'.

[xviii] Haines and Jones, "Padiham Urban District Council, Eighty Years of Local Government" 1994

[xix] Haines and Jones, "Padiham Urban District Council, Eighty Years of Local Government", 1994

[xx] Farrer, William and Brownbill J., (editors) 'The History of the County of Lancashire' Vol., 6

[xxi] A much more detailed account of St Leonard's Church up to 1969 can be found in the excellent little booklet *'Challenge in Stone, St Leonard's Padiham 1869-1969'*. by John Travis and Lilian Carr.

[xxii] Burnley Express 1 June 1940 'The Cause that was Founded by Sabden Pioneers'

[xxiii] Blackburn Standard 31 July 1880, page eight.

[xxiv] Information from 'History of Methodism in Padiham' Burnley reference library.

[xxv] Burnley Express 20 March 1992 article on the history of Methodists in Padiham.

[xxvi] Gill, Tom 'St John's Church Padiham 1881-1981'

[xxvii] Bennett Walter 'History of Burnley, Vol III' page 334

[xxviii] Haines and Jones, "Padiham Urban District Council, Eighty Years of Local Government" 1994

[xxix] Burnley Express 13 June 1967

[xxx] A much more detailed account of the National School at Padiham can be read in an excellent little booklet by Molly Haines and Margaret Jones titled 'A History of Mill Street Padiham 1830-2009' by Burnley and District U3A Local History Group.

[xxxi] Burnley Express 17 October 1888 'Memorial Stone Laying at Padiham'

[xxxii] Burnley Express 2 November 1901 'The Opening of the New Padiham Technical Institute'

[xxxiii] Burnley Express 9 May 1888 'Completion Of A New Weaving Shed, Engine Christened'

[xxxiv] Rothwell, Mike 'Industrial Heritage, Padiham and District' (2005) page 14

[xxxv] Jones, Margaret, Article 'Iron Man who took a healthy interest in his adopted town' Lancashire Evening Telegraph 2 September 2004

[xxxvi] Rothwell, Mike 'Industrial Heritage, Padiham and District' (2005) page 8

[xxxvii] Report in Blackburn Standard Saturday 6 March 1886.

[xxxviii] Rothwell, Mike 'Industrial Heritage, Padiham and District' (2005) page 9.

[xxxix] The Morning Post, Wednesday 30 March 1870 under 'Partnerships Dissolved'

[xl] Report on the fire in Burnley Express 24 March 1965.

[xli] Blackburn Standard Saturday 25 June 1881

[xlii] Burnley Express 11 April 1986 'The Mill Chimney Collector'

[xliii] Rothwell, Mike 'Industrial Heritage, Padiham and District' (2005)

xliv Burnley Advertiser 7 September 1861

[xlv] Bannister, F. 'Annals of the Forest of Trawden' Landy Publishing, 1987

[xlvi] Bennett, Walter 'History of Burnley, Volume II page 91.

[xlvii] Information from George Heys Book in Burnley Reference Library 'The Industrial History of the Burnley Coalfield'.

[xlviii] Burnley Express 12 June 1965, report on the shafts at Bancroft Woods.

[xlix] The obituary to Norman Blezard, Burnley Express 12 October 1901.

[l] Burnley Express 17 July 1901 'The Death of Mr Francis Helm of Padiham'

[li] Rothwell, Mike 'Industrial Heritage, Padiham and District' (2005) page 28

[lii] Rothwell, Mike 'Industrial Heritage, Padiham and District' (2005) page 29

[liii] Most of the information on Hill 'Special' cycles has come from the excellent WebPages constructed by Robin Hatherell and from the Lancashire Evening Gazette 14 January 1981

[liv] The obituary to James Bertwistle, Burnley Gazette 12 November 1910.

[lv] Barrett's Trade directory, 1945

[lvi] The obituary to Ernest Bradshaw, Burnley Express 23 February 1973.

[lvii] Padiham Express 25 September 1998 article 'Tripe's Back in Town'.

[lviii] Bennett Walter, 'History of Burnley Vol., IV pages 117-118

[lix] Haines and Jones, "Padiham Urban District Council, Eighty Years of Local Government" 1994

[lx] Much of the information on the Padiham Power stations came from 'PADIHAM power stations: its role in 100 years of electricity generation in East Lancashire'. By National Power.

[lxi] Haines and Jones, "Padiham Urban District Council, Eighty Years of Local Government" 1994

[lxii] Molly Haines and Margaret Jones 'A History of Mill Street Padiham 1830-2009' by Burnley and District U3A Local History Group. A Piece on the Cinema is by Maureen Knowles.

[lxiii] Urban District Council Minutes September 1928 change of name from Whittaker Street to Park View.

[lxiv] Padiham Historical Assessment Report May 2005, Lancashire County Council.

[lxv] Mid Week Gazette 10 December 1884.

[lxvi] Burnley Express 29 July 1914.

[lxvii] Burnley Gazette 22 September 1866.

[lxviii] Burnley Express 17 and 24 March 1888.

[lxix] Burnley Express 1 March 1950, the obituary of Dr Owen Fenner Joynson.

[lxx] Burnley Express 14 October 2005 'Padiham park stalwart dies' obituary to Mr Donald Harris.

[lxxi] Burnley Express 25 October 1952 'Padiham museum to close'

[lxxii] Much of the information about Padiham Medical Officers of Health comes from Haines and Jones, "Padiham Urban District Council, Eighty Years of Local Government" 1994

INDEX

Albert Mill, 80, 82,
Alexandra Theatre, 189,
Alma Mill, 85,
Bancroft Colliery, 115,
Battle of Read Bridge, 17,
Bendwood Bridge, 180,
Black Bull Inn, 8, 26,
Blacksmiths, 140,
Bowling Greens, 195,
Bridge End Mill (Wonder Mill) 85,
Bridge Inn, 179,
Britannia Mill, 87,
British and Foreign School Society, 64,
Brookfoot, 15,
Burnley Poor Law Union, 23,
Burnley Road Baptist Chapel, 41, 64,
Civil War, 17,
Clay Bank Mill, 89,
Clock Face Inn, 26,
Coal mining, 9,
Commercial Mill, 89,
Co-operative Movement, 202,
Cophurst, 15,
Cornfield Colliery, 116,
County Primary School, 69,
Craggs Colliery, 118,
Craven Bank, 197,
Crime, 27,
Crooked Leaches Colliery, 119,
Cross Bank Chapel, 44,
Cross Bank, 15,
Crossways, 208,
Cuckstool, 10, 11,
Decline Colliery, 120,
Dugdale Colliery, 120,
Dun Horse Inn, 190,
East Pit, 120,
Ebenezer Chapel, 46,
Electricity Supply, 161,

Engineering Industry, 161,
Enterprise & Industry Mill, 90,
Eyses Colliery, 123,
Fire Service, 204,
Foulds House, 7,
Gas Supply, 164,
Gawthorpe Colliery, 124,
Gawthorpe High School, 65,
Gawthorpe, 12,
George and Dragon, 26,
Globe cinema, 190,
Gothic Works (Baxi, Main Morley), 139,
Grand Cinema, 190,
Green Bridge Mill, 95,
Green Brook Bridge, 181,
Green Lane Mill, 97,
Grove Mill, 19, 98,
Guy Street, 14,
Guy Yate Mill, 19,
Hall Hill Chapel, 47,
Hargrove 63,
High Whitaker, 6, 12,
Hill 'Special' Cycles., 141,
Hill's Mineral Waters, 146,
Holme Mill, 99,
Horeb Chapel, 51,
Huntroyde, 8, 16, 18, 22,
Ightenhill Manor House, 10,
Isles House, 18,
Jubilee Mill, 100,
Kingdom Hall, 53,
Knight Hill, 208,
Levant Mill, 102,
Lily of the Valley Mill, 103,
Local Board, 29,
Lomax Colliery, 125,
Markets, 7,
Methodists, 25,
Middlefield Colliery, 125,
Mineral waters and brewing, 144,

INDEX

Mining Disputes, 159,
Mount Zion Chapel, 53,
National School, 63, 67, 75,
Neolithic Period, 6,
Nook I' Th' Holme Colliery, 126,
Old Moss, 16,
Opencast Mining, 127,
Orchard Mill, 104,
Padiham Aerated Waters, 145,
Padiham Bridge, 8, 178,
Padiham Building Company, 25,
Padiham corn mill, 12, 13,
Padiham Green School, 71,
Padiham Liberal Club, 14,
Padiham Memorial Park, 183,
Padiham Old Mill, 106,
Padiham Parish or Charity School, 63,
Padiham Permanent Benefit Building Society, 200,
Padiham Pool, 194,
Padiham rushbearings, 16,
Padiham stocks, 10,
Padiham witch, see Pearson Margaret,
Padiham Workhouse, 22, 23,
Palmerston Street footbridge, 182,
Partridge Hill School, 73,
Partridge Hill, 7,
Pearson Margaret (Padiham witch) 11,
Peel's Mill, 107,
Pendle Street footbridge, 182,
Perseverance Mill, 107,
Pickles Wilfred 62,
Pickup Delph Quarry, 64,
Postal Service, 172,
Quarrying, 132,
Railway Saw Mill, 147,
Railway, 173,
Recreation Ground, 193,

Riverside Mill, 109,
Romans, 6,
Ropewalks, 148,
Salvation Army, 55,
Sewerage Treatment, 171,
Simonstone Colliery, 126,
Slade, 15,
Smithy Gate Mill, 110,
Spa Mill, 111,
St Anne and Elizabeth Church, 39,
St John the Baptist Church, 60, 74,
St Leonard's Church, 30-37,
St Leonard's School, 75,
St Matthew's Church, 37,
St Philip the Apostle Church, 61,
Starkie Arms, 172,
Starkie Arms, 26, 179,
Station Road Bridge, 181,
Stockbridge House, 7, 15, 17,
Strikes and Disputes, 150,
Technical Institute, 77,
Temperance Mission Hall, 56,
Tennis Courts, 195,
Towneley Hall, 17,
Tripe Dressing Works, 149,
Tudor Period, 14,
Unitarian Chapel, 57,
Victoria Foundry, 138,
Victoria Mills, 19, 112,
Wallgreen, 15,
Water clock, 66,
Water Supply, 166,
Wellington Mill, 113,
Wesley, John, 25, 49,
Whalley Abbey, 17,
Whitaker Clough Colliery, 127,
Whitegate Park, 188,
Whitegate Quarry, 64,
Workhouse Farm, 22, 23,
Wyre Street Foundry, 139,

SURNAME INDEX

Adamson, 11, 15, 24, 31, 67, 73,
Aidan, 75,
Ainsworth, 26, 140,
Alcock, 197,
Anderson, 132,
Anderton, 26, 59, 60,
Armistead, 198,
Ashworth, 22, 23,
Bailey, 176,
Bainbridge, 68,
Baldwin, 65,
Bardshaw, 94,
Bear, 86, 94, 107, 108, 111, 205,
Bertwistle, 33, 38, 52, 53, 54, 65, 79, 85, 88, 110, 144, 147, 175, 179, 187, 200,
Bibby, 90,
Bickerstaffe, 127,
Birkbeck, 197,
Birtwell, 66,
Bleasdale, 61,
Blezard, 27, 65, 95, 99, 101, 112, 135, 136, 179, 180, 193,
Booth, 32, 56, 208, 209,
Bowers, 144, 145,
Bradshaw, 149,
Bramley, 68, 164,
Bridge, 27, 200,
Briggs, 195,
Broadley, 40,
Brooks, 74,
Broxup, 204,
Butterworth, 97, 100, 102, 103,
Catlow, 90, 157,
Cave-Browne-Cave, 71,
Chadwick, 172,
Clark, 210,
Clayton, 32, 183, 184, 185, 186, 187,
Claytor, 35,
Clegg, 26, 165,

Cockshutt, 28,
Collins, 114,
Cook, 28, 57,
Cooper, 94, 114, 148,
Coverdale, 75,
Crawshaw, 133, 200,
Cronshaw, 56,
Darney, 25, 47,
Davies, 133,
Dean, 66, 94, 97, 102, 106,
Dearden, 27,
Dewhurst, 97,
Dharmavir, 211,
Dicken, 143,
Diggle, 115,
Dodgeon, 45, 46,
Douglas, 193,
Drew, 186,
Duce, 195,
Dugdale, 11, 33,
Dunne, 69,
Duxbury, 133,
Dwyer, 61,
Dyer, 61,
Earnshaw, 123,
Eastwood, 27,
Eddleston, 13,
Edmondson, 89, 132,
Farnworth, 66,
Fisher, 41,
Fishwick, 80,
Fitzgerald, 61,
Flynn, 197,
Foley, 97,
Forsythe, 211,
Fort, 125,
Foster, 41, 64, 111,
Fox, 34, 38,
Frankland, 95,
Gill, 201,
Glynne, 31,

SURNAME INDEX

Gornall, 39,
Granger, 76, 192, 198,
Gray, 199,
Green, 94, 97, 200,
Greenwood, 35,
Gregson, 96, 171, 174, 204, 205,
Griffin, 42,
Grimshaws, 146,
Grundy, 59,
Hacking, 212,
Haighton, 138,
Hall, 143, 144,
Hallam, 71,
Hargreaves, 32, 54, 88, 89, 90, 96, 116, 125, 127, 160, 192,
Harrison, 165,
Hartley, 63,
Hartnell, 194,
Harvey, 53,
Haworth, 140,
Haydocke, 11,
Hayhurst, 149,
Heap, 19, 23, 110,
Heaton, 85,
Hebbran, 209,
Hefft, 190,
Helm, 15, 19, 25, 27, 45, 98, 99, 103, 107, 110, 111, 112, 138,
Hey, 121,
Heydon, 169,
Heys, 122, 129,
Hill, 141, 142, 146,
Hilliers, 65,
Hindle, 141,
Hirst, 133,
Holgate, 27,
Holker, 26,
Holland, 172,
Hollins, 56,
Holmes, 74,
Holt, 25,

Hopwood, 50,
Horne, 183,
Hoyle, 199,
Hudson, 167,
Hudson, 27,
Hull, 90,
Hutchinson, 174,
Inckle, 196,
Ingham, 80, 81, 82, 90, 140, 150, 157, 203,
Johnstone, 35,
Joynson, 208,
Kay, 95,
Kay-Shuttleworth, 43, 124, 160, 188, 205,
Keighley, 101,
Kelly, 20,
Kenyon, 155,
Kirkham, 20,
Langley, 42,
Langstaff, 77,
Latham, 97,
Lawson, 197,
Laycock, 90, 200,
Lee, 132,
Lees, 32,
Lomax, 114,
Lord, 61,
Lucas, 32, 56, 57,
Mackenzie, 196,
Mann, 155,
Marks, 150,
Marsden, 27,
Marshall, 30, 31, 115,
Massey, 146,
Mawson, 183,
McBride, 43,
McEnery, 61,
Mercer, 90,
Mitchell, 61,
Monk, 49, 90, 110, 145, 170, 200,

SURNAME INDEX

Morris, 139, 196,
Morrisey, 75,
Mountford-Aram, 102,
Mussley, 74,
Muxworthy, 42, 51, 52, 64,
Myers, 148,
Nash, 134,
Naylor, 54,
Neville, 66,
Nuttall, 64,
Oldring, 53,
Ormerod, 65,
Oxley, 56,
Parkinson, 98, 123, 149, 201,
Paslew, 32,
Peart, 197,
Phillipson, 128,
Pickles, 26, 54, 62, 109,
Pickup, 145,
Pilkington, 120,
Pilling, 22, 23, 32, 95,
Pinder, 151, 152,
Pollard, 27, 57, 58, 59, 115,
Preston, 13,
Proctor, 94,
Railton, 55,
Rawstron, 61,
Reeves, 189,
Riley, 74,
Roberts, 159, 160,
Robinson, 19, 26, 57, 58, 59, 66, 68, 69, 87, 90, 114, 157,
Robson, 176,
Roo, 15,
Ross, 74,
Rushworth, 173,
Russell, 190,
Ryan, 27,
Ryden, 86, 95,
Ryder, 42,
Ryley, 14,

Sagar, 26, 27, 94, 97, 100, 103,
Scott, 185,
Sethson, 20,
Shackleton, 123, 175,
Shacklock, 141,
Shaw, 19, 31, 97,
Shepherd, 53, 121,
Sherburn, 32,
Short, 193,
Shuttleworth, 12, 17, 37, 38, 52, 66, 69, 71, 73, 77, 78, 79, 110, 114, 121, 126,
Simpson, 172,
Slater, 95,
Smith, 170,
Sparrow, 46,
Speight, 195,
Standing, 61,
Stanworth, 47,
Starkie, 11, 16, 22, 24, 27, 32, 33, 34, 35, 36, 37, 39, 40, 67, 68, 71, 73, 75, 154, 178, 181, 193,
Stephenson, 26, 97, 98,
Stevenson, 104,
Stocks, 32,
Stuttard, 105, 106, 156,
Suddall, 8,
Tanganika, 175,
Tattersall, 114,
Taylor, 26, 39, 72,
Thompson, 32, 40, 85, 87, 88, 97, 108, 207,
Thoms, 29,
Thornber, 95,
Thornton, 198,
Thursby, 160,
Tickle, 85, 110, 119, 199,
Tomlinson, 133, 134, 135,
Towers, 61,
Towneley, 13, 17, 18,
Tullis, 169,

SURNAME INDEX

Turkington, 191,
Tylas, 77,
Varley, 22,
Vasey, 53,
Verity, 152, 153,
Waddington, 18, 25, 26, 33, 86, 90, 101, 104, 108, 127, 133, 140, 179,
Wade, 16,
Wallington, 64,
Walmsley, 27, 94, 99,
Walton, 8, 14, 19,
Wardleworth, 141,
Watson, 113,
Webster, 15, 26, 44,
Weir, 211,
Wesley, 25, 49,
Whinnerah, 173,
Whitaker, 12, 123,
Whittaker, 26, 54, 91, 97, 111, 113, 127, 155, 156, 178, 197,
Wiggins, 206,
Wilkinson, 13, 15, 24, 36, 89, 90, 91, 95, 118, 141, 153,
Willion, 48,
Wilson, 26, 65,
Winfield, 72,
Witham, 118, 123,
Wood, 41,
Yarnold, 64,
Yates, 155,